HIGHLAND
LIBRARIES

07014594

629.28722

WITHDRAWN

Haynes

THE BOOK ®

Peugeot 406
Service and Repair Manual

Mark Coombs and John S Mead

Models covered   *(3394 - 12AF1 - 320)*
Peugeot 406 Saloon and Estate models
with normally-aspirated four-cylinder petrol engines and Turbo-diesel engines, including special/limited editions;

1580 cc, 1761 cc, & 1998 cc petrol engines
1905 cc & 2088 cc turbo diesel engines

Does not cover 1998 cc Turbo or 2946 cc V6 petrol engines, 1997 cc HDi Turbo-diesel engine or Coupe

© Haynes Publishing 2003   ABCDE   Printed in the USA
                                            FGHIJ

A book in the **Haynes Service and Repair Manual Series**   **Haynes Publishing**
                                                            Sparkford, Yeovil, Somerset, BA22 7JJ, England

All rights reserved. No part of this book may be reproduced or transmitted in any form or by any means, electronic or mechanical, including photocopying, recording or by any information storage or retrieval system, without permission in writing from the copyright holder.

Haynes North America, Inc
861 Lawrence Drive, Newbury Park, California 91320, USA

Editions Haynes
4, Rue de l'Abreuvoir
92415 COURBEVOIE CEDEX, France

ISBN **1 85960 983 X**

British Library Cataloguing in Publication Data
A catalogue record for this book is available from the British Library.

Haynes Publishing Nordiska AB
Box 1504, 751 45 UPPSALA, Sverige

Contents

LIVING WITH YOUR PEUGEOT 406

Roadside repairs

Weekly checks

MAINTENANCE

Routine maintenance and servicing

Contents

The Peugeot 406 Saloon was introduced into the UK in early 1996. At its launch, the 406 was offered with a choice of 1.6 (1580 cc - not available in the UK), 1.8 (1761 cc) and 2.0 litre (1998 cc) petrol engines or a 1.9 litre (1905 cc) turbo diesel engine.

The engines fitted to the 406 range are all versions of the well-proven units which have appeared in many Peugeot/Citroën vehicles over the years. The petrol engines are from the XU engine series, and are of four-cylinder overhead camshaft design; the 1.6 litre engine is a SOHC 8-valve unit and the 1.8 and 2.0 litre engines are DOHC 16-valve units. The diesel engine is from the XUD engine series, and is a SOHC 8-valve unit.

The engine is mounted transversely at the front of vehicle, with the transmission mounted on its left-hand end. All engines are fitted with a manual transmission as standard (an automatic transmission option was introduced at a later date on some engines).

All models have fully-independent front and rear suspension arrangements incorporating shock absorbers and coil springs.

A wide range of standard and optional equipment is available within the range to suit most tastes, including central locking, electric windows and an electric sunroof. An air conditioning system was available as an option on certain models.

In the summer of 1996, a 2.1 litre (2088 cc) turbo diesel engine was introduced into the range (a 2.0 litre petrol turbo model was also introduced, but is not covered by this manual). The new engine is a 12-valve version of the XUD engine which has also been used in other Peugeot/Citroën vehicles.

In early 1997, Peugeot introduced an Estate model, and also introduced the V6 petrol engine (not covered by this manual) into the range. Apart from this, only minor detail changes have been made to the vehicle.

Provided that regular servicing is carried out in accordance with the manufacturer's recommendations, the vehicle should prove reliable and very economical. The engine compartment is well-designed, and most of the items requiring frequent attention are easily accessible.

Peugeot 406 Saloon

Peugeot 406 Estate

The Peugeot 406 Team

Haynes manuals are produced by dedicated and enthusiastic people working in close co-operation. The team responsible for the creation of this book included:

Authors	**Mark Coombs** **John S Mead**
Sub-editor	**Sophie Yar**
Editor & Page Make-up	**Bob Jex**
Workshop manager	**Paul Buckland**
Photo Scans	**John Martin** **Steve Tanswell**
Cover illustration & Line Art	**Roger Healing**
Wiring diagrams	**Matthew Marke**

We hope the book will help you to get the maximum enjoyment from your car. By carrying out routine maintenance as described you will ensure your car's reliability and preserve its resale value.

Your Peugeot 406 manual

The aim of this manual is to help you get the best value from your vehicle. It can do so in several ways. It can help you decide what work must be done (even should you choose to get it done by a garage). It will also provide information on routine maintenance and servicing, and give a logical course of action and diagnosis when random faults occur. However, it is hoped that you will use the manual by tackling the work yourself. On simpler jobs it may even be quicker than booking the car into a garage and going there twice, to leave and collect it. Perhaps most important, a lot of money can be saved by avoiding the costs a garage must charge to cover its labour and overheads.

The manual has drawings and descriptions to show the function of the various components so that their layout can be understood. Tasks are described and photographed in a clear step-by-step sequence.

References to the 'left' and 'right' of the vehicle are in the sense of a person in the driver's seat facing forward.

Acknowledgements

Thanks are due to Draper Tools Limited, who provided some of the workshop tools, and to all those people at Sparkford who helped in the production of this manual.

We take great pride in the accuracy of information given in this manual, but vehicle manufacturers make alterations and design changes during the production run of a particular vehicle of which they do not inform us. No liability can be accepted by the authors or publishers for loss, damage or injury caused by any errors in, or omissions from, the information given.

Working on your car can be dangerous. This page shows just some of the potential risks and hazards, with the aim of creating a safety-conscious attitude.

General hazards

Scalding

• Don't remove the radiator or expansion tank cap while the engine is hot.
• Engine oil, automatic transmission fluid or power steering fluid may also be dangerously hot if the engine has recently been running.

Burning

• Beware of burns from the exhaust system and from any part of the engine. Brake discs and drums can also be extremely hot immediately after use.

Crushing

• When working under or near a raised vehicle, always supplement the jack with axle stands, or use drive-on ramps. *Never venture under a car which is only supported by a jack.*
• Take care if loosening or tightening high-torque nuts when the vehicle is on stands. Initial loosening and final tightening should be done with the wheels on the ground.

Fire

• Fuel is highly flammable; fuel vapour is explosive.
• Don't let fuel spill onto a hot engine.
• Do not smoke or allow naked lights (including pilot lights) anywhere near a vehicle being worked on. Also beware of creating sparks (electrically or by use of tools).
• Fuel vapour is heavier than air, so don't work on the fuel system with the vehicle over an inspection pit.
• Another cause of fire is an electrical overload or short-circuit. Take care when repairing or modifying the vehicle wiring.
• Keep a fire extinguisher handy, of a type suitable for use on fuel and electrical fires.

Electric shock

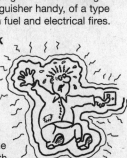

• Ignition HT voltage can be dangerous, especially to people with heart problems or a pacemaker. Don't work on or near the ignition system with the engine running or the ignition switched on.

• Mains voltage is also dangerous. Make sure that any mains-operated equipment is correctly earthed. Mains power points should be protected by a residual current device (RCD) circuit breaker.

Fume or gas intoxication

• Exhaust fumes are poisonous; they often contain carbon monoxide, which is rapidly fatal if inhaled. Never run the engine in a confined space such as a garage with the doors shut.
• Fuel vapour is also poisonous, as are the vapours from some cleaning solvents and paint thinners.

Poisonous or irritant substances

• Avoid skin contact with battery acid and with any fuel, fluid or lubricant, especially antifreeze, brake hydraulic fluid and Diesel fuel. Don't syphon them by mouth. If such a substance is swallowed or gets into the eyes, seek medical advice.
• Prolonged contact with used engine oil can cause skin cancer. Wear gloves or use a barrier cream if necessary. Change out of oil-soaked clothes and do not keep oily rags in your pocket.
• Air conditioning refrigerant forms a poisonous gas if exposed to a naked flame (including a cigarette). It can also cause skin burns on contact.

Asbestos

• Asbestos dust can cause cancer if inhaled or swallowed. Asbestos may be found in gaskets and in brake and clutch linings. When dealing with such components it is safest to assume that they contain asbestos.

Special hazards

Hydrofluoric acid

• This extremely corrosive acid is formed when certain types of synthetic rubber, found in some O-rings, oil seals, fuel hoses etc, are exposed to temperatures above 400ºC. The rubber changes into a charred or sticky substance containing the acid. *Once formed, the acid remains dangerous for years. If it gets onto the skin, it may be necessary to amputate the limb concerned.*
• When dealing with a vehicle which has suffered a fire, or with components salvaged from such a vehicle, wear protective gloves and discard them after use.

The battery

• Batteries contain sulphuric acid, which attacks clothing, eyes and skin. Take care when topping-up or carrying the battery.
• The hydrogen gas given off by the battery is highly explosive. Never cause a spark or allow a naked light nearby. Be careful when connecting and disconnecting battery chargers or jump leads.

Air bags

• Air bags can cause injury if they go off accidentally. Take care when removing the steering wheel and/or facia. Special storage instructions may apply.

Diesel injection equipment

• Diesel injection pumps supply fuel at very high pressure. Take care when working on the fuel injectors and fuel pipes.

⚠️ *Warning: Never expose the hands, face or any other part of the body to injector spray; the fuel can penetrate the skin with potentially fatal results.*

Remember...

DO

• Do use eye protection when using power tools, and when working under the vehicle.

• Do wear gloves or use barrier cream to protect your hands when necessary.

• Do get someone to check periodically that all is well when working alone on the vehicle.

• Do keep loose clothing and long hair well out of the way of moving mechanical parts.

• Do remove rings, wristwatch etc, before working on the vehicle – especially the electrical system.

• Do ensure that any lifting or jacking equipment has a safe working load rating adequate for the job.

DON'T

• Don't attempt to lift a heavy component which may be beyond your capability – get assistance.

• Don't rush to finish a job, or take unverified short cuts.

• Don't use ill-fitting tools which may slip and cause injury.

• Don't leave tools or parts lying around where someone can trip over them. Mop up oil and fuel spills at once.

• Don't allow children or pets to play in or near a vehicle being worked on.

The following pages are intended to help in dealing with common roadside emergencies and breakdowns. You will find more detailed fault finding information at the back of the manual, and repair information in the main chapters.

If your car won't start and the starter motor doesn't turn

- ☐ If it's a model with automatic transmission, make sure the selector is in 'P' or 'N'.
- ☐ Open the bonnet and make sure that the battery terminals are clean and tight.
- ☐ Switch on the headlights and try to start the engine. If the headlights go very dim when you're trying to start, the battery is probably flat. Get out of trouble by jump starting (see next page) using a friend's car.

If your car won't start even though the starter motor turns as normal

- ☐ Is there fuel in the tank?
- ☐ Is there moisture on electrical components under the bonnet? Switch off the ignition, then wipe off any obvious dampness with a dry cloth. Spray a water-repellent aerosol product (WD-40 or equivalent) on ignition and fuel system electrical connectors like those shown in the photos. Pay special attention to the ignition coil wiring connector and HT leads. (Note that diesel engines don't normally suffer from damp.)

A Remove the plastic cover and check the condition and security of the battery connections.

B Check that the fuel/ignition system (as applicable) wiring connectors are securely connected (2.0 litre petrol model shown).

C Check that the alternator wiring connectors are securely connected.

D Check that all fuses are still in good condition and none have blown.

Check that electrical connections are secure (with the ignition switched off) and spray them with a water-dispersant spray like WD-40 if you suspect a problem due to damp.

Jump starting will get you out of trouble, but you must correct whatever made the battery go flat in the first place. There are three possibilities:

1 *The battery has been drained by repeated attempts to start, or by leaving the lights on.*

2 *The charging system is not working properly (alternator drivebelt slack or broken, alternator wiring fault or alternator itself faulty).*

3 *The battery itself is at fault (electrolyte low, or battery worn out).*

When jump-starting a car using a booster battery, observe the following precautions:

✔ Before connecting the booster battery, make sure that the ignition is switched off.

✔ Ensure that all electrical equipment (lights, heater, wipers, etc) is switched off.

✔ Take note of any special precautions printed on the battery case.

Jump starting

✔ Make sure that the booster battery is the same voltage as the discharged one in the vehicle.

✔ If the battery is being jump-started from the battery in another vehicle, the two vehicles MUST NOT TOUCH each other.

✔ Make sure that the transmission is in neutral (or PARK, in the case of automatic transmission).

1 Connect one end of the red jump lead to the positive (+) terminal of the flat battery

2 Connect the other end of the red lead to the positive (+) terminal of the booster battery.

3 Connect one end of the black jump lead to the negative (-) terminal of the booster battery

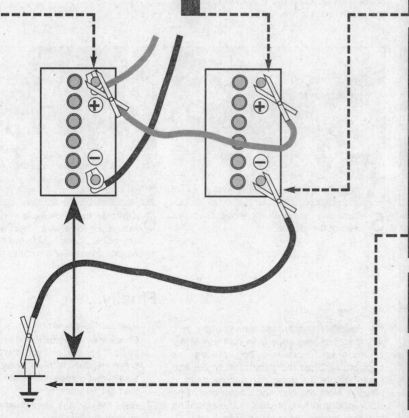

4 Connect the other end of the black jump lead to a bolt or bracket on the engine block, well away from the battery, on the vehicle to be started.

5 Make sure that the jump leads will not come into contact with the fan, drivebelts or other moving parts of the engine.

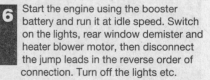

6 Start the engine using the booster battery and run it at idle speed. Switch on the lights, rear window demister and heater blower motor, then disconnect the jump leads in the reverse order of connection. Turn off the lights etc.

Wheel changing

Some of the details shown here will vary according to model. For instance, the location of the spare wheel and jack is not the same on all cars. However, the basic principles apply to all vehicles.

Warning: Do not change a wheel in a situation where you risk being hit by other traffic. On busy roads, try to stop in a lay-by or a gateway. Be wary of passing traffic while changing the wheel – it is easy to become distracted by the job in hand.

Preparation

☐ When a puncture occurs, stop as soon as it is safe to do so.
☐ Park on firm level ground, if possible, and well out of the way of other traffic.
☐ Use hazard warning lights if necessary.

☐ If you have one, use a warning triangle to alert other drivers of your presence.
☐ Apply the handbrake and engage first or reverse gear (or Park on models with automatic transmission.

☐ Chock the wheel diagonally opposite the one being removed – a couple of large stones will do for this.
☐ If the ground is soft, use a flat piece of wood to spread the load under the jack.

Changing the wheel

1 The spare wheel and tools are stored in the luggage compartment. Lift up the carpet/rear family seat (as applicable) and remove the tool kit and jack from the centre of the spare wheel. Unscrew the retainer and remove the spare wheel.

2 Remove the wheel trim/hub cap (as applicable). On models where anti-theft wheel bolts are fitted, pull off the plastic cover then unscrew the anti-theft bolt using the special socket provided.

3 With the vehicle on the ground, slacken each wheel bolt by half a turn.

4 Make sure the jack is located on firm ground, and engage the jack head correctly with the sill.

5 Raise the jack until the wheel is raised clear of the ground.

6 Unscrew the wheel bolts and remove the wheel. Fit the spare wheel and screw in the bolts. Lightly tighten the bolts with the wheelbrace then lower the car to the ground.

7 Securely tighten the wheel bolts in a diagonal sequence then refit the wheel trim/hub cap/wheel bolt covers (as applicable). Stow the punctured wheel and tools back in the boot, and secure them in position. Note that the wheel bolts should be slackened and retightened to the specified torque at the earliest possible opportunity.

Finally...

☐ Remove the wheel chocks.
☐ Check the tyre pressure on the wheel just fitted. If it is low, or if you don't have a pressure gauge with you, drive slowly to the nearest garage and inflate the tyre to the right pressure.
☐ Have the damaged tyre or wheel repaired as soon as possible.

Identifying leaks

Puddles on the garage floor or drive, or obvious wetness under the bonnet or underneath the car, suggest a leak that needs investigating. It can sometimes be difficult to decide where the leak is coming from, especially if the engine bay is very dirty already. Leaking oil or fluid can also be blown rearwards by the passage of air under the car, giving a false impression of where the problem lies.

 Warning: Most automotive oils and fluids are poisonous. Wash them off skin, and change out of contaminated clothing, without delay.

 The smell of a fluid leaking from the car may provide a clue to what's leaking. Some fluids are distinctively coloured. It may help to clean the car and to park it over some clean paper as an aid to locating the source of the leak. Remember that some leaks may only occur while the engine is running.

Sump oil

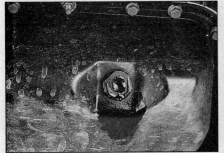

Engine oil may leak from the drain plug...

Oil from filter

...or from the base of the oil filter.

Gearbox oil

Gearbox oil can leak from the seals at the inboard ends of the driveshafts.

Antifreeze

Leaking antifreeze often leaves a crystalline deposit like this.

Brake fluid

A leak occurring at a wheel is almost certainly brake fluid.

Power steering fluid

Power steering fluid may leak from the pipe connectors on the steering rack.

Towing

When all else fails, you may find yourself having to get a tow home – or of course you may be helping somebody else. Long-distance recovery should only be done by a garage or breakdown service. For shorter distances, DIY towing using another car is easy enough, but observe the following points:

☐ Use a proper tow-rope – they are not expensive. The vehicle being towed must display an 'ON TOW' sign in its rear window.

☐ Always turn the ignition key to the 'on' position when the vehicle is being towed, so that the steering lock is released, and so that the direction indicator and brake lights will work.

☐ The towing eye is supplied in the vehicle toolkit which is stored in the luggage compartment with the spare wheel (see "Wheel changing"). To fit the eye, unclip the access cover from the relevant bumper and screw the eye firmly into position

☐ Before being towed, release the handbrake and select neutral on the transmission.

☐ Note that greater-than-usual pedal pressure will be required to operate the brakes, since the vacuum servo unit is only operational with the engine running.

☐ On models with power steering, greater-than-usual steering effort will also be required.

☐ The driver of the car being towed must

keep the tow-rope taut at all times to avoid snatching.

☐ Make sure that both drivers know the route before setting off.

☐ Only drive at moderate speeds and keep the distance towed to a minimum. Drive smoothly and allow plenty of time for slowing down at junctions.

Caution: On models with automatic transmission, do not tow the car at speeds in excess of 45 mph (75 kmh) or for a distance of greater than 60 miles (100 km). If towing speed/distance are to exceed these limits, then the car must be towed with its front wheels off the ground.

Introduction

There are some very simple checks which need only take a few minutes to carry out, but which could save you a lot of inconvenience and expense.

These "Weekly checks" require no great skill or special tools, and the small amount of time they take to perform could prove to be very well spent, for example;

☐ Keeping an eye on tyre condition and pressures, will not only help to stop them wearing out prematurely, but could also save your life.

☐ Many breakdowns are caused by electrical problems. Battery-related faults are particularly common, and a quick check on a regular basis will often prevent the majority of these.

☐ If your car develops a brake fluid leak, the first time you might know about it is when your brakes don't work properly. Checking the level regularly will give advance warning of this kind of problem.

☐ If the oil or coolant levels run low, the cost of repairing any engine damage will be far greater than fixing the leak, for example.

Underbonnet check points

◀ **2.0 litre petrol (1.8 litre similar)**

A Engine oil level dipstick
B Engine oil filler cap
C Coolant expansion tank
D Brake fluid reservoir
E Screen washer fluid reservoir
F Battery
G Power steering fluid reservoir

◀ **1.9 litre diesel**

A Engine oil level dipstick
B Engine oil filler cap
C Coolant expansion tank
D Brake fluid reservoir
E Screen washer fluid reservoir
F Battery
G Power steering fluid reservoir

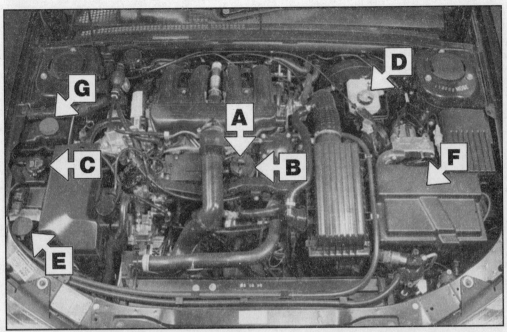

A Engine oil level dipstick
B Engine oil filler cap
C Coolant expansion tank
D Brake fluid reservoir
E Screen washer fluid reservoir
F Battery
G Power steering fluid reservoir

Engine oil level

Before you start

✔ Make sure that your car is on level ground.
✔ Check the oil level before the car is driven, or at least 5 minutes after the engine has been switched off.

HAYNES HiNT *If the oil level is checked immediately after driving the vehicle, some of the oil will remain in the upper engine components, resulting in an inaccurate reading on the dipstick!*

The correct oil

Modern engines place great demands on their oil. It is very important that the correct oil for your car is used (See "Lubricants, fluids and tyre pressures").

Car care

● If you have to add oil frequently, you should check whether you have any oil leaks. Place some clean paper under the car overnight, and check for stains in the morning. If there are no leaks, the engine may be burning oil.

● Always maintain the level between the upper and lower dipstick marks (see photo 3). If the level is too low severe engine damage may occur. Oil seal failure may result if the engine is overfilled by adding too much oil.

1 The dipstick is located at the front of the engine (see "Underbonnet check points" for exact location); the dipstick end is brightly coloured for easy identification. Withdraw the dipstick.

2 Using a clean rag or paper towel remove all oil from the dipstick. Insert the clean dipstick into the tube as far as it will go, then withdraw it again.

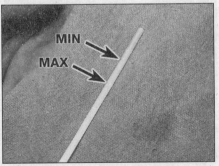

MIN
MAX

3 Note the oil level on the end of the dipstick, which should be between the upper ("MAX") mark and lower ("MIN") mark. Approximately 1.0 litre of oil will raise the level from the lower mark to the upper mark.

4 Oil is added through the filler cap. Unscrew the cap and top-up the level; a funnel may help to reduce spillage. Add the oil slowly, checking the level on the dipstick often. Don't overfill (see "Car care" left).

Coolant level

Warning: DO NOT attempt to remove the expansion tank pressure cap when the engine is hot, as there is a very great risk of scalding. Do not leave open containers of coolant about, as it is poisonous.

Car care

● Adding coolant should not be necessary on a regular basis. If frequent topping-up is required, it is likely there is a leak. Check the radiator, all hoses and joint faces for signs of staining or wetness, and rectify as necessary.

● It is important that antifreeze is used in the cooling system all year round, not just during the winter months. Don't top-up with water alone, as the antifreeze will become too diluted.

1 The coolant level must be checked with the engine cold. Remove the pressure cap (see Warning) from the expansion tank which is located on the right-hand side of the engine compartment.

2 The coolant level should be between the MAX and MIN marks on the expansion tank neck insert. The MIN mark is the thin bar at the base of the neck and the MAX mark is the slot approximately halfway up the neck.

3 If topping-up is necessary, remove the expansion tank cap and add a mixture of water and antifreeze to the expansion tank until the coolant level is between the level marks. Once the level is correct, securely refit the cap.

Brake fluid level

Warning:
● *Brake fluid can harm your eyes and will damage painted surfaces, so use extreme caution when handling and pouring it.*
● *Do not use fluid that has been standing open for some time, as it absorbs moisture from the air, which can cause a dangerous loss of braking effectiveness.*

HAYNES HINT • *Make sure that your car is on level ground.*
• *The fluid level in the reservoir will drop slightly as the brake pads wear down, but the fluid level must never be allowed to drop below the "MIN" mark.*

Safety first!

● If the reservoir requires repeated topping-up this is an indication of a fluid leak somewhere in the system, which should be investigated immediately.
● If a leak is suspected, the car should not be driven until the braking system has been checked. Never take any risks where brakes are concerned.

1 The upper (MAX) and lower (DANGER) fluid level markings are on the side of the reservoir, which is located in the left-hand rear corner of the engine compartment. The fluid level must always be kept between these two marks.

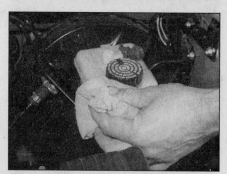

2 If topping-up is necessary, first wipe clean the area around the filler cap with a clean cloth, then unscrew the cap and remove it along with the rubber diaphragm.

3 Carefully add fluid, avoiding spilling it on the surrounding paintwork. Use only the specified hydraulic fluid. After filling the correct level, refit the cap and diaphragm and tighten it securely. Wipe off any spilt fluid.

Power steering fluid level

Before you start:
✔ Park the vehicle on level ground.
✔ Set the steering wheel straight-ahead.
✔ The engine should be turned off.

For the check to be accurate, the steering must not be turned once the engine has been stopped.

Safety first!
● The need for frequent topping-up indicates a leak, which should be investigated immediately.

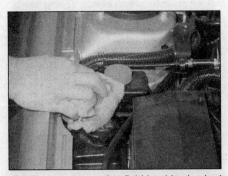

1 The power steering fluid level is checked in the fluid reservoir on the right-hand side of the engine compartment. With the engine cold, wipe clean the area around the reservoir cap.

2 Unscrew the reservoir cap, and check the fluid level is between the upper (MAXI) and lower (MINI) level indicators which are visible inside the reservoir.

3 Top-up the reservoir with the specified type of the fluid. Once the level is between the level marks, securely refit the reservoir cap. Do not overfill the reservoir.

Washer fluid level

Screenwash additives not only keep the winscreen clean during foul weather, they also prevent the washer system freezing in cold weather - which is when you are likely to need it most. Don't top up using plain water as the screenwash will become too diluted, and will freeze during cold weather. *On no account use coolant antifreeze in the washer system - this could discolour or damage paintwork.*

1 The washer fluid reservoir is located in the right-hand front corner of the engine compartment. To check the fluid level, remove the filler cap whilst holding a finger over the cap hole. The tube attached to the cap has level markings on it, and the fluid level can be clearly be seen through the clear tube.

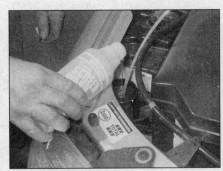

2 If topping-up is necessary, add water and a screenwash additive in the quantities recommended on the bottle.

Tyre condition and pressure

It is very important that tyres are in good condition, and at the correct pressure - having a tyre failure at any speed is highly dangerous. Tyre wear is influenced by driving style - harsh braking and acceleration, or fast cornering, will all produce more rapid tyre wear. As a general rule, the front tyres wear out faster than the rears. Interchanging the tyres from front to rear ("rotating" the tyres) may result in more even wear. However, if this is completely effective, you may have the expense of replacing all four tyres at once! Remove any nails or stones embedded in the tread before they penetrate the tyre to cause deflation. If removal of a nail does reveal that the tyre has been punctured, refit the nail so that its point of penetration is marked. Then immediately change the wheel, and have the tyre repaired by a tyre dealer.

Regularly check the tyres for damage in the form of cuts or bulges, especially in the sidewalls. Periodically remove the wheels, and clean any dirt or mud from the inside and outside surfaces. Examine the wheel rims for signs of rusting, corrosion or other damage. Light alloy wheels are easily damaged by "kerbing" whilst parking; steel wheels may also become dented or buckled. A new wheel is very often the only way to overcome severe damage.

New tyres should be balanced when they are fitted, but it may become necessary to re-balance them as they wear, or if the balance weights fitted to the wheel rim should fall off. Unbalanced tyres will wear more quickly, as will the steering and suspension components. Wheel imbalance is normally signified by vibration, particularly at a certain speed (typically around 50 mph). If this vibration is felt only through the steering, then it is likely that just the front wheels need balancing. If, however, the vibration is felt through the whole car, the rear wheels could be out of balance. Wheel balancing should be carried out by a tyre dealer or garage.

1 Tread Depth - visual check

The original tyres have tread wear safety bands (B), which will appear when the tread depth reaches approximately 1.6 mm. The band positions are indicated by a triangular mark on the tyre sidewall (A).

2 Tread Depth - manual check

Alternatively, tread wear can be monitored with a simple, inexpensive device known as a tread depth indicator gauge.

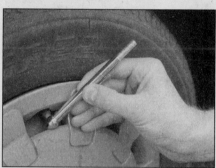

3 Tyre Pressure Check

Check the tyre pressures regularly with the tyres cold. Do not adjust the tyre pressures immediately after the vehicle has been used, or an inaccurate setting will result.

Tyre tread wear patterns

Shoulder Wear

Underinflation (wear on both sides)
Under-inflation will cause overheating of the tyre, because the tyre will flex too much, and the tread will not sit correctly on the road surface. This will cause a loss of grip and excessive wear, not to mention the danger of sudden tyre failure due to heat build-up.
Check and adjust pressures
Incorrect wheel camber (wear on one side)
Repair or renew suspension parts
Hard cornering
Reduce speed!

Centre Wear

Overinflation
Over-inflation will cause rapid wear of the centre part of the tyre tread, coupled with reduced grip, harsher ride, and the danger of shock damage occurring in the tyre casing.
Check and adjust pressures

If you sometimes have to inflate your car's tyres to the higher pressures specified for maximum load or sustained high speed, don't forget to reduce the pressures to normal afterwards.

Uneven Wear

Front tyres may wear unevenly as a result of wheel misalignment. Most tyre dealers and garages can check and adjust the wheel alignment (or "tracking") for a modest charge.
Incorrect camber or castor
Repair or renew suspension parts
Malfunctioning suspension
Repair or renew suspension parts
Unbalanced wheel
Balance tyres
Incorrect toe setting
Adjust front wheel alignment
Note: *The feathered edge of the tread which typifies toe wear is best checked by feel.*

Wiper blades

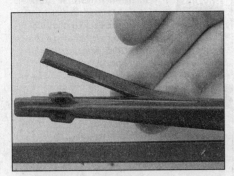

1 Check the condition of the wiper blades: if they are cracked or show signs of deterioration, or if the glass swept area is smeared, renew them. For maximum clarity of vision, wiper blades should be renewed annually.

2 To remove a windscreen wiper blade, lift the arm locking clip then raise the wiper arm slightly away from the screen.

3 Disengage the blade from the wiper arm and remove it from the vehicle, taking care not to allow the arm to damage the windscreen.

Battery

Caution: Before carrying out any work on the vehicle battery, read the precautions given in "Safety first" at the start of this manual.

✔ Make sure that the battery tray is in good condition, and that the clamp is tight. Corrosion on the tray, retaining clamp and the battery itself can be removed with a solution of water and baking soda. Thoroughly rinse all cleaned areas with water. Any metal parts damaged by corrosion should be covered with a zinc-based primer, then painted.

✔ Periodically (approximately every three months), check the charge condition of the battery as described in Chapter 5A.

✔ If the battery is flat, and you need to jump start your vehicle, see *Roadside Repairs*.

1 Remove the plastic cover to gain access to the battery, which is located at the front left-hand corner of the engine compartment. The exterior of the battery should be inspected periodically for damage such as a cracked case or cover.

2 Check the battery lead clamps for tightness to ensure good electrical connections, and check the leads for signs of damage.

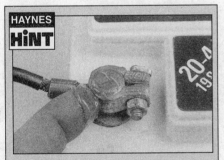

HAYNES HINT

Battery corrosion can be kept to a minimum by applying a layer of petroleum jelly to the clamps and terminals after they are reconnected.

3 If corrosion (white, fluffy deposits) is evident, remove the cables from the battery terminals, clean them with a small wire brush, then refit them. Automotive stores sell a tool for cleaning the battery post . . .

4 . . . as well as the battery cable clamps

Bulbs and fuses

✔ Check all external lights and the horn. Refer to the appropriate Sections of Chapter 12 for details if any of the circuits are found to be inoperative.

✔ Visually check all accessible wiring connectors, harnesses and retaining clips for security, and for signs of chafing or damage.

 If you need to check your brake lights and indicators unaided, back up to a wall or garage door and operate the lights. The reflected light should show if they are working properly.

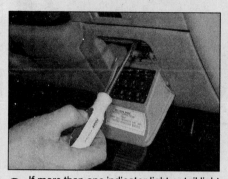

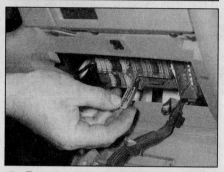

1 If a single indicator light, stop-light, sidelight or headlight has failed, it is likely that a bulb has blown, and will need to be replaced. Refer to Chapter 12 for details. If both stop-lights have failed, it is possible that the switch has failed (see Chapter 9).

2 If more than one indicator light or tail light has failed, it is likely that either a fuse has blown or that there is a fault in the circuit (see Chapter 12). The fuses are located behind the cover on the driver's side lower facia panel, release the retaining clip(s) and lower the cover. Additional fuses and relays are located in the left-hand side of the engine compartment fusebox.

3 To replace a blown fuse, simply pull it out and fit a new fuse of the correct rating (see Chapter 12). If the fuse blows again, it is important that you find out why - a complete checking procedure is given in Chapter 12.

Lubricants and fluids

Engine:

Petrol	Multigrade engine oil, viscosity SAE 5W/40 to 10W/40, to API SJ or SJ-EC and ACEA-A3.98
Diesel	Multigrade engine oil, viscosity SAE 5W/40 to 10W/40, to API CF or CF-EC and ACEA-B3.98
Cooling system	Procor 3000 antifreeze and soft water
Manual transmission	SAE 75W/80 gear oil
Automatic transmission	ESSO LT 71141 automatic transmission fluid only
Braking system	Hydraulic fluid to SAE J1703F or DOT 4
Power steering	Dexron type IID ATF

Choosing your engine oil

Engines need oil, not only to lubricate moving parts and minimise wear, but also to maximise power output and to improve fuel economy.

HOW ENGINE OIL WORKS

• Beating friction

Without oil, the moving surfaces inside your engine will rub together, heat up and melt, quickly causing the engine to seize. Engine oil creates a film which separates these moving parts, preventing wear and heat build-up.

• Cooling hot-spots

Temperatures inside the engine can exceed 1000° C. The engine oil circulates and acts as a coolant, transferring heat from the hot-spots to the sump.

• Cleaning the engine internally

Good quality engine oils clean the inside of your engine, collecting and dispersing combustion deposits and controlling them until they are trapped by the oil filter or flushed out at oil change.

OIL CARE - FOLLOW THE CODE

To handle and dispose of used engine oil safely, always:

OIL BANK LINE
0800 66 33 66
www.oilbankline.org.uk

• *Avoid skin contact with used engine oil. Repeated or prolonged contact can be harmful.*
• *Dispose of used oil and empty packs in a responsible manner in an authorised disposal site. Call 0800 663366 to find the one nearest to you. Never tip oil down drains or onto the ground.*

Tyre pressures

Note 1: *The tyre pressures for each specific vehicle are given on a label attached to the rear edge of the driver's door. On models with a space-saver spare wheel, a separate pressure is given for the spare tyre, and care must be taken not to misread the sticker; the space-saver wheel is inflated to a lot higher pressure than the standard tyres (typically 60 psi). On models with a space-saver spare wheel, note that the spare is for temporary use only; whilst the spare is fitted, the vehicle should not be driven at speeds in excess of 50 mph (80 kmh).*
Note 2: *Pressures on the sticker apply to original-equipment tyres listed, and may vary if any other make or type of tyre is fitted; check with the tyre manufacturer or supplier for correct pressures if necessary.*
Note 3: *Tyre pressures must always be checked with the tyres cold to ensure accuracy.*

Saloon models (typical)	Front (psi)	Rear (psi)
185/70 R14 tyres, 195/65 R15 tyres	33	33
205/60 R15 tyres	35	35
Estate models (typical)		
185/70 R14 tyres	35	36
195/65 R15 tyres	33	35
205/60 R15 tyres	35	35

Advanced driving

Many people see the words 'advanced driving' and believe that it won't interest them or that it is a style of driving beyond their own abilities. Nothing could be further from the truth. Advanced driving is straightforward safe, sensible driving - the sort of driving we should all do every time we get behind the wheel.

An average of 10 people are killed every day on UK roads and 870 more are injured, some seriously. Lives are ruined daily, usually because somebody did something stupid. Something like 95% of all accidents are due to human error, mostly driver failure. Sometimes we make genuine mistakes - everyone does. Sometimes we have lapses of concentration. Sometimes we deliberately take risks.

For many people, the process of 'learning to drive' doesn't go much further than learning how to pass the driving test because of a common belief that good drivers are made by 'experience'.

Learning to drive by 'experience' teaches three driving skills:

☐ Quick reactions. (Whoops, that was close!)
☐ Good handling skills. (Horn, swerve, brake, horn).
☐ Reliance on vehicle technology. (Great stuff this ABS, stop in no distance even in the wet...)

Drivers whose skills are 'experience based' generally have a lot of near misses and the odd accident. The results can be seen every day in our courts and our hospital casualty departments.

Advanced drivers have learnt to control the risks by controlling the position and speed of their vehicle. They avoid accidents and near misses, even if the drivers around them make mistakes.

The key skills of advanced driving are **concentration,** effective all-round **observation, anticipation** and **planning.** When **good vehicle handling** is added to these skills, all driving situations can be approached and negotiated in a safe, methodical way, leaving nothing to chance.

Concentration means applying your mind to safe driving, completely excluding anything that's not relevant. Driving is usually the most dangerous activity that most of us undertake in our daily routines. It deserves our full attention.

Observation means not just looking, but seeing and seeking out the information found in the driving environment.

Anticipation means asking yourself what is happening, what you can reasonably expect to happen and what could happen unexpectedly. (One of the commonest words used in compiling accident reports is 'suddenly'.)

Planning is the link between seeing something and taking the appropriate action. For many drivers, planning is the missing link.

If you want to become a safer and more skilful driver and you want to enjoy your driving more, contact the Institute of Advanced Motorists on 0208 994 4403 or write to IAM House, Chiswick High Road, London W4 4HS for an information pack.

Chapter 1 Part A:
Routine maintenance & servicing - petrol models

Contents

Degrees of difficulty

| Easy, suitable for novice with little experience | Fairly easy, suitable for beginner with some experience | Fairly difficult, suitable for competent DIY mechanic 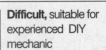 | Difficult, suitable for experienced DIY mechanic | Very difficult, suitable for expert DIY or professional |

Lubricants and fluids
Refer to "Weekly checks"

Capacities

Engine oil (including oil filter)
All engines:
Steel sump	4.75 litres
Aluminium sump	4.25 litres

Cooling system
All engines (approximate)	8.0 litres

Transmission
Manual transmission:
BE3	2.0 litres
ML5T	1.9 litres

Automatic transmission:
4 HP 20:
Drain and refill	3.0 litres
Total capacity (including torque converter)	8.3 litres

AL4:
Drain and refill	3.0 litres
Total capacity (including torque converter)	5.8 litres

Fuel tank	70 litres

Engine
Auxiliary drivebelt tension (for use with Peugeot electronic tool - see text):
New belt	120 SEEM units
Used belt	90 SEEM units

Cooling system
Antifreeze mixture:
50% antifreeze	Protection down to -37°C (5°F)
55% antifreeze	Protection down to -45°C (-22°F)

Note: Refer to antifreeze manufacturer for latest recommendations.

Ignition system
Spark plugs	Bosch FR 7 DE
Electrode gap	0.9 mm

Brakes
Brake pad friction material minimum thickness	2.0 mm
Brake shoe friction material minimum thickness	1.5 mm

Tyre pressures
See end of "Weekly checks"

Torque wrench settings

	Nm	lbf ft
Auxiliary drivebelt tensioner pulley assembly retaining bolts (models without air conditioning):		
1.6 and 1.8 litre engines	30	22
2.0 litre engines	20	15
Auxiliary drivebelt automatic tensioner assembly retaining bolts (models with air conditioning)	20	15
Manual transmission filler/level plug	20	15
Spark plugs	25	18
Roadwheel bolts	90	66

The maintenance intervals in this manual are provided with the assumption that you, not the dealer, will be carrying out the work. These are the minimum maintenance intervals recommended by us for vehicles driven daily. If you wish to keep your vehicle in peak condition at all times, you may wish to perform some of these procedures more often. We encourage frequent maintenance, because it enhances the efficiency, performance and resale value of your vehicle.

When the vehicle is new, it should be serviced by a factory-authorised dealer service department, in order to preserve the factory warranty.

Weekly, or every 250 miles (400 km)

☐ Refer to *"Weekly checks"*

Every 9000 miles (15 000 km) or 12 months - whichever comes first

☐ Renew the engine oil and filter (Section 3)
☐ Check the 4 HP 20 automatic transmission fluid level, and top up if necessary (Section 4)
☐ Check all underbonnet components and hoses for fluid leaks (Section 5)
☐ Renew the pollen filter (where fitted) (Section 6)
☐ Check the operation of the clutch (Section 7)
☐ Check the condition of the driveshaft rubber gaiters (Section 8)
☐ Check the steering and suspension components for condition and security (Section 9)
☐ Lubricate all hinges and locks (Section 10)

Every 18 000 miles (30 000 km)

In addition to all the items listed above, carry out the following:
☐ Check the condition of the front brake pads, and renew if necessary (Section 11)
☐ Check the condition of the rear brake pads and renew if necessary - rear disc brake models (Section 12)
☐ Check the operation of the handbrake (Section 13)
☐ Carry out a road test (Section 14)

Every 18 000 miles (30 000 km) or 2 years, whichever comes first

☐ Renew the 4 HP 20 automatic transmission fluid (Chapter 7B)

Every 36 000 miles (60 000 km)

In addition to all the items listed above, carry out the following:
☐ Renew the spark plugs (Section 15)
☐ Renew the air filter (Section 16)
☐ Renew the fuel filter (Section 17)
☐ Check the condition of the auxiliary drivebelt, and renew if necessary (Section 18)
☐ Check the manual transmission oil level, and top-up if necessary (Section 19)
☐ Check the AL4 automatic transmission fluid level, and top up if necessary (Section 4)
☐ Check the condition of the rear brake shoes and renew if necessary - rear drum brake models (Section 20)

Every 36 000 miles (60 000 km) or 2 years, whichever comes first

☐ Renew the brake fluid (Section 21)

Every 72 000 miles (120 000 km)

In addition to all the items listed above, carry out the following:
☐ Renew the timing belt (Section 22)

Note: It is strongly recommended that the timing belt renewal interval is halved to 36 000 miles (60 000 km) on vehicles which are subjected to intensive use, ie. mainly short journeys or a lot of stop-start driving. The actual belt renewal interval is therefore very much up to the individual owner, but bear in mind that severe engine damage will result if the belt breaks.

Every 72 000 miles (120 000 km) or 2 years, whichever comes first

☐ Renew the coolant (Section 23)

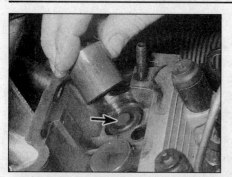

11.14a Lift out the follower and remove the shim (arrowed)

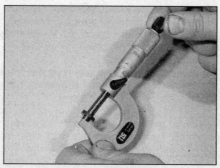

11.14b Using a micrometer to measure shim thickness

allow it to drop out as the follower is removed. Remove all traces of oil from the shim, and measure its thickness with a micrometer **(see illustrations)**. The shims usually carry thickness markings, but wear may have reduced the original thickness.

15 Refer to the clearance recorded for the valve concerned. If the clearance was more than that specified, the shim thickness must be *increased* by the difference recorded (2). If the clearance was less than that specified, the thickness of the shim must be *decreased* by the difference recorded (2).

16 Draw three more lines beneath each valve on the calculation paper, as shown in illustration 11.6. On line (4), note the measured thickness of the shim, then add or deduct the difference from line (2) to give the final shim thickness required on line (5).

17 Shims are available in thicknesses between 2.225 mm and 3.550 mm, in steps of 0.025 mm. Clean new shims before measuring or fitting them.

18 Repeat the procedure given in paragraphs 14 to 16 on the remaining valves, keeping each follower identified for position.

19 When reassembling, oil the shim, and fit it on the valve stem with the size marking face downwards. Oil the follower, and lower it onto the shim. Do not raise the follower after fitting, as the shim may become dislodged.

20 When all the followers are in position, complete with their shims, refit the camshaft as described in Section 10. Recheck the valve clearances before refitting the cylinder head cover, to make sure they are correct.

12 Cylinder head - removal and refitting

Removal

1 Disconnect the battery negative terminal.

2 Drain the cooling system as described in Chapter 1A.

3 Align the engine assembly/valve timing holes as described in Section 3, locking both the camshaft sprocket(s) and crankshaft pulley in position, and proceed as described under the relevant sub-heading. *Do not*

attempt to rotate the engine whilst the pins are in position.

1.6 litre models

4 Remove the cylinder head cover as described in Section 4.

5 Remove the air cleaner-to-throttle housing duct as described in Chapter 4A.

6 Note that the following text assumes that the cylinder head will be removed with both inlet and exhaust manifolds attached; this is easier, but makes it a bulky and heavy assembly to handle. If it is wished first to remove the manifolds, proceed as described in Chapter 4A.

7 Working as described in Chapter 4A, disconnect the exhaust system front pipe from the manifold. Where necessary, disconnect or release the lambda sensor wiring, so that it is not strained by the weight of the exhaust.

8 Carry out the following operations as described in Chapter 4A:

a) *Depressurise the fuel system, and disconnect the fuel feed and return hoses. Plug all openings, to prevent loss of fuel and the entry of dirt into the system.*

b) *Disconnect the accelerator cable.*

c) *Disconnect the vacuum servo unit vacuum hose, and all the other relevant vacuum/breather hoses, from the inlet manifold and throttle housing. Release the hoses from the retaining clips on the manifold.*

d) *Disconnect all the electrical connector plugs from the throttle housing.*

e) *Disconnect the wiring connectors from the fuel injectors, and free the wiring loom from the manifold.*

9 Slacken the retaining clips, and disconnect the coolant hoses from the thermostat housing (on the left-hand end of the cylinder head).

10 Depress the retaining clip(s), and disconnect the wiring connector(s) from the electrical switch(es) and/or sensor(s) which are screwed into the thermostat housing, or into the left-hand end of the cylinder head (as appropriate).

11 Slacken and remove the bolt securing the engine oil dipstick tube to the left-hand end of the cylinder head, and withdraw the tube from the cylinder block.

12 Disconnect the wiring connector from the ignition HT coil. If the cylinder head is to be dismantled for overhaul, remove the ignition HT coil as described in Chapter 5B. Note that the HT leads should be disconnected from the spark plugs instead of the coil, and the coil and leads removed as an assembly. If the cylinder numbers are not already marked on the HT leads, number each lead, to avoid the possibility of the leads being incorrectly connected on refitting.

13 Release the timing belt tensioner and disengage the timing belt from the camshaft sprocket as described in Section 8.

1.8 and 2.0 litre models

14 Remove the air cleaner assembly and intake ducting as described in Chapter 4A.

15 Remove the cylinder head cover as described in Section 4.

16 Remove the inlet manifold as described in Chapter 4A.

17 Working as described in Chapter 4A, disconnect the exhaust system front pipe from the manifold. Where necessary, disconnect or release the lambda sensor wiring, so that it is not strained by the weight of the exhaust.

18 Disconnect the radiator hose from the coolant outlet elbow.

19 Disconnect all remaining vacuum/breather hoses, and all electrical connector plugs from the cylinder head.

20 Release the timing belt tensioner and disengage the timing belt from the camshaft sprocket as described in Section 8.

All models

21 Working in the *reverse* of the sequence shown in illustration 12.38, progressively slacken the ten cylinder head bolts by half a turn at a time, until all bolts can be unscrewed by hand. Remove the bolts along with their washers, noting the correct location of the spacer fitted to the front left-hand bolt on 1.6 litre models.

22 With all the cylinder head bolts removed, the joint between the cylinder head and gasket and the cylinder block/crankcase must now be broken. On wet-liner engines, there is a risk of coolant and foreign matter leaking into the sump if the cylinder head is lifted carelessly. If care is not taken and the liners are moved, there is also a possibility of the bottom seals being disturbed, causing leakage after refitting the head.

23 To break the joint, obtain two L-shaped metal bars which fit into the cylinder head bolt holes, and gently "rock" the cylinder head free towards the front of the car. *Do not* try to swivel the head on the cylinder block/crankcase; it is located by dowels.

24 When the joint is broken, lift the cylinder head away. Seek assistance if possible, as it is a heavy assembly, especially if it is complete with the manifolds. Remove the gasket from the top of the block, noting the two locating dowels. If the locating dowels are a loose fit, remove them and store them with

12.25 Cylinder liners clamped in position using suitable bolts and large flat washers

the head for safe-keeping. Do not discard the gasket; it will be needed for identification purposes.

25 On wet-liner engines, *do not* attempt to turn the crankshaft with the cylinder head removed, otherwise the liners may be displaced. Operations that require the crankshaft to be turned (eg cleaning the piston crowns), should only be carried out once the cylinder liners are firmly clamped in position. In the absence of the special Peugeot liner clamps, the liners can be clamped in position as follows. Use large flat washers positioned underneath suitable-length bolts, or temporarily refit the original head bolts, with suitable spacers fitted to their shanks **(see illustration)**.

26 If the cylinder head is to be dismantled for overhaul, remove the camshaft(s) as described in Section 10, then refer to Part C of this Chapter.

Preparation for refitting

27 The mating faces of the cylinder head and cylinder block/crankcase must be perfectly clean before refitting the head. Use a hard plastic or wooden scraper to remove all traces of gasket and carbon; also clean the piston crowns. On wet-liner engines, refer to paragraph 25 before turning the engine. Take particular care on these models, as the soft aluminium alloy is easily damaged. On all models, make sure that the carbon is not allowed to enter the oil and water passages - this is particularly important for the lubrication system, as carbon could block the oil supply to the engine's components. Using adhesive tape and paper, seal the water, oil and bolt holes in the cylinder block/crankcase. To prevent carbon entering the gap between the pistons and bores, smear a little grease in the gap. After cleaning each piston, use a small brush to remove all traces of grease and carbon from the gap, then wipe away the remainder with a clean rag. Clean all the pistons in the same way.

28 Check the mating surfaces of the cylinder block/crankcase and the cylinder head for nicks, deep scratches and other damage. If slight, they may be removed carefully with a file, but if excessive, machining may be the only alternative to renewal. If warpage of the cylinder head gasket surface is suspected,

use a straight-edge to check it for distortion. Refer to Part C of this Chapter if necessary.

29 On wet-liner engines, check the cylinder liner protrusion as described in Part C of this Chapter.

30 When purchasing a new cylinder head gasket, it is essential that a gasket of the correct thickness is obtained. On some models only one thickness of gasket is available, so this is not a problem. However on other models, there are two different thicknesses available - the standard gasket which is fitted at the factory, and a slightly thicker "repair" gasket (+ 0.2 mm), for use once the head gasket face has been machined. If the cylinder head has been machined, it should have the letter "R" stamped adjacent to the No 3 exhaust port, and the gasket should also have the letter "R" stamped adjacent to No 3 cylinder on its front upper face. The gaskets can also be identified as described in the following paragraph, using the cut-outs on the left-hand end of the gasket.

31 With the gasket fitted the correct way up on the cylinder block, there will be either a single hole, or a series of holes, punched in the tab on the left-hand end of the gasket. The standard (1.2 mm) gasket has only one hole punched in it; the slightly thicker (1.4 mm) gasket has either two or three holes punched in it, depending on its manufacturer. Identify the gasket type, and ensure that the new gasket obtained is of the correct thickness. Note that modifications to the cylinder head gasket material, type, and manufacturer are constantly taking place; seek the advice of a Peugeot dealer as to the latest recommendations.

32 Check the condition of the cylinder head bolts, and particularly their threads, whenever they are removed. Wash the bolts in a suitable solvent, and wipe them dry. Check each bolt for any sign of visible wear or damage, renewing them if necessary. Measure the length of each bolt (without the washer fitted) from the underside of its head to the end of the bolt. If all bolts are less than 176.5 mm on 1.6 litre models, less than 160 mm on 1.8 litre models, and less than 112 mm on 2.0 litre models, they may be re-used. However, if any one bolt is longer than the specified length, *all* of the bolts should be renewed as a complete set. Considering the stress which the cylinder head bolts are under, it is highly recommended that they are renewed, regardless of their apparent condition.

Refitting

33 Wipe clean the mating surfaces of the cylinder head and cylinder block/crankcase. Check that the two locating dowels are in position at each end of the cylinder block/crankcase surface. Where applicable, remove the cylinder liner clamps.

34 Position a new gasket on the cylinder block/crankcase surface, ensuring that its identification holes or the projecting tongue are at the left-hand end of the gasket.

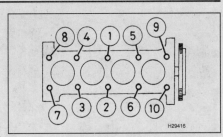

12.38 Cylinder head bolt tightening sequence

1.6 litre models

35 Check that the crankshaft pulley and camshaft sprocket are still locked in position with their respective pins. With the aid of an assistant, carefully refit the cylinder head assembly to the block, aligning it with the locating dowels.

36 Apply a smear of grease to the threads, and to the underside of the heads, of the cylinder head bolts. Peugeot recommend the use of Molykote G Rapid Plus (available from your Peugeot dealer); in the absence of the specified grease, any good-quality high-melting-point grease may be used.

37 Carefully enter each bolt and washer into its relevant hole (*do not drop it in*) and screw it in finger-tight, not forgetting to fit the spacer to the front left-hand bolt.

38 Working progressively and in the sequence shown, tighten the cylinder head bolts to their Stage 1 torque setting, using a torque wrench and a suitable socket **(see illustration)**.

39 Once all the bolts have been tightened to their Stage 1 torque, fully slacken all the head bolts, working in the reverse of the tightening sequence. Once the bolts are loose, tighten all bolts to their Stage 2 specified torque setting, again following the specified sequence.

40 With all the bolts tightened to their Stage 2 setting, working again in the specified sequence, angle-tighten the bolts through the specified Stage 3 angle, using a socket and extension bar. It is recommended that an angle-measuring gauge is used during this stage of tightening, to ensure accuracy. If a gauge is not available, use white paint to make alignment marks between the bolt head and cylinder head prior to tightening; the marks can then be used to check that the bolt has rotated sufficiently.

41 Once the cylinder head bolts are correctly tightened, reconnect the wiring connector to the ignition HT coil. Otherwise, if the head was stripped for overhaul, refit the HT coil as described in Chapter 5B.

42 Fit the timing belt over the camshaft sprocket. Refit the mounting bracket to the end of the cylinder head, and securely tighten its retaining bolts. Refit the engine right-hand mounting bracket, and tighten its retaining nuts to the specified torque. The jack can then be removed from underneath the engine.

43 Refit the timing belt to the camshaft sprocket as described in Section 8, and tension the belt as described in Section 7.

44 The remainder of the refitting procedure is a reversal of removal, noting the following points:

a) *Ensure that all wiring is correctly routed, and that all connectors are securely reconnected to the correct components.*

b) *Ensure that the coolant hoses are correctly reconnected, and that their retaining clips are securely tightened.*

c) *Ensure that all vacuum/breather hoses are correctly reconnected.*

d) *Refit the cylinder head cover as described in Section 4.*

e) *Reconnect the exhaust system to the manifold, refit the air cleaner housing and ducts, and adjust the accelerator cable, as described in Chapter 4A. If the manifolds were removed, refit these as described in Chapter 4A.*

f) *On completion, refill the cooling system as described in Chapter 1A, and reconnect the battery.*

1.8 and 2.0 litre models

45 Refit the cylinder head as described above in paragraphs 35 to 37, ignoring the remark about the spacer fitted to the front left-hand bolt.

46 Working progressively and in the sequence shown in illustration 12.38, tighten the cylinder head bolts, to their Stage 1 torque setting.

47 Once all the bolts have been tightened to their Stage 1 torque setting, fully slacken all the head bolts, working in the reverse of the tightening sequence. Once the bolts are loose, tighten all bolts to their Stage 2 specified torque setting, again following the specified sequence.

48 With all the bolts tightened to their Stage 2 setting, working again in the specified sequence, angle-tighten the bolts through the specified Stage 3 angle, using a socket and extension bar. It is recommended that an angle-measuring gauge is used during this stage of tightening, to ensure accuracy. If a gauge is not available, use white paint to make alignment marks between the bolt head and cylinder head prior to tightening; the marks can then be used to check that the bolt has rotated sufficiently.

49 Refit the timing belt to the camshaft sprocket as described in Section 8, and tension the belt as described in Section 7.

50 The remainder of the refitting procedure is a reversal of removal, noting the points made in paragraph 44.

13 Sump - removal and refitting

Removal

1 Disconnect the battery negative terminal.
2 Chock the rear wheels, jack up the front of the vehicle and support it on axle stands.

3 Drain the engine oil as described in Chapter 1A, then clean and refit the engine oil drain plug, tightening it securely. If the engine is nearing its service interval when the oil and filter are due for renewal, it is recommended that the filter is also removed, and a new one fitted. After reassembly, the engine can then be refilled with fresh oil. Refer to Chapter 1A for further information.

4 Where necessary, disconnect the wiring connector from the oil temperature sender unit, which is screwed into the sump.

5 Remove the auxiliary drivebelt as described in Chapter 1A.

6 On models with air conditioning, where the compressor is located on the side of the sump, unbolt the compressor and position it clear of the sump. Support the weight of the compressor by tying it to the vehicle, to prevent any excess strain being placed on the compressor lines. *Do not* disconnect the refrigerant lines from the compressor (refer to the warnings given in Chapter 3).

7 Progressively slacken and remove all the sump retaining bolts. Since the sump bolts vary in length, remove each bolt in turn, and store it in its correct fitted order by pushing it through a clearly-marked cardboard template. This will avoid the possibility of installing the bolts in the wrong locations on refitting.

8 Break the joint by striking the sump with the palm of your hand. Lower the sump, and withdraw it from underneath the vehicle. Remove the gasket (where fitted), and discard it; a new one must be used on refitting. While the sump is removed, take the opportunity to check the oil pump pick-up/strainer for signs of clogging or splitting. If necessary, remove the pump as described in Section 14, and clean or renew the strainer.

9 On some models, a large spacer plate is fitted between the sump and the base of the cylinder block/crankcase. If this plate is fitted, undo the two retaining screws from diagonally-opposite corners of the plate. Remove the plate from the base of the engine, noting which way round it is fitted.

Refitting

10 Clean all traces of sealant/gasket from the mating surfaces of the cylinder block/crankcase and sump, then use a clean rag to wipe out the sump and the engine's interior.

11 Where a spacer plate is fitted, remove all traces of sealant/gasket from the spacer plate, then apply a thin coating of suitable sealant (see paragraph 14) to the plate upper mating surface. Offer up the plate to the base of the cylinder block/crankcase, and securely tighten its retaining screws.

12 On models where the sump was fitted without a gasket, ensure that the sump mating surfaces are clean and dry, then apply a thin coating of suitable sealant to the sump mating surface.

13 On models where the sump was fitted with a gasket, ensure that all traces of the old

gasket have been removed, and that the sump mating surfaces are clean and dry. Position the new gasket on the top of the sump, using a dab of grease to hold it in position.

14 Offer up the sump to the cylinder block/crankcase. Refit its retaining bolts, ensuring that each is screwed into its original location. Tighten the bolts evenly and progressively to the specified torque setting.

15 On models with air conditioning, refit the compressor to the side of the sump and tighten the bolts.

16 Refit the auxiliary drivebelt (see Chapter 1A) and the pressure regulator accumulator.

17 Reconnect the wiring connector to the oil temperature sensor (where fitted).

18 Lower the vehicle to the ground, then refill the engine with oil as described in Chapter 1A and reconnect the battery negative terminal.

14 Oil pump - removal, inspection and refitting

Removal

1 Remove the sump (see Section 13).
2 Undo the two retaining screws, and slide the sprocket cover off the front of the oil pump.
3 Slacken and remove the three bolts securing the oil pump to the base of the cylinder block/crankcase. Disengage the pump sprocket from the chain, and remove the oil pump **(see illustration)**. Where necessary, also remove the spacer plate which is fitted behind the oil pump.

Inspection

4 Examine the oil pump sprocket for signs of damage and wear, such as chipped or missing teeth. If the sprocket is worn, the pump assembly must be renewed, since the sprocket is not available separately. It is also recommended that the chain and drive sprocket, fitted to the crankshaft, be renewed at the same time. To renew the chain and drive sprocket, first remove the crankshaft timing belt sprocket as described in Section 8. Unbolt the oil seal carrier from the cylinder block. The sprocket, spacer (where fitted) and chain can

14.3 Removing the oil pump

14.5a Remove the oil pump cover retaining bolts . . .

14.5b . . . then lift off the cover and remove the spring . . .

14.5c . . . and the relief valve piston, noting which way round it is fitted

then be slid off the end of the crankshaft. Refer to Part C for further information.

5 Slacken and remove the bolts (along with the baffle plate, where fitted) securing the strainer cover to the pump body. Lift off the strainer cover, and take off the relief valve piston and spring, noting which way round they are fitted (see illustrations).

6 Examine the pump rotors and body for signs of wear ridges or scoring. If worn, the complete pump assembly must be renewed.

7 Examine the relief valve piston for signs of wear or damage, and renew if necessary. The condition of the relief valve spring can only be measured by comparing it with a new one; if there is any doubt about its condition, it should also be renewed. Both the piston and spring are available individually.

8 Thoroughly clean the oil pump strainer with a suitable solvent, and check it for signs of clogging or splitting. If the strainer is damaged, the strainer and cover assembly must be renewed.

9 Locate the relief valve spring and piston in the strainer cover. Refit the cover to the pump body, aligning the relief valve piston with its bore in the pump. Refit the baffle plate (where fitted) and the cover retaining bolts, and tighten them securely.

Refitting

10 Offer up the spacer plate (where fitted), then locate the pump sprocket with its drive chain. Seat the pump on the base of the cylinder block/crankcase. Refit the pump retaining bolts, and tighten them to the specified torque setting.

11 Where necessary, slide the sprocket cover into position on the pump. Refit its retaining bolts, tightening them securely.

12 Refit the sump as described in Section 13.

13 Before starting the engine, prime the oil pump as follows. Disconnect the fuel injector wiring connectors, then spin the engine on the starter until the oil pressure light goes out. Reconnect the injector wiring on completion.

15 Oil cooler - removal and refitting

Removal

1 Firmly apply the handbrake, then jack up the front of the vehicle and support it on axle stands.

2 Drain the cooling system as described in Chapter 1A. Alternatively, clamp the oil cooler coolant hoses directly above the cooler, and be prepared for some coolant loss as the hoses are disconnected.

3 Position a suitable container beneath the oil filter. Unscrew the filter using an oil filter removal tool if necessary, and drain the oil into the container. If the oil filter is damaged or distorted during removal, it must be renewed. Given the low cost of a new oil filter relative to the cost of repairing the damage which could result if a re-used filter springs a leak, it is probably a good idea to renew the filter in any case.

4 Release the hose clips, and disconnect the coolant hoses from the oil cooler.

5 Unscrew the oil cooler/oil filter mounting bolt from the cylinder block, and withdraw the cooler. Note the locating notch in the cooler flange, which fits over the lug on the cylinder block (see illustration). Discard the oil cooler sealing ring; a new one must be used on refitting.

15.5 Oil cooler/oil filter mounting bolt (A) and locating notch (B)

Refitting

6 Fit a new sealing ring to the recess in the rear of the cooler, then offer the cooler to the cylinder block.

7 Ensure that the locating notch in the cooler flange is correctly engaged with the lug on the cylinder block, then refit the mounting bolt and tighten it securely.

8 Fit the oil filter, then lower the vehicle to the ground. Top-up the engine oil level as described in "Weekly Checks".

9 Refill or top-up the cooling system as described in "Weekly Checks" (as applicable). Start the engine, and check the oil cooler for signs of leakage.

16 Crankshaft oil seals - renewal

Right-hand oil seal

1 Remove the crankshaft sprocket and (where fitted) spacer, referring to Section 8. Secure the timing belt clear of the working area, so that it cannot be contaminated with oil. Make a note of the correct fitted depth of the seal in its housing.

2 Punch or drill two small holes opposite each other in the seal. Screw a self-tapping screw into each, and pull on the screws with pliers to extract the seal. Alternatively, the seal can be levered out of position. Use a flat-bladed screwdriver, and take great care not to damage the crankshaft shoulder or seal housing.

3 Clean the seal housing, and polish off any burrs or raised edges, which may have caused the seal to fail in the first place.

4 Lubricate the lips of the new seal with clean engine oil, and carefully locate the seal on the end of the crankshaft. Note that its sealing lip must be facing inwards. Take care not to damage the seal lips during fitting.

5 Fit the new seal using a suitable tubular drift, such as a socket, which bears only on the hard outer edge of the seal. Tap the seal into position, to the same depth in the housing as the original was prior to removal.

6 Wash off any traces of oil, then refit the crankshaft sprocket as described in Section 8.

Left-hand oil seal

7 Remove the flywheel/driveplate as described in Section 17. Make a note of the correct fitted depth of the seal in its housing.
8 Punch or drill two small holes opposite each other in the seal. Screw a self-tapping screw into each, and pull on the screws with pliers to extract the seal.
9 Clean the seal housing, and polish off any burrs or raised edges, which may have caused the seal to fail in the first place.
10 Lubricate the lips of the new seal with clean engine oil, and carefully locate the seal on the end of the crankshaft.
11 Fit the new seal using a suitable tubular drift, which bears only on the hard outer edge of the seal. Drive the seal into position, to the same depth in the housing as the original was prior to removal.
12 Wash off any traces of oil, then refit the flywheel/driveplate as described in Section 17.

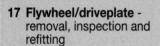

17 Flywheel/driveplate - removal, inspection and refitting

Removal

Flywheel (models with manual transmission)

1 Remove the transmission as described in Chapter 7A, then remove the clutch assembly as described in Chapter 6.
2 Prevent the flywheel from turning by locking the ring gear teeth with a similar arrangement to that shown in illustration 5.2. Alternatively, bolt a strap between the flywheel and the cylinder block/crankcase. *Do not* attempt to lock the flywheel in position using the crankshaft pulley locking pin described in Section 3.
3 Slacken and remove the flywheel retaining bolts, and remove the flywheel from the end of the crankshaft. Be careful not to drop it; it is heavy. If the flywheel locating dowel is a loose fit in the crankshaft end, remove it and store it with the flywheel for safe-keeping. Discard the flywheel bolts; new ones must be used on refitting.

Driveplate (models with automatic transmission)

4 Remove the transmission as described in Chapter 7B. Lock the driveplate as described in paragraph 2. Mark the relationship between the torque converter plate and the driveplate, and slacken all the driveplate retaining bolts.
5 Remove the retaining bolts, along with the torque converter plate and (where fitted) the two shims (one fitted on each side of the torque converter plate). Note that the shims are of different thickness, the thicker one

17.10 If the new flywheel bolt threads are not supplied with their threads pre-coated, apply a suitable locking compound to them . . .

being on the outside of the torque converter plate. Discard the driveplate retaining bolts; new ones must be used on refitting.
6 Remove the driveplate from the end of the crankshaft. If the locating dowel is a loose fit in the crankshaft end, remove it and store it with the driveplate for safe-keeping.

Inspection

7 On models with manual transmission, examine the flywheel for scoring of the clutch face, and for wear or chipping of the ring gear teeth. If the clutch face is scored, the flywheel may be surface-ground, but renewal is preferable. Seek the advice of a Peugeot dealer or engine reconditioning specialist to see if machining is possible. If the ring gear is worn or damaged, the flywheel must be renewed, as it is not possible to renew the ring gear separately.
8 On models with automatic transmission, check the torque converter driveplate carefully for signs of distortion. Look for any hairline cracks around the bolt holes or radiating outwards from the centre, and inspect the ring gear teeth for signs of wear or chipping. If any sign of wear or damage is found, the driveplate must be renewed.

Refitting

Flywheel (models with manual transmission)

9 Clean the mating surfaces of the flywheel and crankshaft. Remove any remaining locking compound from the threads of the crankshaft holes, using the correct-size tap, if available.

 If a suitable tap is not available, cut two slots into the threads of one of the old flywheel bolts and use the bolt to remove the locking compound from the threads.

10 If the new flywheel retaining bolts are not supplied with their threads already pre-coated, apply a suitable thread-locking compound to the threads of each bolt **(see illustration)**.

17.12 . . . then refit the flywheel, and tighten the bolts to the specified torque

11 Ensure the locating dowel is in position. Offer up the flywheel, locating it on the dowel, and fit the new retaining bolts.
12 Lock the flywheel using the method employed on dismantling, and tighten the retaining bolts to the specified torque **(see illustration)**.
13 Refit the clutch as described in Chapter 6. Remove the flywheel locking tool, and refit the transmission as described in Chapter 7A.

Driveplate (models with automatic transmission)

14 Carry out the operations described above in paragraphs 9 and 10, substituting "driveplate" for all references to the flywheel.
15 Locate the driveplate on its locating dowel.
16 Offer up the torque converter plate, with the thinner shim positioned behind the plate and the thicker shim on the outside, and align the marks made prior to removal.
17 Fit the new retaining bolts, then lock the driveplate using the method employed on dismantling. Tighten the retaining bolts to the specified torque wrench setting.
18 Remove the driveplate locking tool, and refit the transmission as described in Chapter 7B.

18 Engine/transmission mountings - inspection and renewal

Inspection

1 If improved access is required, raise the front of the car and support it securely on axle stands.
2 Check the mounting rubber to see if it is cracked, hardened or separated from the metal at any point; renew the mounting if any such damage or deterioration is evident.
3 Check that all the mounting's fasteners are securely tightened; use a torque wrench to check if possible.
4 Using a large screwdriver or a crowbar, check for wear in the mounting by carefully levering against it to check for free play. Where this is not possible, enlist the aid of an

assistant to move the engine/transmission unit back and forth, or from side to side, while you watch the mounting. While some free play is to be expected even from new components, excessive wear should be obvious. If excessive free play is found, check first that the fasteners are correctly secured, then renew any worn components as described below.

Renewal

Right-hand mounting -
1.6 litre models

5 Disconnect the battery negative terminal. Release all the relevant hoses and wiring from their retaining clips, and position clear of the mounting so that they do not hinder the removal procedure.
6 Place a jack beneath the engine, with a block of wood on the jack head. Raise the jack until it is supporting the weight of the engine.
7 Slacken and remove the three nuts securing the right-hand mounting bracket to the engine unit and the single nut securing the bracket to the mounting rubber.
8 Undo the bolt securing the upper engine movement limiter to the right-hand mounting bracket, and the four bolts securing the movement limiter mounting bracket to the body. Lift away the right-hand mounting bracket and the movement limiter assembly.
9 Lift the rubber buffer plate off the mounting rubber stud, then unscrew the mounting rubber from the body and remove it from the vehicle. If necessary, the mounting bracket can be unbolted and removed from the side of the cylinder head.
10 Check all components carefully for signs of wear or damage, and renew them where necessary.
11 On reassembly, screw the mounting rubber into the vehicle body, and tighten it to the specified torque. Refit the mounting bracket to the side of the cylinder head, apply a drop of locking compound to the retaining bolts and tighten them to the specified torque.
12 Refit the engine movement limiter assembly to the engine mounting bracket and to the body and tighten the bolts to the specified torque.
13 Refit the rubber buffer plate to the mounting rubber stud, and install the mounting bracket.
14 Tighten the mounting bracket retaining nuts to the specified torque setting.

15 Remove the jack from underneath the engine, and reconnect the battery negative terminal.

Right-hand mounting -
1.8 and 2.0 litre models

16 Disconnect the battery negative terminal. Release all the relevant hoses and wiring from their retaining clips. Place the hoses/wiring clear of the mounting so that the removal procedure is not hindered.
17 Place a jack beneath the engine, with a block of wood on the jack head. Raise the jack until it is supporting the weight of the engine.
18 Slacken and remove the two nuts and two bolts securing the right-hand engine/transmission mounting bracket to the engine. Remove the single nut securing the bracket to the mounting rubber.
19 Undo the bolt securing the upper engine movement limiter to the right-hand mounting bracket, and the four bolts securing the movement limiter mounting bracket to the body. Lift away the right-hand mounting bracket and the movement limiter assembly.
20 Lift the rubber buffer plate off the mounting rubber stud, then unscrew the mounting rubber from the body and remove it from the vehicle. If necessary, the mounting bracket can be unbolted and removed from the front of the cylinder block.
21 Check all components carefully for signs of wear or damage, and renew as necessary.
22 On reassembly, screw the mounting rubber into the vehicle body, and tighten it securely. Refit the mounting bracket to the front of the cylinder head, and securely tighten its retaining bolts.
23 Refit the engine movement limiter assembly to the engine mounting bracket and to the body and tighten the bolts to the specified torque.
24 Refit the rubber buffer plate to the mounting rubber stud, and install the mounting bracket.
25 Tighten the mounting bracket retaining nuts to the specified torque setting. Remove the jack from underneath the engine and reconnect the battery.

Left-hand mounting

26 Remove the air cleaner assembly, as described in Chapter 4A.
27 Place a jack beneath the transmission, with a block of wood on the jack head. Raise

the jack until it is supporting the weight of the transmission.
28 Slacken and remove the centre nut and washer from the left-hand mounting, then undo the nuts securing the mounting in position and remove it from the engine compartment.
29 If necessary, slide the spacer (where fitted) off the mounting stud, then unscrew the stud from the top of the transmission housing, and remove it along with its washer. If the mounting stud is tight, a universal stud extractor can be used to unscrew it.
30 Check all components carefully for signs of wear or damage, and renew as necessary.
31 Clean the threads of the mounting stud, and apply a coat of thread-locking compound to its threads. Refit the stud and washer to the top of the transmission, and tighten it to the specified torque setting.
32 Slide the spacer (where fitted) onto the mounting stud, then refit the rubber mounting. Tighten both the mounting-to-body bolts and the mounting centre nut to their specified torque settings, and remove the jack from underneath the transmission.
33 Refit the air cleaner assembly, then refit the battery as described in Chapter 5A.

Lower engine movement limiter

34 If not already done, chock the rear wheels, then jack up the front of the vehicle and support it securely on axle stands.
35 Unscrew and remove the bolt securing the movement limiter link to the driveshaft intermediate bearing housing.
36 Remove the bolt securing the link to the subframe. Withdraw the link.
37 To remove the intermediate bearing housing assembly it will first be necessary to remove the right-hand driveshaft as described in Chapter 8.
38 With the driveshaft removed, undo the retaining bolts and remove the bearing housing from the rear of the cylinder block.
39 Check carefully for signs of wear or damage on all components, and renew them where necessary.
40 On reassembly, fit the bearing housing assembly to the rear of the cylinder block, and tighten its retaining bolts securely. Refit the driveshaft as described in Chapter 8.
41 Refit the movement limiter link, and tighten both its bolts to their specified torque settings.
42 Lower the vehicle to the ground.

Chapter 2 Part B:
Diesel engine in-car repair procedures

Contents

Degrees of difficulty

Easy, suitable for novice with little experience	Fairly easy, suitable for beginner with some experience	Fairly difficult, suitable for competent DIY mechanic 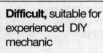	Difficult, suitable for experienced DIY mechanic	Very difficult, suitable for expert DIY or professional

Specifications

General

Designation:
1.9 litre (1905 cc engine)	XUD9
2.1 litre (2088 cc engine)	XUD11

Engine codes*:
1.9 litre engine	DHX (XUD9BTF/Y/L3)
2.1 litre engine	P8C (XUD11BTE/Y/L/L3)

Bore:
1.9 litre engine	83.00 mm
2.1 litre engine	85.00 mm

Stroke:
1.9 litre engine	88.00 mm
2.1 litre engine	92.00 mm

Direction of crankshaft rotation	Clockwise (viewed from the right-hand side of vehicle)
No 1 cylinder location	At the transmission end of block

Compression ratio:
1.9 litre engine	21.8 : 1
2.1 litre engine	21.5 : 1

*The engine code is stamped on a plate attached to the front of the cylinder block. This is the code most often used by Peugeot. The code given in brackets is the factory identification number, and is not often referred to by Peugeot or this manual.

Compression pressures (engine hot, at cranking speed)

Normal	25 to 30 bars (363 to 435 psi)
Minimum	18 bars (261 psi)
Maximum difference between any two cylinders	5 bars (73 psi)

Camshaft

Drive	Toothed belt

No of bearings:
1.9 litre engine	3
2.1 litre engine	5

Endfloat:
1.9 litre engine	0.07 to 0.16 mm
2.1 litre engine	Not available at time of writing

Valve clearances (1.9 litre engine)

Inlet .... 0.15 ± 0.08 mm
Exhaust .... 0.30 ± 0.08 mm

Lubrication system

Oil pump type .... Gear-type, chain-driven off the crankshaft right-hand end
Minimum oil pressure at 90°C .... 4.9 bars at 4000 rpm
Oil pressure warning switch operating pressure .... 0.8 bars

Torque wrench settings

	Nm	lbf ft
1.9 litre engines		
Big-end bearing cap nuts:		
Stage 1	20	15
Stage 2	Tighten through a further 70°	
Camshaft bearing cap nuts	20	15
Camshaft sprocket bolt	45	33
Crankshaft pulley bolt:		
Stage 1	40	30
Stage 2	Tighten through a further 51°	
Crankshaft front oil seal housing bolts	16	12
Cylinder head bolts:		
Stage 1	20	15
Stage 2	60	44
Stage 3	Tighten through a further 220°	
Cylinder head cover bolts	10	7
Flywheel/driveplate bolts	50	37
Injection pump sprocket puller retaining screws	10	7
Injection pump sprocket nut	50	37
Left-hand engine/transmission mounting:		
Mounting bracket-to-body	30	22
Rubber mounting-to-bracket bolts	30	22
Mounting stud-to-transmission	60	44
Centre nut	65	48
Lower engine movement limiter-to-driveshaft intermediate bearing housing	50	37
Lower engine movement limiter-to-subframe	85	62
Main bearing cap bolts:		
Stage 1	15	11
Stage 2	Tighten through a further 60°	
Oil pump mounting bolts	13	10
Piston oil jet spray tube bolt	10	7
Right-hand engine/transmission mounting:		
Mounting bracket-to-engine nuts	45	33
Mounting bracket-to-rubber mounting nut	45	33
Rubber mounting-to-body nut	40	29
Upper engine movement limiter bolts	50	37
Sump bolts	16	12
Timing belt cover bolts	8	6
Timing belt tensioner adjustment bolt	20	15
Timing belt tensioner pivot nut	20	15
2.1 litre engines		
Big-end bearing cap nuts:		
Stage 1	20	15
Stage 2	Tighten through a further 70°	
Camshaft carrier bolts	25	18
Camshaft sprocket bolt	50	37
Crankshaft front oil seal housing bolts	16	12
Crankshaft pulley bolt:		
Stage 1	40	30
Stage 2	Tighten through a further 60°	
Cylinder head cover bolts	8	6
Cylinder head bolts:		
Stage 1	70	52
Stage 2	Tighten through a further 150°	
Warm up engine and allow to cool for 3.5 hours. Slacken bolts, then tighten to:		
Stage 3	70	52
Stage 4	Tighten through a further 150°	

Torque wrench settings (continued)

	Nm	lbf ft
2.1 litre engines (continued)		
Flywheel/driveplate bolts	50	37
Injection pump sprocket puller retaining screws	10	7
Injection pump sprocket nut	50	37
Left-hand engine/transmission mounting:		
Mounting bracket-to-body	30	22
Rubber mounting-to-bracket bolts	30	22
Mounting stud-to-transmission	60	44
Centre nut	65	48
Lower engine movement limiter-to-driveshaft intermediate bearing		
housing	50	37
Lower engine movement limiter-to-subframe	85	62
Main bearing cap bolts:		
Stage 1	15	11
Stage 2	Tighten through a further 60°	
Oil pump mounting bolts	13	10
Piston oil jet spray tube bolt	10	7
Right-hand engine/transmission mounting:		
Mounting bracket-to-engine nuts	45	33
Mounting bracket-to-rubber mounting nut	45	33
Rubber mounting-to-body nut	40	29
Upper engine movement limiter bolts	50	37
Sump bolts	16	12
Timing belt idler pulley	37	27
Timing belt tensioner nut/bolt	10	7

1 General information

How to use this Chapter

This Part of Chapter 2 describes the repair procedures that can reasonably be carried out on the engine while it remains in the vehicle. If the engine has been removed from the vehicle and is being dismantled as described in Part C, any preliminary dismantling procedures can be ignored.

Note that, while it may be possible physically to overhaul items such as the piston/connecting rod assemblies while the engine is in the car, such tasks are not usually carried out as separate operations. Usually, several additional procedures are required (not to mention the cleaning of components and oilways); for this reason, all such tasks are classed as major overhaul procedures, and are described in Part C of this Chapter.

Part C describes the removal of the engine/transmission from the car, and the full overhaul procedures that can then be carried out.

XUD engine description

The engine is a turbocharged four-cylinder overhead camshaft design, mounted transversely, with the transmission mounted on the left-hand side.

An aluminium alloy cylinder head is fitted, incorporating eight valves on 1.9 litre models, and twelve valves on 2.1 litre versions. On 1.9 litre models, the valve clearances are adjusted by shims, positioned between the followers and the tip of the valve stem; on 2.1 litre models the valve clearances are self-adjusting by means of hydraulic tappets fitted to the cam followers.

The camshaft is supported by three bearings machined directly in the cylinder head on 1.9 litre models, and by five bearings within a separate carrier on 2.1 litre models. A toothed timing belt drives the camshaft, fuel injection pump and coolant pump.

The crankshaft runs in five main bearings of the usual shell type. Endfloat is controlled by thrustwashers either side of No 2 main bearing.

The pistons are selected to be of matching weight, and incorporate fully-floating gudgeon pins retained by circlips.

The oil pump is chain-driven from the front of the crankshaft. An oil cooler is fitted to all engines.

Throughout the manual, it is often necessary to identify the engines not only by their cubic capacity, but also by their engine code. The engine code consists of three letters (eg. DHX). The code is stamped on a plate attached to the front of the cylinder block.

Repair operations - precaution

Both the 1.9 and 2.1 litre engines are complex units with numerous accessories and ancillary components. The design of the 406 engine compartment is such that every conceivable space has been utilised, and access to virtually all of the engine components is extremely limited. In many cases, ancillary components will have to be removed, or moved to one side, and wiring, pipes and hoses will have to be disconnected or removed from various cable clips and support brackets.

When working on these engines, read through the entire procedure first, look at the car and engine at the same time, and establish whether you have the necessary tools, equipment, skill and patience to proceed. Allow considerable time for any operation, and be prepared for the unexpected. Any major work on these engines is not for the faint-hearted!

Because of the limited access, many of the photographs appearing in this Chapter were, by necessity, taken with the engine removed from the vehicle.

Repair operations possible with the engine in the vehicle

The following operations can be carried out without having to remove the engine from the vehicle:

1.9 litre models

a) Removal and refitting of the cylinder head.
b) Removal and refitting of the timing belt and sprockets.
c) Removal and refitting of the camshaft.
d) Removal and refitting of the sump.
e) Removal and refitting of the big-end bearings, connecting rods and pistons*.
f) Removal and refitting of the oil pump.
g) Renewal of the engine/transmission mountings.
h) Removal and refitting of the flywheel/driveplate.

*Although it is possible to remove these components with the engine in place, for reasons of access and cleanliness it is recommended that the engine is removed.

2.1 litre models

a) *Removal and refitting of the timing belt and sprockets.*

b) *Removal and refitting of the camshaft and hydraulic tappets.*

c) *Removal and refitting of the sump.*

d) *Removal and refitting of the oil pump.*

e) *Renewal of the engine/transmission mountings.*

f) *Removal and refitting of the flywheel/driveplate.*

Note: *On 2.1 litre models, access between the cylinder head and engine compartment bulkhead, and to the rear underside of the engine is so restricted that it is impossible to remove the cylinder head with the engine in the car. Cylinder head removal and refitting procedures are therefore contained in Part C, assuming that the engine/transmission has been removed from the vehicle.*

---

2 Compression and leakdown tests - description and interpretation

Compression test

Note: *A compression tester specifically designed for diesel engines must be used for this test.*

1 When engine performance is down, or if misfiring occurs which cannot be attributed to the fuel system, a compression test can provide diagnostic clues as to the engine's condition. If the test is performed regularly, it can give warning of trouble before any other symptoms become apparent.

2 A compression tester specifically intended for diesel engines must be used, because of the higher pressures involved. The tester is connected to an adapter which screws into the glow plug or injector hole. On these models, an adapter suitable for use in the injector holes will be required, due to the limited access to the glow plug holes **(see illustration)**. It is unlikely to be worthwhile buying such a tester for occasional use, but it may be possible to borrow or hire one - if not, have the test performed by a garage.

3 Unless specific instructions to the contrary

2.2 Performing a compression test

are supplied with the tester, observe the following points:

a) *The battery must be in a good state of charge, the air filter must be clean, and the engine should be at normal operating temperature.*

b) *All the injectors or glow plugs should be removed before starting the test. If removing the injectors, also remove the flame shield washers, otherwise they may be blown out.*

c) *On 1.9 litre models, the stop solenoid must be disconnected, to prevent the engine from running or fuel from being discharged. On 2.1 litre models it is normally sufficient to disconnect the fuel injection multi-function relay located in the ECU module box, but the advice of a dealer should be sought.*

4 There is no need to hold the accelerator pedal down during the test, because the diesel engine air inlet is not throttled.

5 The actual compression pressures measured are not so important as the balance between cylinders. Values are given in the "Specifications".

6 The cause of poor compression is less easy to establish on a diesel engine than on a petrol one. The effect of introducing oil into the cylinders ("wet" testing) is not conclusive, because there is a risk that the oil will sit in the swirl chamber or in the recess on the piston crown instead of passing to the rings. However, the following can be used as a rough guide to diagnosis.

7 All cylinders should produce very similar pressures; any difference greater than that specified indicates the existence of a fault. Note that the compression should build up quickly in a healthy engine; low compression on the first stroke, followed by gradually-increasing pressure on successive strokes, indicates worn piston rings. A low compression reading on the first stroke, which does not build up during successive strokes, indicates leaking valves or a blown head gasket (a cracked head could also be the cause). Deposits on the undersides of the valve heads can also cause low compression.

8 A low reading from two adjacent cylinders is almost certainly due to the head gasket having blown between them; the presence of coolant in the engine oil will confirm this.

9 If the compression reading is unusually high, the cylinder head surfaces, valves and pistons are probably coated with carbon deposits. If this is the case, the cylinder head should be removed and decarbonised (see Part C).

Leakdown test

10 A leakdown test measures the rate at which compressed air fed into the cylinder is lost. It is an alternative to a compression test, and in many ways it is better, since the escaping air provides easy identification of where pressure loss is occurring (piston rings, valves or head gasket).

11 The equipment needed for leakdown testing is unlikely to be available to the home mechanic. If poor compression is suspected, have the test performed by a suitably-equipped garage.

---

3 Engine assembly/valve timing holes - general information and usage

Note: *Do not attempt to rotate the engine whilst the crankshaft/camshaft/injection pump are locked in position. If the engine is to be left in this state for a long period of time, it is a good idea to place suitable warning notices inside the vehicle, and in the engine compartment. This will reduce the possibility of the engine being accidentally cranked on the starter motor, which is likely to cause damage with the locking pins in place.*

1 On all models, timing holes are drilled in the camshaft sprocket, injection pump sprocket and flywheel. The holes are used to align the crankshaft, camshaft and injection pump and to prevent the possibility of the valves contacting the pistons when refitting the cylinder head, or when refitting the timing belt. When the holes are aligned with their corresponding holes in the cylinder head and cylinder block (as appropriate), suitable diameter bolts/pins can be inserted to lock both the camshaft, injection pump and crankshaft in position, preventing them from rotating unnecessarily. Proceed as follows.

Note: *With the timing holes aligned, No 4 cylinder is at TDC on its compression stroke.*

2 Remove the upper timing belt covers as described in Section 6.

3 The crankshaft must now be turned until the bolt holes in the camshaft and injection pump sprockets (one hole in the camshaft sprocket, one or two holes in the injection pump sprocket) are aligned with the corresponding holes in the engine front plate. The crankshaft can be turned by using a spanner on the pulley bolt. To gain access to the pulley bolt, from underneath the front of the car, prise out the retaining clips and remove the screws, then withdraw the plastic wheel arch liner from the wing valance, to gain access to the crankshaft pulley bolt. Where necessary, unclip the coolant hoses from the bracket, to improve access further. The crankshaft can then be turned using a suitable socket and extension bar fitted to the pulley bolt. Note that the crankshaft must always be turned in a clockwise direction (viewed from the right-hand side of the vehicle).

4 Insert an 8 mm diameter rod or drill through the hole in the left-hand flange of the cylinder block by the starter motor; if necessary, carefully turn the crankshaft either way until the rod enters the timing hole in the flywheel/driveplate **(see illustrations)**. On 2.1 litre models, access is very restricted, and it may be easier to remove the starter motor (see Chapter 5A) to be able to locate the hole.

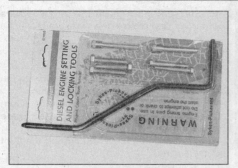

3.4a Suitable tools available for locking engine in position

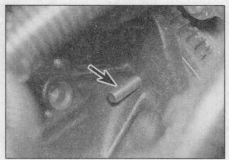

3.4b Rod (arrowed) inserted through cylinder block into timing hole in flywheel/driveplate

3.5a Bolt (arrowed) inserted through timing hole in camshaft sprocket on 1.9 litre models . . .

3.5b . . . and on 2.1 litre models

3.5c Two bolts (arrowed) inserted through timing holes in fuel injection pump sprocket on 1.9 litre models . . .

3.5d . . . and single bolt inserted through the pump sprocket on 2.1 litre models

5 Insert one 8 mm bolt through the hole in the camshaft sprocket, and two (1.9 litre models) or one (2.1 litre models) bolt(s) through the fuel injection pump sprocket, and screw them into the engine finger-tight **(see illustrations)**.

6 The crankshaft, camshaft and injection pump are now locked in position, preventing unnecessary rotation.

4 Cylinder head cover - removal and refitting

Removal

1.9 litre models

1 Disconnect the breather hose from the front of the cylinder head cover and remove the air cleaner inlet ducts as necessary for access.

2 Unscrew the securing bolt and remove the fuel hose bracket from the right-hand end of the cylinder head cover **(see illustration)**.

3 Disconnect the vacuum hose from the fast idle control diaphragm unit, then undo the two bolts and move the unit to one side.

4 Note the locations of any brackets secured by the three cylinder head cover retaining bolts, then unscrew the bolts. Recover the metal and fibre washers under each bolt **(see illustration)**.

5 Carefully move any hoses clear of the cylinder head cover.

6 Lift off the cover, and recover the rubber seal. Examine the seal for signs of damage and deterioration, and if necessary, renew it.

2.1 litre models

7 Remove the timing belt upper cover as described in Section 6.

8 Remove the inlet manifold upper part as described in Chapter 4B.

9 Disconnect the breather hose from the front of the cylinder head cover.

10 Note the locations of any brackets secured by the cylinder head cover retaining bolts, then unscrew the eleven bolts in a progressive spiral sequence.

11 Carefully move any hoses clear of the cylinder head cover.

12 Lift off the cover, and recover the rubber seal **(see illustration)**. Examine the seal for signs of damage and deterioration, and if necessary, renew it.

4.2 Removing the fuel hose bracket from the cylinder head cover

4.4 Remove the cylinder head cover retaining bolts and washers

4.12 Lifting off the cylinder head cover on 2.1 litre models

Refitting

13 Refitting is a reversal of removal, bearing in mind the following points:
   a) *Refit any brackets in their original positions noted before removal.*
   b) *Refit the inlet manifold (2.1 litre models) and air inlet ducts described in Chapter 4B.*

---

5 Crankshaft pulley - removal and refitting

1 Refer to Chapter 2A, Section 5. Although not strictly necessary, due to its tightening sequence, it is recommended that the retaining bolt is renewed whenever it is disturbed. **Note:** *If the engine is in the car and it proves impossible to hold on the brakes, remove the starter motor and use the locking tool shown to retain the flywheel* **(see illustration).**

---

6 Timing belt covers - removal and refitting

Removal - 1.9 litre models

Upper front cover

1 Slacken and remove the retaining screw and nut, and remove the front cover from the engine.

Upper rear cover

2 Remove the front cover as described in paragraph 1.

6.12 Undo the single retaining bolt (arrowed), located in the centre of the upper cover on 2.1 litre models

6.16 Removing the centre cover from the front of the injection pump on 2.1 litre models

---

5.1 Notched tool (arrowed) positioned on ring gear teeth to lock flywheel

3 Chock the rear wheels of the car, firmly apply the handbrake, then jack up the front of the car and support it on axle stands. Remove the right-hand front roadwheel and inner wheel arch liner.
4 Remove the auxiliary drivebelt as described in Chapter 1B.
5 From underneath the vehicle, slacken and remove the nuts and bolts securing the engine lower roll restrictor mounting to the subframe and engine, and remove the link.
6 Remove the right-hand engine mounting as described in Section 9.
7 Undo the securing clips and remove the air outlet hose from the turbocharger.
8 Undo the retaining bolts and remove the rear cover from the engine.

Lower cover

9 Remove the crankshaft pulley (see Section 5).
10 Remove both upper covers as described previously.

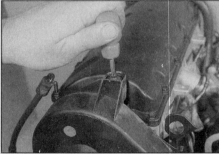
6.13 On 2.1 litre models, turn the fastener clockwise to release the cover locking peg

6.20 Removing the lower timing belt cover on 2.1 litre models

---

11 Slacken and remove the retaining nuts and bolts, and remove the lower cover.

Removal - 2.1 litre models

Upper cover

12 Undo the single retaining bolt, located in the centre of the cover **(see illustration).**
13 Turn the upper fastener a quarter of a turn clockwise to release the locking peg **(see illustration).**
14 Manipulate the cover up and off the front of the engine.

Centre cover

15 Remove the auxiliary drivebelt as described in Chapter 1B.
16 Undo the two bolts and remove the centre cover from the front of the injection pump **(see illustration).**

Lower cover

17 Remove the crankshaft pulley as described in Section 5.
18 Remove the right-hand engine mounting assembly as described in Section 19.
19 Remove both upper covers as described previously.
20 Slacken and remove the retaining bolts, and remove the lower cover **(see illustration).**

Refitting

21 Refitting is a reversal of the relevant removal procedure, ensuring that each cover section is correctly located, and that the cover retaining nuts and/or bolts are tightened to the specified torque.

---

7 Timing belt - removal, inspection, refitting and tensioning

---

General

1 The timing belt drives the camshaft, injection pump, and coolant pump from a toothed sprocket on the front of the crankshaft. If the belt breaks or slips in service, the pistons are likely to hit the valve heads, resulting in expensive damage.
2 The timing belt should be renewed at the specified intervals, or earlier if it is contaminated with oil, or at all noisy in operation (a "scraping" noise due to uneven wear).
3 If the timing belt is being removed, it is a wise precaution to check the condition of the coolant pump at the same time (check for signs of coolant leakage). This may avoid the need to remove the timing belt again at a later stage, should the coolant pump fail.

Removal

1.9 litre models

4 Align the engine assembly/valve timing holes as described in Section 3, and lock the camshaft sprocket, injection pump sprocket and flywheel in position. *Do not* attempt to rotate the engine whilst the pins are in position. Disconnect the battery negative terminal.

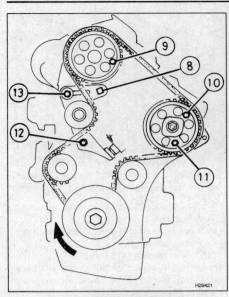

7.6 Removing the timing belt - 1.9 litre models

8 Square hole	12 Tensioner
9 Bolt	pivot nut
10 Bolt	13 Adjustment bolt
11 Bolt	

5 Remove the remaining timing belt covers as described in Section 6.

6 Remove the right-hand engine mounting and mounting bracket as described in Section 9, then loosen the timing belt tensioner pivot nut and adjustment bolt, then turn the tensioner bracket anti-clockwise to release the tension. Retighten the adjustment bolt to hold the tensioner in the released position. If available, use a 10 mm square drive extension in the hole provided, to turn the tensioner bracket against the spring tension **(see illustration)**.

7 Mark the timing belt with an arrow to indicate its running direction, if it is to be re-used. Remove the belt from the sprockets.

2.1 litre models

8 Align the engine assembly/valve timing holes as described in Section 3, and lock the camshaft sprocket, injection pump sprocket

7.11 On 2.1 litre models, slacken the timing belt tensioner locking bolt using a 5 mm Allen key

and flywheel in position. *Do not* attempt to rotate the engine whilst the pins are in position. Disconnect the battery negative terminal.

9 Remove the remaining timing belt covers as described in Section 6.

10 Slacken the timing belt tensioner pulley retaining nut, situated just to the left of the engine mounting carrier bracket.

11 Using a 5 mm Allen key inserted through the hole in the engine mounting carrier bracket, slacken the timing belt tensioner locking bolt **(see illustration)**.

12 Using a 10 mm socket or box spanner inserted through the same hole, retract the tensioner by turning its shaft clockwise to the extent of its travel **(see illustrations)**.

13 Mark the timing belt with an arrow to indicate its running direction, if it is to be re-used. Remove the belt from the sprockets **(see illustration)**.

Inspection

14 Check the timing belt carefully for any signs of uneven wear, split or oil contamination. Pay particular attention to the roots of the teeth. Renew it if there is the slightest doubt about its condition. If the engine is undergoing an overhaul, and has covered more than 36 000 miles (60 000 km) with the existing belt fitted, renew the belt as a matter of course, regardless of its apparent condition. The cost of a new belt is nothing compared with the cost of repairs, should the belt break in service. If signs of oil contamination are found, trace the source of the oil leak and rectify it. Wash down

the engine timing belt area and all related components, to remove all traces of oil. Check that the tensioner and idler pulley rotates freely, without any sign of roughness. If necessary, renew as described in Sections 9 and 10 (as applicable).

Refitting and tensioning

1.9 litre models

15 Commence refitting by ensuring that the 8 mm bolts are still fitted to the camshaft and fuel injection pump sprockets, and that the rod/drill is positioned in the timing hole in the flywheel.

16 Locate the timing belt on the crankshaft sprocket, making sure that, where applicable, the direction of rotation arrow is facing the correct way.

17 Engage the timing belt with the crankshaft sprocket, hold it in position, then feed the belt over the remaining sprockets in the following order:

  a) Idler roller.
  b) Fuel injection pump.
  c) Camshaft.
  d) Tensioner roller.
  e) Coolant pump.

18 Be careful not to kink or twist the belt. To ensure correct engagement, locate only a half-width on the injection pump sprocket before feeding the timing belt onto the camshaft sprocket, keeping the belt taut and fully engaged with the crankshaft sprocket. Locate the timing belt fully onto the sprockets.

19 Unscrew and remove the bolts from the camshaft and fuel injection pump sprockets and remove the rod/drill from the timing hole in the flywheel.

20 With the pivot nut loose, slacken the tensioner adjustment bolt while holding the bracket against the spring tension. Slowly release the bracket until the roller presses against the timing belt. Retighten the adjustment bolt and the pivot nut.

21 Rotate the crankshaft through two complete turns in the normal running direction (clockwise). **Do not** rotate the crankshaft backwards, as the timing belt must be kept tight between the crankshaft, fuel injection pump and camshaft sprockets.

7.12a Timing belt tensioner pulley retaining nut (A) and locking bolt (B) on 2.1 litre models

7.12b Timing belt tensioner arrangement on 2.1 litre models showing tensioner 10 mm shaft (arrowed)

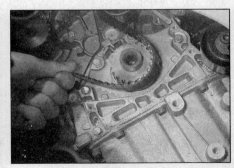

7.13 Removing the timing belt

22 Loosen the tensioner adjustment bolt and the pivot nut to allow the tensioner spring to push the roller against the timing belt, then tighten both the adjustment bolt and pivot nut to the specified torque.

23 Check that the timing holes are all correctly positioned by reinserting the sprocket locking bolts and the rod/drill in the flywheel timing hole, as described in Section 3. If the timing holes are not correctly positioned, the timing belt has been incorrectly fitted (possibly one tooth out on one of the sprockets) - in this case, repeat the refitting procedure from the beginning.

24 The remaining refitting procedure is a reversal of removal.

2.1 litre models

25 Commence refitting by ensuring that the 8 mm bolts are still fitted to the camshaft and fuel injection pump sprockets, and that the rod/drill is positioned in the timing hole in the flywheel.

26 Ensure that the timing belt tensioner is still retracted, then tighten the tensioner pulley retaining nut. Using the 10 mm socket or box spanner, release the tensioner by turning it anti-clockwise to the extent of its travel.

27 Locate the timing belt on the crankshaft sprocket, making sure that, where applicable, the direction of rotation arrow is facing the correct way.

28 Engage the timing belt with the crankshaft sprocket, hold it in position, then feed the belt over the remaining sprockets in the following order:

   a) Idler roller.
   b) Fuel injection pump.
   c) Camshaft.
   d) Coolant pump.
   e) Tensioner roller.

29 Be careful not to kink or twist the belt. To ensure correct engagement, locate only a half-width on the injection pump sprocket before feeding the timing belt onto the camshaft sprocket, keeping the belt taut and fully engaged with the crankshaft sprocket. Locate the timing belt fully onto the sprockets.

30 Slacken the tensioner pulley retaining nut to allow the tensioner to tension the belt.

31 Unscrew and remove the bolts from the camshaft and fuel injection pump sprockets and remove the rod/drill from the timing hole in the flywheel.

32 Rotate the crankshaft through two complete turns in the normal running direction (clockwise). **Do not** rotate the crankshaft backwards, as the timing belt must be kept tight between the crankshaft, fuel injection pump and camshaft sprockets.

33 Slacken the tensioner pulley retaining nut, then rotate the crankshaft through a further two complete turns in the normal running direction, stopping at the timing setting position.

34 Slacken the tensioner pulley retaining nut one turn to allow the tensioner to finally tension the belt. Tighten tensioner pulley retaining nut and the timing belt tensioner locking bolt to the specified torque.

TOOL TIP

A sprocket holding tool can be made from two lengths of steel strip bolted together to form a forked end. Bend the ends of the strip through 90° to form the fork "prongs"

35 Check that the timing holes are all correctly positioned by reinserting the sprocket locking bolts and the rod/drill in the flywheel timing hole, as described in Section 3. If the timing holes are not correctly positioned, the timing belt has been incorrectly fitted (possibly one tooth out on one of the sprockets) - in this case, repeat the refitting procedure from the beginning.

36 The remaining refitting procedure is a reversal of removal.

8 Timing belt sprockets - removal and refitting

Camshaft sprocket

Removal

1 Remove the timing belt (see Section 7).

2 Slacken the camshaft sprocket retaining bolt and remove it, along with its washer. To prevent the camshaft rotating as the bolt is slackened, a sprocket holding tool will be required **(see Tool Tip)**. *Do not* attempt to use the sprocket locking pin to prevent the sprocket from rotating whilst the bolt is slackened. Alternatively on 1.9 litre models, remove the cylinder head cover as described in Section 4. Prevent the camshaft from turning by holding it with a suitable spanner on the lug between Nos 3 and 4 camshaft lobes **(see illustration)**.

8.5 Withdrawing the camshaft sprocket

8.2 Holding the camshaft using a spanner on the lug between Nos 3 and 4 lobes

3 Remove the camshaft sprocket retaining bolt and washer.

4 Unscrew and remove the locking bolt from the camshaft sprocket.

5 With the retaining bolt removed, slide the sprocket off the end of the camshaft **(see illustration)**. Recover the Woodruff key from the end of the camshaft if it is loose. Examine the camshaft oil seal for signs of oil leakage and, if necessary, renew it (see Section 16).

Refitting

6 Refit the Woodruff key to the end of the camshaft, then refit the camshaft sprocket. Note that the sprocket will only fit one way round (with the protruding centre boss against the camshaft), as the end of the camshaft is tapered.

7 Refit the sprocket retaining bolt and washer. Tighten the bolt to the specified torque, preventing the camshaft from turning as during removal.

8 Where applicable, refit the cylinder head cover as described in Section 4.

9 Align the holes in the camshaft sprocket and the engine front plate, and refit the 8 mm bolt to lock the camshaft in position.

10 Refit it the timing belt as described in Section 7.

11 Refit the timing belt covers as described in Section 6.

Crankshaft sprocket

Removal

12 Remove the timing belt (see Section 7).

13 Slide the sprocket off the end of the crankshaft **(see illustration)**.

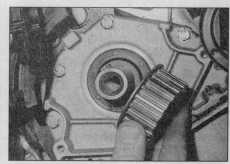

8.13 Withdrawing the crankshaft sprocket

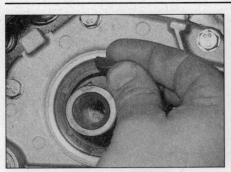

8.14 Removing the Woodruff key from the end of the crankshaft

8.21 Using a home-made tool to prevent the fuel injection pump sprocket turning

8.23 Home-made puller fitted to fuel injection pump sprocket

14 Remove the Woodruff key from the crankshaft, and store it with the sprocket for safe-keeping **(see illustration)**.
15 Examine the crankshaft oil seal for signs of oil leakage and, if necessary, renew it as described in Section 16.

Refitting

16 Refit the Woodruff key to the end of the crankshaft, then refit the crankshaft sprocket (with the flange nearest the cylinder block).
17 Refit the timing belt as described in Section 7.

Fuel injection pump sprocket

Removal

18 Remove the timing belt as described in Section 7.
19 Remove the 8 mm bolt(s) securing the fuel injection pump sprocket in the TDC position.
20 On certain models, the sprocket may be fitted with a built-in puller, which consists of a plate bolted to the sprocket. The plate contains a captive nut (the sprocket securing nut), which is screwed onto the fuel injection pump shaft. On models not fitted with the built-in puller, a suitable puller can be made up using a short length of bar, and two M7 bolts screwed into the holes provided in the sprocket.
21 The fuel injection pump shaft must be prevented from turning as the sprocket nut is unscrewed, and this can be achieved using a tool similar to that shown **(see illustration)**. Use the tool to hold the sprocket stationary by means of the holes in the sprocket.
22 On models with a built-in puller, unscrew the sprocket securing nut until the sprocket is freed from the taper on the pump shaft, then withdraw the sprocket. Recover the Woodruff key from the end of the pump shaft if it is loose. If desired, the puller assembly can be removed from the sprocket by removing the two securing screws and washers.
23 On models not fitted with a built-in puller, partially unscrew the sprocket securing nut, then fit the improvised puller, and tighten the two bolts (forcing the bar against the sprocket nut), until the sprocket is freed from the taper on the pump shaft **(see illustration)**. Withdraw the sprocket and recover the Woodruff key from the end of the pump shaft if it is loose. Remove the puller from the sprocket.

Refitting

24 Refit the Woodruff key to the pump shaft, ensuring that it is correctly located in its groove.
25 Where applicable, if the built-in puller assembly has been removed from the sprocket, refit it, and tighten the two securing screws securely ensuring that the washers are in place.
26 Refit the sprocket, then tighten the securing nut to the specified torque, preventing the pump shaft from turning as during removal.
27 Make sure that the 8 mm bolts are fitted to the camshaft and fuel injection pump sprockets, and that the rod/drill is positioned in the flywheel timing hole.
28 Fit the timing belt around the fuel injection pump sprocket, ensuring that the marks made on the belt and sprocket before removal are aligned.
29 Tension the timing belt as described in Section 7.
30 Refit the upper timing belt covers as described in Section 6.

Coolant pump sprocket

31 The coolant pump sprocket is integral with the pump, and cannot be removed.

---

9 Right-hand engine mount & timing belt tensioner (1.9 litre models) - removal and refitting

General

1 The timing belt tensioner is operated by a spring and plunger housed in the right-hand engine mounting bracket, which is bolted to the end face of the engine. The engine mounting is attached to the mounting on the body via the engine mounting-to-body bracket.

Right-hand engine mounting-to-body bracket

Removal

2 Before removing the bracket, the engine must be supported, preferably using a suitable hoist and lifting tackle attached to the lifting bracket at the right-hand end of the

engine. Alternatively, the engine can be supported using a trolley jack and interposed block of wood beneath the sump. In which case, be prepared for the engine to tilt backwards when the bracket is removed.
3 Release the retaining clips and position all the relevant hoses and cables clear of the engine mounting assembly and suspension top mounting.
4 Unscrew the three nuts securing the bracket to the engine mounting, and the single nut securing the bracket to the body, then lift off the bracket. *Note: On later models undo the bolt and nut securing the upper roll restrictor linkage.*

Refitting

5 Refitting is a reversal of removal. Tighten the retaining nuts and bolts to the specified torque.

Timing belt tensioner and right-hand engine mounting bracket

Note: A suitable tool will be required to retain the timing belt tensioner plunger during this operation.

Removal

6 Remove the engine mounting-to-body bracket as described previously in this Section, and remove the auxiliary drivebelt as described in Chapter 1B.
7 If not already done, support the engine with a trolley jack and interposed block of wood beneath the sump.
8 Where applicable, disconnect the hoist and lifting tackle supporting the engine from the right-hand lifting bracket (this is necessary because the lifting bracket is attached to the engine mounting bracket, and must be removed).
9 Unscrew the two retaining bolts and remove the engine lifting bracket.
10 Align the engine assembly/valve timing holes as described in Section 3, and lock the camshaft sprocket, injection pump sprocket and flywheel in position. *Do not* attempt to rotate the engine whilst the pins are in position.
11 Loosen the timing belt tensioner pivot nut and adjustment bolt, then turn the tensioner bracket anti-clockwise until the adjustment bolt is in the middle of the slot, and retighten

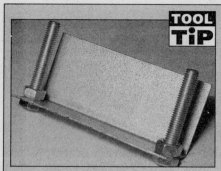

Fabricated tool for holding tensioner plunger in engine mounting bracket

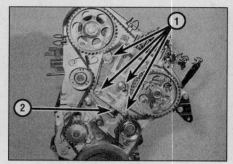

9.15a View of timing belt end of engine
1 *Engine mounting bracket retaining bolts*
2 *Timing belt tensioner plunger*

9.15b Tool in place to hold tensioner plunger in engine mounting bracket - timing belt removed for clarity

the adjustment bolt. If available, use a 10 mm square drive extension in the hole provided, to turn the tensioner bracket against the spring tension.

12 Mark the timing belt with an arrow to indicate its running direction, if it is to be re-used. Remove the belt from the sprockets.

13 A tool must now be obtained in order to hold the tensioner plunger in the engine mounting bracket.

14 The Peugeot tool is designed to slide in the two lower bolt holes of the mounting bracket. It should be straightforward to fabricate a similar tool out of sheet metal, and using 10 mm bolts and nuts instead of metal dowel rods **(see Tool Tip)**.

15 Unscrew the two lower engine mounting bracket bolts, then fit the special tool. Grease the inner surface of the tool, to prevent any damage to the end of the tensioner plunger **(see illustrations)**. Unscrew the pivot nut and adjustment bolt, and withdraw the tensioner assembly.

16 Remove the two remaining engine mounting bracket bolts, and withdraw the bracket.

17 Compress the tensioner plunger into the engine mounting bracket, remove the special tool, then withdraw the plunger and spring.

Refitting

18 Refitting is a reversal of removal, bearing in mind the following points:
a) *Tighten all fixings to the specified torque.*
b) *Refit and tension the timing belt as described in Section 7.*
c) *Refit and tighten the auxiliary drivebelt as described in Chapter 1B.*

10 Timing belt idler roller - removal and refitting

Removal

1.9 litre models

1 Remove the auxiliary drivebelt as described in Chapter 1B.
2 Align the engine assembly/valve timing

holes as described in Section 3, and lock the camshaft sprocket, injection pump sprocket and flywheel in position. *Do not* attempt to rotate the engine whilst the pins are in position.

3 Loosen the timing belt tensioner pivot nut and adjustment bolt, then turn the tensioner bracket anti-clockwise to release the tension, and retighten the adjustment bolt to hold the tensioner in the released position. If available, use a 10 mm square drive extension in the hole provided, to turn the tensioner bracket against spring pressure.

4 Unscrew the two bolts and the stud securing the idler roller assembly to the cylinder block, noting that the upper bolt also secures the engine mounting bracket.

5 Slightly loosen the remaining four engine mounting bolts, noting that the uppermost bolt is on the inside face of the engine front plate, and also secures the engine lifting bracket. Slide out the idler roller assembly.

2.1 litre models

6 Remove the timing belt as described in Section 7.

7 Unscrew the idler roller centre bolt and remove it from the engine.

Refitting

8 Refitting is a reversal of removal, bearing in mind the following points:
a) *Tighten all fixings to the specified torque.*
b) *Refit and/or tension the timing belt as described in Section 7.*
c) *Refit and tension the auxiliary drivebelt as described in Chapter 1B.*

11 Camshaft and followers - removal, inspection and refitting

Removal

1.9 litre models

1 Remove the cylinder head cover as described in Section 4.
2 Remove the camshaft sprocket as described in Section 8.

3 Remove the braking system vacuum pump as described in Chapter 9.

4 The camshaft bearing caps should be numbered from the flywheel end of the engine **(see illustration)**. If the caps are not already numbered, identify them, numbering them from the flywheel end of the engine, and making the marks on the manifold side.

5 Progressively unscrew the nuts, then remove the bearing caps.

6 Lift the camshaft from the cylinder head. Remove the oil seal from the timing belt end of the camshaft. Discard the seal, a new one should be used on refitting.

7 Obtain eight small, clean plastic containers, and number them 1 to 8; alternatively, divide a larger container into eight compartments. Using a rubber sucker, withdraw each follower in turn, and place it in its respective container. Do not interchange the cam followers, or the rate of wear will be much-increased. If necessary, also remove the shim from the top of the valve stem, and store it with its respective follower. Note that the shim may stick to the inside of the follower as it is withdrawn. If this happens, take care not to allow it to drop out as the follower is removed.

2.1 litre models

8 Remove the cylinder head cover as described in Section 4.

9 Remove the camshaft sprocket as described in Section 8.

10 Remove the braking system vacuum pump as described in Chapter 9. Recover the

11.4 Camshaft bearing cap identification mark (arrowed)

11.10 Recover the vacuum pump oil feed tube on 2.1 litre models

11.14 On 2.1 litre models, lift the camshaft carrier, complete with camshaft, upwards off the locating dowels

11.16 Undo the two bolts securing the camshaft thrust plate (arrowed)

11.18a Lift off the rockers . . .

11.18b . . . and their guides and place them in their respective containers

11.19 Remove the oil filter tube from its cylinder head location

vacuum pump oil feed tube from the end of the camshaft **(see illustration)**.

11 Refer to Chapter 4B and remove the fuel supply and leak-off pipes from the fuel injectors.

12 Disconnect the oil return hose from the front of the camshaft carrier.

13 Working in a spiral sequence, progressive slacken and remove the sixteen camshaft carrier retaining bolts.

14 Lift the camshaft carrier, complete with camshaft, upwards off the locating dowels **(see illustration)**.

15 Extract the oil seal from the end of the camshaft carrier.

16 Undo the two bolts securing the camshaft thrust plate, and carefully slide the camshaft out of the carrier **(see illustration)**.

17 Obtain twelve clean plastic containers, and number them inlet 1 to 8, and exhaust 1 to 4; alternatively, divide a larger container into twelve compartments.

18 Lift off the rockers and their guides and place them in their respective containers **(see illustrations)**. Withdraw each hydraulic tappet in turn, and place it in its respective container. Do not interchange the tappets, or the rate of wear will be much-increased.

19 Remove the oil filter tube from its location in the cylinder head **(see illustration)**.

Inspection

20 Examine the camshaft bearing surfaces and cam lobes for signs of wear ridges and scoring. Renew the camshaft if any of these conditions are apparent. Examine the condition of the bearing surfaces, both on the camshaft journals and in the cylinder head/camshaft carrier/bearing caps. If the bearing surfaces are worn excessively, the cylinder head/camshaft carrier will need to be renewed.

21 Examine the cam follower/tappet bearing surfaces which contact the camshaft lobes or rockers for wear ridges and scoring. Renew any component on which these conditions are apparent. If a follower/tappet bearing surface is badly scored, also examine the corresponding rocker or lobe on the camshaft for wear, as it is likely that both will be worn. Renew worn components as necessary.

Refitting

1.9 litre models

22 Where removed, refit each shim to the top of its original valve stem. *Do not* interchange the shims, as this will upset the valve clearances (see Section 12).

23 Liberally oil the cylinder head cam follower bores and the followers. Carefully refit the followers to the cylinder head, ensuring that each follower is refitted to its original bore. Some care will be required to enter the followers squarely into their bores.

24 Lubricate the cam lobes and bearing journals with clean engine oil of the specified grade.

25 Temporarily refit the sprocket to the end

of the camshaft and note the position of the timing hole in relation to the timing hole in the cylinder head - the lobes of No 4 cylinder should be facing upwards. Remove the sprocket, then position the camshaft in the cylinder head passing it through the engine front plate and keeping No 4 cylinder lobes facing upwards. Ensure that the crankshaft is still locked in position (see Section 3).

26 Fit the centre bearing cap the correct way round as previously noted, then screw on the nuts and tighten them two or three turns.

27 Apply sealing compound to the end bearing caps on the areas shown **(see illustration)**. Fit them in the correct positions, and tighten the nuts two or three turns.

28 Tighten all the nuts progressively to the specified torque, making sure that the camshaft remains correctly positioned.

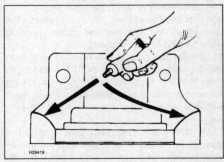

11.27 Apply sealing compound to the end camshaft bearing caps on the areas shown

11.29 Checking the camshaft endfloat using a feeler blade

11.37 Lubricate each hydraulic tappet and place it in its bore

11.38a Position the guides . . .

11.38b . . . and rockers over their respective valves

11.40a Lubricate the lips of a new camshaft oil seal and fit the seal to the camshaft carrier . . .

11.40b . . . tap the seal into position using a suitable socket

29 Check that the camshaft endfloat is as given in the Specifications, using a feeler blade. If not, the camshaft and/or the cylinder head must be renewed. To check the endfloat, push the camshaft fully towards one end of the cylinder head, and insert a feeler blade between the thrust faces of one of the camshaft lobes and a bearing cap (see illustration).

30 If the original camshaft is being refitted, and it is known that the valve clearances are correct, proceed to the next paragraph. Otherwise, check and adjust the valve clearances as described in Section 12. Note that, because the timing belt is still disconnected at this stage, the crankshaft *must* be turned one quarter-turn (either way) from the TDC position, so that all the pistons are halfway down the cylinders. This will prevent the valves striking the pistons when the camshaft is rotated. Remove the rod/drill from the flywheel timing hole, and release the timing belt from the injection pump sprocket while turning the crankshaft.

31 Smear the lips of the new oil seal with clean engine oil and fit it onto the camshaft end, making sure its sealing lip is facing inwards. Press the oil seal in until it is flush with the end face of the camshaft bearing cap.

32 If the crankshaft has been turned a quarter-turn from TDC to prevent the valves from hitting the pistons, turn it back by the same amount so that pistons 1 and 4 are again at TDC. Do not turn the engine more

than a quarter-turn, otherwise pistons 2 and 3 will pass their TDC positions, and will strike the valves.

33 Refit the rod/drill to the flywheel timing hole.

34 Refit the camshaft sprocket as described in Section 8.

35 Refit the cylinder head cover as described in Section 4.

2.1 litre models

36 Liberally lubricate the camshaft and the camshaft bearing journals in the carrier and slide the camshaft into the carrier. Refit the thrust plate and secure with the two bolts.

37 Liberally lubricate each hydraulic tappet and place it in its respective bore (see illustration).

38 Lubricate the guides and rockers and place all twelve over their respective valves (see illustrations). Ensure that the guides are fitted with their slots facing upwards, and that the rockers engage with the guide slots.

39 Insert a new oil filter tube to its bore in the cylinder head.

40 Liberally lubricate the lips of a new camshaft oil seal and fit the seal to the camshaft carrier. Tap the seal into position using a socket of suitable diameter, or the old seal (see illustrations).

41 Apply a bead of silicone sealant to the space between the groove and the outer edge of the camshaft carrier (see illustration). Ensure that the sealant is applied all around the two bolt holes at the timing belt end of the carrier.

42 Locate the assembled camshaft carrier on the cylinder head, taking care not to dislodge the rockers and guides.

43 Refit the retaining bolts, then working in a spiral sequence from the centre outward, progressively tighten the camshaft carrier retaining bolts to the specified torque.

44 Reconnect the oil return hose to the front of the carrier.

45 Refit the fuel supply and leak-off pipes to the fuel injectors with reference to Chapter 4B.

46 Ensure that the oil feed tube is in place, then refit the braking system vacuum pump as described in Chapter 9.

47 Refit the camshaft sprocket as described in Section 8.

48 Refit the cylinder head cover as described in Section 4.

11.41 Apply a bead of silicone sealant to the space between the groove and the outer edge of the camshaft carrier

12 Valve clearances (1.9 litre models) - checking and adjustment

Checking

1 The importance of having the valve clearances correctly adjusted cannot be overstressed, as they vitally affect the performance of the engine. Checking should not be regarded as a routine operation, however. It should only be necessary when the valve gear has become noisy, after engine overhaul, or when trying to trace the cause of power loss. The clearances are checked as follows. The engine must be cold for the check to be accurate.

2 Apply the handbrake, then jack up the front of the car and support it on axle stands. Remove the right-hand front roadwheel.

3 From underneath the front of the car, remove the wheel arch liner from the wing valance to gain access to the crankshaft sprocket bolt.

4 The engine can now be turned over using a suitable socket and extension bar fitted to the crankshaft pulley bolt. **Note:** *The engine will be easier to turn if the fuel injectors or glow plugs are removed.*

5 Remove the cylinder head cover as described in Section 4.

6 On a piece of paper, draw the outline of the engine with the cylinders numbered from the flywheel end. Show the position of each valve, together with the specified valve clearance. Above each valve, draw two lines for noting (1) the actual clearance and (2) the amount of adjustment required **(see illustration)**.

7 Turn the crankshaft until the inlet valve of No 1 cylinder (nearest the transmission) is fully closed, with the tip of the cam facing directly away from the bucket tappet.

8 Using feeler blades, measure the clearance

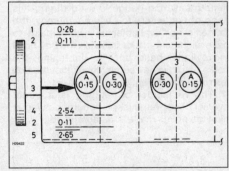

12.6 Example of valve shim thickness calculation

A   Inlet
E   Exhaust
1   Measured clearance
2   Difference between 1 and 3
3   Specified clearance
4   Thickness of shim fitted
5   Thickness of shim required

between the base of the cam and the bucket tappet. Record the clearance on line (1).

9 Repeat the measurement for the other seven valves, turning the crankshaft as necessary so that the cam lobe in question is always facing directly away from the relevant tappet.

10 Calculate the difference between each measured clearance and the desired value, and record it on line (2). Since the clearance is different for inlet and exhaust valves, make sure that you are aware which valve you are dealing with. The valve sequence from either end of the engine is:

In - Ex - Ex - In - In - Ex - Ex - In

11 If all the clearances are within tolerance, refit the cylinder head cover with reference to Section 4, and where applicable, lower the vehicle to the ground. If any clearance measured is outside the specified tolerance, adjustment must be carried out as described in the following paragraphs.

Adjustment

12 Remove the camshaft as described in Section 11.

13 Withdraw the first follower and its shim. Be careful that the shim does not fall out of the tappet. Clean the shim, and measure its thickness with a micrometer. The shims carry thickness markings, but wear may have reduced the original thickness, so be sure to check.

14 Refer to the clearance recorded for the valve concerned. If the clearance was more than that specified, the shim thickness must be increased by the difference recorded (2). If the clearance was less than that specified, the thickness of the shim must be decreased by the difference recorded (2).

15 Draw three more lines beneath each valve on the calculation paper, as shown in illustration 12.6. On line (4) note the measured thickness of the shim, then add or deduct the difference from line (2) to give the final shim thickness required on line (5).

16 Repeat the procedure given in paragraphs 13 to 15 on the remaining valves, keeping each tappet identified for position.

17 When reassembling, oil the shim and fit it into the valve retainer, with the size marking face downwards. Oil the follower and lower it onto the shim. Do not raise the follower after fitting, as the shim may become dislodged.

18 When all the followers are in position, complete with their shims, refit the camshaft as described in Section 11. Recheck the valve clearances before refitting the cylinder head cover, to make sure they are correct.

13 Cylinder head (1.9 litre models) - removal and refitting

Note 1: *This is an involved procedure, and it is suggested that the Section is read thoroughly before starting work. To aid refitting, make*

notes on the locations of all relevant brackets and the routing of hoses and cables before removal.

Note 2: *Due to the limited access, it is necessary to remove the engine/transmission from the car to remove and refit the cylinder head on 2.1 litre models. Refer to Part C for the full procedure.*

Removal

1 Disconnect the battery negative terminal

2 Drain the cooling system as described in Chapter 1B.

3 Remove the inlet and exhaust manifolds as described in Chapter 4B. Alternatively, remove the inlet manifold as described in Chapter 4B, then unscrew the exhaust manifold securing nuts, remove the spacers, and remove the manifold studs from the cylinder head (using a stud extractor or two nuts locked together). The exhaust manifold can then be left in place complete with the turbocharger.

4 Ensure that the manifold and turbocharger are adequately supported, taking particular care not to strain the turbocharger oil feed pipe.

5 Disconnect and remove the fuel injector leak-off hoses.

6 Disconnect the fuel pipes from the fuel injectors and the fuel injection pump, and remove the pipes as described in Chapter 4B.

7 Unscrew the securing nut and disconnect the feed wire from the relevant glow plug. Recover the washers.

8 Disconnect the coolant hose from the rear, left-hand end of the cylinder head.

9 Disconnect the small coolant hose from the front timing belt end of the cylinder head.

10 Unclip the fuel return hose from the brackets on the cylinder head, and move it to one side.

11 Disconnect the accelerator cable from the fuel injection pump (with reference to Chapter 4B if necessary), and move the cable clear of the cylinder head.

12 Remove the fuel filter/thermostat housing as described in Chapter 3.

13 Unscrew the nut or stud securing the coolant hose bracket and the engine lifting bracket to the transmission end of the cylinder head.

14 Remove the camshaft sprocket as described in Section 8.

15 Remove the timing belt tensioner and the right-hand engine mounting bracket as described in Section 9.

16 Remove the timing belt idler roller as described in Section 10.

17. Remove the bolt securing the engine front plate to the fuel injection pump mounting bracket.

18 Remove the nut and bolt securing the engine front plate and the alternator mounting bracket to the fuel injection pump mounting bracket, then remove the engine front plate.

19 Progressively unscrew the cylinder head bolts, in the reverse order to that shown in

Chapter 4 Part A:
Fuel and exhaust system - petrol models

Contents

Degrees of difficulty

Easy, suitable for novice with little experience		Fairly easy, suitable for beginner with some experience		Fairly difficult, suitable for competent DIY mechanic		Difficult, suitable for experienced DIY mechanic		Very difficult, suitable for expert DIY or professional	❧

Specifications

System type
1.6 litre models .... Magneti Marelli 8P
1.8 litre models .... Bosch Motronic MP5.1.1
2.0 litre models .... Bosch Motronic MP5.1.1 or MP5.2

Fuel system data
Fuel pump type .... Electric, immersed in tank
Fuel pump regulated constant pressure (at specified idle speed):
  Bosch system .... 3.0 ± 0.2 bars
  Magneti Marelli system .... 2.5 ± 0.2 bars
Specified idle speed .... 850 ± 50 rpm (not adjustable - controlled by ECU)
Idle mixture CO content .... Less than 0.4 % (not adjustable- controlled by ECU)

Recommended fuel
Minimum octane rating .... 95 RON unleaded (UK unleaded premium). Leaded fuel must **not** be used on models equipped with a catalytic converter

Torque wrench settings

	Nm	lbf ft
Inlet manifold nuts	20	15
Exhaust manifold nuts	35	26

1 General information and precautions

The fuel supply system consists of a fuel tank (which is mounted under the rear of the car, with an electric fuel pump immersed in it), a fuel filter, fuel feed and return lines. The fuel pump supplies fuel to the fuel rail, which acts as a reservoir for the four fuel injectors which inject fuel into the inlet tracts. The fuel filter incorporated in the feed line from the pump to the fuel rail ensures that the fuel supplied to the injectors is clean.

Refer to Section 6 for further information on the operation of each fuel injection system. Throughout this Section, it is also occasionally necessary to identify vehicles by their engine codes rather than by engine capacity alone. Refer to the relevant Part of Chapter 2 for further information on engine code identification.

 Warning: Many of the procedures in this Chapter require the removal of fuel lines and connections, which may result in some fuel spillage. Before carrying out any operation on the fuel system, refer to the precautions given in 'Safety first!' at the beginning of this manual, and follow them implicitly. Petrol is a highly dangerous and volatile liquid, and the precautions necessary when handling it cannot be overstressed.

Note: *Residual pressure will remain in the fuel lines long after the vehicle was last used. When disconnecting any fuel line, first depressurise the fuel system (see Section 7).*

2 Air cleaner assembly and intake ducts - removal and refitting

Removal

1.6 litre models

1 Slacken the retaining clip(s) and disconnect the breather hose(s) from the side of the air cleaner-to-throttle housing duct. Slacken the duct retaining clips, then disconnect it from the air cleaner and throttle housing, and remove it from the vehicle. Where necessary, recover the rubber sealing ring from the throttle housing.

2 Release the two retaining clips, then slacken and remove the two retaining screws from the front of the cylinder head cover, and remove the air cleaner element cover from the head. Withdraw the air cleaner element.

3 To remove the inlet duct, undo the bolt securing the rear section of the duct to the end of the cylinder head, then slacken the retaining clip and disconnect the duct from the cylinder head cover. Undo the bolt securing the front of the duct to the crossmember and manoeuvre the duct out of the engine compartment.

2.4 Slacken the clip (arrowed) and disconnect the intake duct from the throttle housing

1.8 and 2.0 litre models

4 Slacken the retaining clips and disconnect the intake duct from the throttle housing and air cleaner housing lid **(see illustration)**.

5 Undo the screws securing the lid to the air cleaner housing body. Lift off the lid and take out the filter element.

6 Lift the housing body upward to disengage it from the lower locating lugs. On some models, as the housing is lifted up, it will be necessary to disengage a small plastic retaining tag at the front securing the housing to the cold air intake duct underneath.

7 To remove the cold air intake duct, undo the air cleaner housing mounting bracket bolts and withdraw the bracket. Release the cold air intake from the bracket as it is removed.

8 Release the other end of the cold air intake from its body attachments and manipulate the duct from the car.

Refitting

9 Refitting is a reversal of the removal procedure, ensuring that all hoses are properly reconnected, and that all ducts are correctly seated and securely held by their retaining clips.

3 Accelerator cable - removal, refitting and adjustment

Removal

1 Working in the engine compartment, free the accelerator inner cable from the cam on the throttle housing, then pull the outer cable out from its mounting bracket rubber grommet. Slide the flat washer off the end of the cable, and remove the spring clip **(see illustration)**.

2 Working back along the length of the cable, free it from any retaining clips or ties, noting its correct routing.

3 Working from inside the vehicle, open up the engine immobiliser key pad, then rotate the fastener through 90° and lower the fusebox cover. Disconnect the wiring connector from the key pad then slacken and

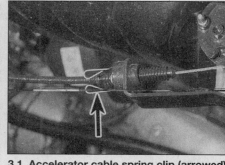

3.1 Accelerator cable spring clip (arrowed)

remove the retaining screws and remove the driver's side lower panel from the facia.

4 Release the retaining clip, and detach the inner cable from the top of the accelerator pedal.

5 Release the outer cable from its retainer on the pedal mounting bracket, then tie a length of string to the end of the cable.

6 Return to the engine compartment, release the cable grommet from the bulkhead and withdraw the cable. When the end of the cable appears, untie the string and leave it in position - it can then be used to draw the cable back into position on refitting.

Refitting

7 Tie the string to the end of the cable, then use the string to draw the cable into position through the bulkhead. Once the cable end is visible, untie the string, then clip the outer cable into its pedal bracket retainer, and clip the inner cable into position in the pedal end.

8 Check that the cable is securely retained, then refit the lower panel to the facia.

9 Within the engine compartment, ensure the outer cable is correctly seated in the bulkhead grommet, then work along the cable, securing it in position with the retaining clips and ties, and ensuring the cable is correctly routed.

10 Slide the flat washer onto the cable end, and refit the spring clip.

11 Pass the outer cable through the mounting bracket grommet on the throttle housing, and reconnect the inner cable to the throttle cam. Adjust the cable as described below.

Adjustment

12 Remove the spring clip from the accelerator outer cable. Ensuring that the throttle cam is fully against its stop, gently pull the cable out of its grommet until all free play is removed from the inner cable.

13 With the cable held in this position, refit the spring clip to the last exposed outer cable groove in front of the rubber grommet and washer. When the clip is refitted and the outer cable is released, there should be only a small amount of free play in the inner cable.

14 Have an assistant depress the accelerator pedal, and check that the throttle cam opens fully and returns smoothly to its stop.

4 Accelerator pedal - removal and refitting

Removal

1 Disconnect the accelerator cable from the pedal as described in Section 3.

2 According to type either remove the screws from the pedal pivot bush, or unscrew the nut (or remove the spring clip) from the end of the pedal pivot shaft. Where a pivot shaft and nut arrangement is used, unscrew the nut whilst retaining the pivot shaft with an open-ended spanner on the flats provided.

3 Remove the pedal, or pull the pedal and pivot shaft assembly from the support bracket according to type.

Refitting

4 Refitting is a reversal of the removal procedure, applying a little multi-purpose grease to the pedal pivot point. On completion, adjust the accelerator cable as described in Section 3.

5 Unleaded petrol - general information and usage

Note: *The information given in this Chapter is correct at the time of writing. If updated information is thought to be required, check with a Peugeot dealer. If travelling abroad, consult one of the motoring organisations (or a similar authority) for advice on the fuel available.*

1 The fuel recommended by Peugeot is given in the Specifications Section of this Chapter, followed by the equivalent petrol currently on sale in the UK.

2 All Peugeot 406 petrol models are designed to run on unleaded fuel with a minimum octane rating of 95 (RON). However not all models have a catalytic converter - 2.0 litre R6E2 engines and certain other export models not available in the UK, are not fitted with a catalytic converter. On models not fitted with a catalytic converter, it is permissible to use leaded fuel. All catalytic converter models must be run on unleaded fuel **only**. Under no circumstances should leaded fuel (UK "4-star") be used, as this may damage the converter.

3 Super unleaded petrol (98 RON) can also be used in all models if wished, though there is no advantage in doing so.

6 Fuel injection systems - general information

Note: *The fuel injection ECU is of the "self-learning" type, meaning that as it operates, it also monitors and stores the settings which*

give optimum engine performance under all operating conditions. When the battery is disconnected, these settings are lost and the ECU reverts to the base settings programmed into its memory at the factory. On restarting, this may lead to the engine running/idling roughly for a short while, until the ECU has re-learned the optimum settings. This process is best accomplished by taking the vehicle on a road test (for approximately 15 minutes), covering all engine speeds and loads, concentrating mainly in the 2,500 to 3,500 rpm region.

Magneti Marelli 8P and Bosch Motronic MP5.1.1 systems

1 The Magneti Marelli 8P system is fitted to 1.6 litre (BFZ) engines, and the Bosch Motronic MP5.1.1 system is fitted to 1.8 litre (LFY) engines and 2.0 litre (RFV) engines. Both systems are full engine management (fuel injection/ignition) systems incorporating both a closed-loop catalytic converter and evaporative emission control to comply with the very latest emission standards. Refer to Chapter 5 for information on the ignition side of the system; the fuel side of both systems is very similar and operates as follows.

2 The fuel pump (which is immersed in the fuel tank) supplies fuel from the tank to the fuel rail, via a filter mounted underneath the rear of the vehicle. Fuel supply pressure is controlled by the pressure regulator in the fuel rail. When the optimum operating pressure of the fuel system is exceeded, the regulator allows excess fuel to return to the tank.

3 The electrical control system consists of the ECU, along with the following sensors:

a) *Throttle potentiometer - informs the ECU of the throttle position, and the rate of throttle opening/closing.*

b) *Coolant temperature sensor - informs the ECU of engine temperature.*

c) *Inlet air temperature sensor - informs the ECU of the temperature of the air passing through the throttle housing.*

d) *Lambda (oxygen) sensor - informs the ECU of the oxygen content of the exhaust gases (explained in greater detail in Part C of this Chapter).*

e) *Crankshaft (RPM) sensor - informs the ECU of the crankshaft position and speed of rotation.*

f) *Manifold Absolute Pressure (MAP) sensor - informs the ECU of the load on the engine (expressed in terms of inlet manifold vacuum).*

g) *Vehicle speed sensor - informs the ECU of the vehicle speed.*

h) *Knock sensor - informs the ECU of pre-ignition (detonation) within the cylinders. Fitted to Motronic systems only.*

4 All the above signals are analysed by the ECU which selects the fuelling response appropriate to those values. The ECU controls the fuel injectors (varying the pulse width - the length of time the injectors are held open - to

provide a richer or weaker mixture, as appropriate). The mixture is constantly varied by the ECU, to provide the best setting for cranking, starting (with either a hot or cold engine), warm-up, idle, cruising and acceleration.

5 The ECU also has full control over the engine idle speed via a stepper motor fitted to the throttle housing. The motor has a pushrod controlling the opening of an air passage which bypasses the throttle valve. When the throttle valve is closed, the ECU controls the movement of the motor pushrod, which regulates the amount of air which flows through the throttle housing passage, so controlling the idle speed. The bypass passage is also used as an additional air supply during cold starting.

6 The ECU also controls the exhaust and evaporative emission control systems, which are described in detail in Part C of this Chapter.

7 An electric heating element is fitted to the throttle housing; the heater is supplied with current by the ECU, and warms the throttle housing on cold starts to prevent possible icing of the throttle valve.

8 If there is an abnormality in any of the readings obtained from either the coolant temperature sensor, the inlet air temperature sensor or the lambda sensor, the ECU enters its back-up mode. In this event, it ignores the abnormal sensor signal and assumes a pre-programmed value which will allow the engine to continue running (albeit at reduced efficiency). If the ECU enters this back-up mode, the warning light on the instrument panel will come on, and the relevant fault code will be stored in the ECU memory.

9 If the warning light comes on, the vehicle should be taken to a Peugeot dealer at the earliest opportunity. A complete test of the engine management system can then be carried out, using a special electronic diagnostic test unit which is simply plugged into the system's diagnostic connector located near the fusebox on the facia.

Bosch Motronic MP5.2 system

10 The Bosch Motronic MP5.2 engine management (fuel injection/ignition) system is fitted to 2.0 litre models without a catalytic converter (R6E engine). Refer to Chapter 5B for information on the ignition side of the system.

11 The system is similar in operation to the MP5.1.1 system described above, however on this system there is no lambda (oxygen) sensor and no evaporative emission control system.

12 At the time of writing there was very little information available on the MP5.2 system, but the component layout within the engine compartment is similar, and the majority of the procedures described for the other two systems will be applicable.

7 Fuel injection system - depressurisation

Note: *Refer to the warning note in Section 1 before proceeding.*

⚠️ *Warning: The following procedure will merely relieve the pressure in the fuel system - remember that fuel will still be present in the system components and take precautions accordingly before disconnecting any of them.*

1 The fuel system referred to in this Section is defined as the tank-mounted fuel pump, the fuel filter, the fuel injectors, the fuel rail and the pressure regulator, and the metal pipes and flexible hoses of the fuel lines between these components. All these contain fuel which will be under pressure while the engine is running, and/or while the ignition is switched on. The pressure will remain for some time after the ignition has been switched off, and must be relieved in a controlled fashion when any of these components are disturbed for servicing work.
2 Disconnect the battery negative terminal.
3 Place a container beneath the connection/ union to be disconnected, and have a large rag ready to soak up any escaping fuel not being caught by the container.
4 Slowly loosen the connection or union nut to avoid a sudden release of pressure, and position the rag around the connection, to catch any fuel spray which may be expelled. Once the pressure is released, disconnect the fuel line. Plug the pipe ends, to minimise fuel loss and prevent the entry of dirt into the fuel system.

8 Fuel pump - removal and refitting

Note: *Refer to the warning note in Section 1 before proceeding.*

Removal

1 Disconnect the battery negative terminal.
2 For access to the fuel pump, remove the rear seat as described in Chapter 11.
3 Using a screwdriver, carefully prise the plastic access cover from the floor to expose the fuel pump.
4 Disconnect the wiring connector from the top of the fuel pump **(see illustration)**.

 HAYNES HiNT *Tape the connector to the vehicle body in order to prevent it from disappearing behind the tank.*

5 Mark the hoses for identification purposes, then slacken the feed and return hose retaining clips. Where the crimped-type Peugeot hose clips are fitted, cut the clips and

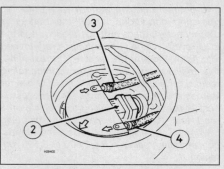

8.4 Fuel pump wiring connector (2), fuel feed hose (3) and return hose (4)

discard them; use standard worm-drive hose clips on refitting. Disconnect both hoses from the top of the pump, and plug the hose ends.
6 Noting the relationship of the notch and alignment pin on the tank and pump, and the arrow on the pump cover, unscrew the locking ring and remove it from the tank. Although Peugeot recommend the use of tool 1336 to unscrew the locking ring, this can be accomplished by using a screwdriver on the raised studs of the locking ring. Carefully tap the screwdriver to turn the ring anti-clockwise and release it. Once the locking ring is released, it will be necessary to position it to one side and lay it on the top of the fuel tank; the diameter of the ring is larger than that of the opening in the floor.
7 Lift the fuel pump assembly out of the fuel tank, taking great care not to damage the float arm, or to spill fuel inside the car.
8 Note that the fuel pump is only available as a complete assembly - no components are available separately.

Refitting

9 Carefully manoeuvre the pump assembly into the fuel tank, ensuring that the arrow on the pump cover and the notch and pin are in alignment as noted during removal. Refit the locking ring and securely tighten it using the same method as for removal..
10 Reconnect the feed and return hoses to the top of the fuel pump, using the marks made on removal to ensure that they are correctly reconnected, and securely tighten their retaining clips.

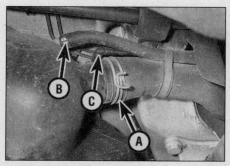

10.6 Fuel filler pipe (A), breather pipe (B) and vapour collection pipe (C) attachments at the fuel tank

11 Reconnect the pump wiring connector.
12 Reconnect the battery negative terminal and start the engine. Check the fuel pump feed and return hoses unions for signs of leakage.
13 If all is well, refit the plastic access cover. Refit the rear seat as described in Chapter 11.

9 Fuel gauge sender unit - removal and refitting

The fuel gauge sender unit is incorporated in the fuel pump - refer to Section 8.

10 Fuel tank - removal and refitting

Note: *Refer to the warning note in Section 1 before proceeding.*

Removal

1 Before removing the fuel tank, all fuel must be drained from the tank. Since a fuel tank drain plug is not provided, it is therefore preferable to carry out the removal operation when the tank is nearly empty. Before proceeding, disconnect the battery negative terminal and syphon or hand-pump the remaining fuel from the tank.
2 Disconnect the fuel pump wiring connector and the fuel feed and return hoses at the pump outlets as described in Section 8.
3 Jack up the rear of the car and support on axle stands.
4 Remove the exhaust system from the catalytic converter rearward (see Section 17).
5 Unbolt and remove the exhaust heat shield from the underbody.
6 Disconnect the fuel filler pipe, breather pipe and vapour collection pipe at their tank attachments **(see illustration)**. Where the crimped-type Peugeot hose clips are fitted, cut the clips and discard them; use standard worm-drive hose clips on refitting.
7 Disconnect the fuel supply and return pipes at their fuel tank connections **(see illustration)**.
8 Unclip the handbrake cable and move it aside as far as possible.

10.7 Fuel supply and return pipe connections at the fuel tank

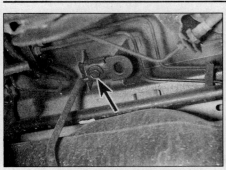

10.10 Fuel tank cradle mounting bolt (arrowed)

9 Place a trolley jack with an interposed block of wood beneath the tank, then raise the jack until it is supporting the weight of the tank. Position the jack so as to allow room to remove the fuel tank cradle.

10 Unscrew the fuel tank cradle mounting bolts and remove the cradle (see illustration).

11 Lower the fuel tank and remove it from under the car.

12 If the tank is contaminated with sediment or water, remove the fuel pump and swill the tank out with clean fuel. The tank is injection-moulded from a synthetic material - if seriously damaged, it should be renewed. However, in certain cases, it may be possible to have small leaks or minor damage repaired. Seek the advice of a specialist before attempting to repair the fuel tank.

Refitting

13 Refitting is the reverse of the removal procedure, noting the following points:

a) *When lifting the tank back into position, take care to ensure none of the hoses get trapped between the tank and body.*

b) *Ensure that all pipes and hoses are correctly routed, and securely held in position with their retaining clips.*

c) *On completion, refill the tank with a small amount of fuel, and check for signs of leakage prior to taking the vehicle out on the road.*

11 Fuel injection system - testing

Testing

1 If a fault appears in the fuel injection system (including the ignition system and engine management system as a whole), first ensure that all the system wiring connectors are securely connected and free of corrosion. Ensure that the fault is not due to poor maintenance; ie, check that the air cleaner filter element is clean, the spark plugs are in good condition and correctly gapped, the cylinder compression pressures are correct, and that the engine breather hoses are clear and undamaged, referring to the relevant Parts of Chapters 1, 2 and 5 for further information.

2 If these checks fail to reveal the cause of the problem, it is possible that a fault exists and a fault code may be stored in the system ECU. A diagnostic socket is incorporated in the engine management circuit, into which a fault code reader can be plugged. The socket is located next to the fusebox under the facia; to gain access, open up the engine immobiliser key pad, then rotate the fastener through 90° and lower the fusebox cover. If a fault code reader is available, follow the instructions supplied with the reader for connection and operation of the unit.

3 Although a fault code reader will identify the likely component or area in which a fault may lie, and can often provide the answer to a peculiar fault quickly, bear in mind that certain faults may not generate a fault code, and may not be detectable by the reader. In this instance (and even in cases where a fault code has been recorded) further testing to actually pinpoint the precise problem may be necessary, and additional test equipment will usually be required to do this. Tests of this nature are complex and outside the scope of this manual. For more detailed information about fuel injection system testing, Haynes Publishing produce a book in the Techbook series called "*Automotive Engine Management And Fuel Injection Systems Manual*". This incorporates information on all aspects of fuel injection and engine management diagnostics and testing.

Fault code read-out

4 Having accessed any stored fault codes by means of the fault code reader, it is now necessary to interpret the meaning of the codes. Given in the accompanying tables are the possible fuel/ignition fault codes for the Bosch Motronic 5.1.1 and Magneti Marelli 8P systems and the component or area in the system where the fault is likely to be found. Note that at the time of writing, no specific fault codes were available for the Motronic 5.2 system but they are likely to be similar to those for the 5.1.1 system.

Motronic 5.1.1 system

Fault code	Interpretation
11	End of diagnosis - no faults detected
12	Initiation of diagnosis
13	Inlet air temperature sensor
14	Coolant temperature sensor
15	Fuel pump relay
21	Throttle potentiometer sensor - idle contact
31	Idle switch
32	Mixture regulation - manifold leakage or low/high fuel pressure
33	Carbon canister solenoid valve - circuit fault
34	Carbon canister solenoid valve
35	Throttle position sensor - full load contact
41	Crankshaft position (RPM) sensor
42	Injectors
43	Knock regulation - knock sensor/engine temperature/spark plugs/etc.
44	Knock regulation - other
51	Lambda (oxygen) sensor - circuit fault
52	Mixture control - supply voltage/air/exhaust leak
53	Battery voltage
54	ECU - ECU supply/injection relay
56	Immobiliser system
71	No 1 injector control
72	No 2 injector control
73	No 3 injector control
74	No 4 injector control

Magneti Marelli 8P system

Fault code	Interpretation
11	End of diagnosis - no faults detected
12	Initiation of diagnosis
13	Inlet air temperature sensor
14	Coolant temperature sensor
15	Fuel pump control
21	Throttle position sensor
22	Idle speed stepper motor
27	Vehicle speed sensor
31	Lambda (oxygen) sensor - circuit fault
33	Manifold absolute pressure sensor
34	Carbon canister solenoid valve - circuit fault
41	Crankshaft position (RPM) sensor
42	Injector control
44	Knock sensor
45	Ignition coil control (coil one)
52	Lambda (oxygen) sensor - circuit fault
53	Battery voltage
54	ECU
57	Ignition coil control (coil one)

13.2 Fuel pressure regulator vacuum pipe (arrowed)

13.6 Fuel rail retaining bolts (arrowed)

13.13 Throttle potentiometer wiring connector (arrowed)

12 Throttle housing - removal and refitting

Removal

1 Disconnect the battery negative terminal.
2 Remove the air cleaner-to-throttle housing duct as described in Section 2.
3 Disconnect the accelerator inner cable from the throttle cam then withdraw the outer cable from the mounting bracket along with its flat washer and spring clip.
4 Depress the retaining clips, and disconnect the wiring connectors from the throttle potentiometer, the electric heating element, the inlet air temperature sensor and idle speed control stepper motor (as applicable).
5 Release the retaining clips (where fitted), and disconnect all the relevant vacuum and breather hoses from the throttle housing. Make identification marks on the hoses, to ensure that they are connected correctly on refitting.
6 Where necessary, undo the bolts or screws and release the accelerator cable bracket and housing support bracket.
7 Slacken and remove the retaining screws, and remove the throttle housing from the inlet manifold. Remove the O-ring from the manifold, and discard it - a new one must be used on refitting.

Refitting

8 Refitting is a reversal of the removal procedure, noting the following points:
  a) Fit a new O-ring to the manifold, then refit the throttle housing and securely tighten its retaining nuts or screws (as applicable).
  b) Ensure that all hoses are correctly reconnected and, where necessary, are securely held in position by the retaining clips.
  c) Ensure that all wiring is correctly routed, and that the connectors are securely reconnected.
  d) On completion, adjust the accelerator cable as described in Section 3.

13 Bosch Motronic MP5.1.1 system components - removal and refitting

Fuel rail and injectors

Note: *Refer to the warning note in Section 1 before proceeding.*
Note: *If a faulty injector is suspected, before condemning the injector, it is worth trying the effect of one of the proprietary injector-cleaning treatments.*
1 Disconnect the battery negative terminal.
2 Disconnect the vacuum pipe from the fuel pressure regulator **(see illustration)**.
3 Bearing in mind the information given in Section 7, slacken the retaining clips and disconnect the fuel feed and return hoses from the fuel rail. Where the original crimped-type Peugeot hose clips are still fitted, cut them and discard; replace them with standard worm-type hose clips on refitting.
4 Open the retaining clips and release the wiring and hoses running along the front of the fuel rail.
5 Depress the retaining tangs and disconnect the wiring connectors from the four injectors.
6 Slacken and remove the fuel rail retaining bolts then carefully ease the fuel rail and injector assembly out from the inlet manifold and remove it from the vehicle **(see illustration)**. Remove the O-rings from the end of each injector and discard them; they must be renewed whenever they are disturbed.
7 Slide out the retaining clip(s) and remove the relevant injector(s) from the fuel rail. Remove the upper O-ring from each disturbed injector and discard; all disturbed O-rings must be renewed.
8 Refitting is a reversal of the removal procedure, noting the following points.
  a) Fit new O-rings to all disturbed injector unions.
  b) Apply a smear of engine oil to the O-rings to aid installation then ease the injectors and fuel rail into position ensuring that none of the O-rings are displaced.
  c) On completion start the engine and check for fuel leaks.

Fuel pressure regulator

Note: *Refer to the warning note in Section 1 before proceeding.*
9 Disconnect the battery negative terminal.
10 Disconnect the vacuum pipe from the regulator.
11 Place a wad of rag over the regulator, to catch any fuel spray which may be released, then remove the retaining clip and ease the regulator out from the fuel rail.
12 Refitting is a reversal of the removal procedure. Examine the regulator seal for signs of damage or deterioration and renew if necessary.

Throttle potentiometer

13 Depress the retaining clip and disconnect the wiring connector from the throttle potentiometer located beneath the throttle housing **(see illustration)**.
14 Slacken and remove the two retaining screws then disengage the potentiometer from the throttle valve spindle and remove it from the vehicle.
15 Refitting is a reverse of the removal procedure ensuring that the potentiometer is correctly engaged with the throttle valve spindle.

Electronic Control Unit (ECU)

16 The ECU is located in a plastic box which is mounted on the right-hand front wheel arch.
17 Ensure that the ignition is switched off then lift off the ECU module box lid. On automatic transmission models there will be two ECU's in the box; the fuel injection/ignition ECU is the unit nearest to the engine.
18 Release the wiring connector by lifting the locking lever on top of the connector upwards. Lift the connector at the rear, disengage the tag at the front and carefully withdraw the connector from the ECU pins.
19 Lift the ECU upwards and remove it from its location.
20 Refitting is a reversal of removal. Note that if a new ECU has been fitted, the vehicle should be taken on an extensive road test. Initially, engine performance may be less than acceptable, but should improve as the ECU control circuitry adapts to the engine parameters.

Idle speed control stepper motor

21 The idle speed control stepper motor is located on the side of the throttle housing assembly.
22 Release the retaining clip, and disconnect the wiring connector from the motor.
23 Slacken and remove the two retaining screws, and withdraw the motor from the throttle housing.
24 Refitting is a reversal of the removal procedure.

Manifold absolute pressure (MAP) sensor

25 The MAP sensor is situated on the inlet manifold.
26 Disconnect the wiring connector and vacuum hose and remove the MAP sensor from the manifold.
27 Refitting is the reverse of the removal procedure.

Coolant temperature sensor

28 Refer to Chapter 3.

Inlet air temperature sensor

29 The inlet air temperature sensor is screwed into the underside of the inlet manifold.
30 Disconnect the wiring connector then unscrew the sensor and remove it from the vehicle.
31 Refitting is the reverse of removal.

Crankshaft (RPM) sensor

35 The crankshaft sensor is situated on the front face of the transmission clutch housing.
36 Trace the wiring back from the sensor to the wiring connector and disconnect it from the main harness.
37 Prise out the rubber grommet then undo the retaining bolt and withdraw the sensor from the transmission.
38 Refitting is the reverse of the removal procedure ensuring that the sensor retaining bolt is securely tightened and the grommet is correctly seated in the transmission housing.

Vehicle speed sensor

39 The vehicle speed sensor is an integral part of the transmission speedometer drive assembly. Refer to the relevant Part of Chapter 7 for removal and refitting details.

Knock sensor

40 The knock sensor is screwed into the front face of the cylinder block.
41 To gain access to the sensor, apply the handbrake then jack up the front of the car and support it on axle stands. Remove the splash guard from under the engine.
42 Trace the wiring back from the sensor to its wiring connector, and disconnect it from the main loom.
43 Undo the bolt securing the sensor to the cylinder block, and remove it from under the vehicle.
44 Refitting is a reversal of the removal procedure.

Fuel injection system relay unit

45 The relay unit is located in the ECU module box which is mounted on the right-hand front wheel arch.
46 Ensure that the ignition is switched off then lift off the ECU module box lid.
47 Disconnect the wiring connector and remove the relay unit from the mounting plate.
48 Refitting is the reverse of removal.

14 Magneti Marelli 8P system components - removal and refitting

Fuel injectors

Note: Refer to the warning note in Section 1 before proceeding. If a faulty injector is suspected, before condemning the injector, it is worth trying the effect of one of the proprietary injector-cleaning treatments.

1 Disconnect the battery negative terminal.
2 Remove the air cleaner-to-throttle housing duct as described in Section 2.
3 Undo the two bolts securing the wiring tray to the top of the manifold, and position the tray clear of the injectors.
4 Depress the retaining clip(s), and disconnect the wiring connector(s) from the injector(s).
5 Slacken the retaining screw, and remove the injector retaining plate; Nos 1 and 2 injectors are retained by one plate, Nos 3 and 4 by another.
6 Place a wad of clean rag over the injector, to catch any fuel spray which may be released, then carefully ease the relevant injector(s) out of the manifold. Remove the O-rings from the end of each disturbed injector, and discard them - these must be renewed whenever they are disturbed.
7 On refitting the injectors, fit a new O-rings to the end of each injector. Apply a smear of engine oil to the O-ring, to aid installation, then ease the injector(s) back into position in the manifold.
8 Ensure each injector connector is correctly positioned, then refit the retaining plate and securely tighten its retaining screw. Reconnect the wiring connector(s) to the injector(s).

9 Refit the wiring tray to the top of the manifold, and securely tighten its bolts.
10 Refit the air cleaner-to-throttle body duct, and reconnect the battery. Start the engine, and check the injectors for signs of leakage.

Fuel pressure regulator

11 Refer to Section 13.

Throttle potentiometer

12 The throttle potentiometer is fitted to the right-hand side of the throttle housing.
13 Depress the retaining clip, and disconnect the potentiometer wiring connector (see illustration).
14 Slacken and remove the two retaining screws, and remove the potentiometer from the throttle housing.
15 Refitting is the reverse of removal, ensuring that the potentiometer is correctly engaged with the throttle valve spindle.

Electronic Control Unit (ECU)

16 Refer to Section 13.

Idle speed control stepper motor

17 The idle speed control stepper motor is located on the front of the throttle housing assembly.
18 Release the retaining clip, and disconnect the wiring connector from the motor (see illustration).
19 Slacken and remove the two retaining screws, and withdraw the motor from the throttle housing.
20 Refitting is a reversal of the removal procedure.

Manifold absolute pressure (MAP) sensor

21 The MAP sensor is located at the front of the ECU module box which is mounted on the right-hand front wheel arch.
22 Ensure that the ignition is switched off then lift off the ECU module box lid.
23 Undo the retaining nut(s) or clips and free the MAP sensor from the module box.
24 Disconnect the wiring connector and vacuum hose and remove the MAP sensor from the engine compartment.
25 Refitting is the reverse of the removal procedure.

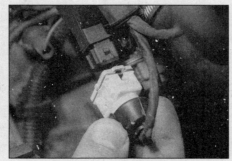

14.13 Disconnecting the wiring from the throttle potentiometer

14.18 Disconnecting the idle speed control stepper motor wiring

Coolant temperature sensor

26 Refer to Chapter 3.

Inlet air temperature sensor

27 The inlet air temperature sensor is located in the throttle housing.

28 To remove the sensor, first remove the throttle potentiometer as described in paragraphs 12 to 14.

29 Depress the retaining clip, and disconnect the wiring connector from the air temperature sensor.

30 Remove the screw securing the sensor connector to the top of the throttle housing, then carefully ease the sensor out of position and remove it from the throttle housing. Examine the sensor O-ring for signs of damage or deterioration, and renew if necessary.

31 Refitting is a reversal of the removal procedure, using a new O-ring where necessary, and ensuring that the throttle potentiometer is correctly engaged with the throttle valve spindle.

Crankshaft (RPM) sensor

32 Refer to Section 13.

Fuel injection system relay unit

33 Refer to Section 13.

Vehicle speed sensor

34 Refer to Section 13.

15 Inlet manifold - removal and refitting

Removal

1 Disconnect the battery negative terminal and proceed as described under the relevant sub-heading.

1.6 litre models

2 Remove the air cleaner-to-throttle housing duct as described in Section 2.

3 Disconnect the accelerator inner cable from the throttle cam then withdraw the outer cable from the mounting bracket along with its flat washer and spring clip.

4 Undo the two bolts securing the wiring tray to the top of the manifold, and position the tray, and its associated wiring and hoses, clear of the manifold so that it does not hinder removal.

5 Depress the retaining clips, and disconnect the wiring connectors from the four fuel injectors.

6 Bearing in mind the information given in Section 7, slacken the retaining clips, and disconnect the fuel feed and return hoses from either side of the manifold. Where the original crimped-type Peugeot hose clips are still fitted, cut them off and discard them; use standard worm-drive hose clips on refitting.

7 Slacken the retaining clip(s), and disconnect

the braking system vacuum servo unit hose, and all the relevant vacuum/ breather hoses, from the top of the manifold. Where necessary, make identification marks on the hoses, to ensure that they are correctly reconnected on refitting.

8 Undo the manifold retaining nuts, and withdraw the manifold from the engine compartment. Recover the two manifold seals, and discard them - new ones must be used on refitting.

1.8 and 2.0 litre models

9 Remove the throttle housing as described in Section 12 and the fuel rail and injectors as described in Section 13.

10 Slacken the retaining clip(s), and disconnect the braking system vacuum servo unit hose, and all the relevant vacuum/ breather hoses, from the manifold. Where necessary, make identification marks on the hoses, to ensure that they are correctly reconnected on refitting.

11 Where applicable, slacken and remove the bolt securing the dipstick tube to the side of the manifold.

12 Undo the nuts and bolts securing the manifold to the cylinder head, and remove the manifold from the engine compartment. Recover the manifold gasket/seals, and discard them - new ones must be used on refitting.

Refitting

13 Refitting is a reverse of the relevant removal procedure, noting the following points:

a) Ensure that the manifold and cylinder head mating surfaces are clean and dry, then locate the new gasket/seals on the manifold. Refit the manifold and tighten its retaining nuts and bolts to the specified torque setting.

b) Ensure that all relevant hoses are reconnected to their original positions and are securely held (where necessary) by the retaining clips.

c) Adjust the accelerator cable as described in Section 3.

16 Exhaust manifold - removal and refitting

Removal

1 Disconnect the hot-air inlet hose from the manifold shroud and remove it from the vehicle.

2 Slacken and remove the three retaining screws, and remove the shroud from the top of the exhaust manifold.

3 Chock the rear wheels, then jack up the front of the vehicle and support it on axle stands.

4 Where necessary, disconnect the wiring from the lambda (oxygen) sensor. Alternatively,

support the exhaust front pipe, to avoid any strain being placed on the sensor wiring.

5 Undo the nuts securing the exhaust front pipe to the manifold and recover the springs. Where applicable, remove the bolt securing the front pipe to its mounting bracket. Disconnect the front pipe from the manifold, and recover the gasket.

6 Undo the retaining nuts securing the manifold to the cylinder head. Manoeuvre the manifold out of the engine compartment, and discard the manifold gaskets.

Refitting

7 Refitting is the reverse of the removal procedure, noting the following points:

a) Examine all the exhaust manifold studs for signs of damage and corrosion; remove all traces of corrosion, and repair or renew any damaged studs.

b) Ensure that the manifold and cylinder head sealing faces are clean and flat, and fit the new manifold gasket(s). Tighten the manifold retaining nuts to the specified torque setting.

c) Reconnect the front pipe to the manifold, using the information given in Section 17.

17 Exhaust system - general information, removal and refitting

General information

1 A multi-section exhaust system is fitted. All exhaust sections are joined by a flanged joint. The downpipe to manifold joint is secured by nuts and bolts with a centre sealing ring. The joint is of the spring-loaded ball type, to allow for movement in the exhaust system. Other joints in the system are secured by a clamping ring.

2 Where fitted the catalytic converter is located on the front section of the exhaust.

3 The system is suspended throughout its entire length by rubber mountings.

Removal

4 Each exhaust section can be removed individually, or the system can be removed complete, then separated after removal.

5 To remove part of the system, first jack up the front or rear of the car and support it on axle stands. Alternatively, position the car over an inspection pit or on car ramps.

Front pipe

6 Undo the nuts and bolts securing the front pipe flange joint to the manifold, and recover the springs **(see illustration)**. Separate the joint and recover the sealing ring.

7 Loosen the clamp bolt securing the front pipe flange joint to the intermediate pipe/rear pipe and separate the joint. Withdraw the front pipe from underneath the vehicle, and recover the sealing ring.

17.6 Exhaust front pipe-to-manifold retaining nuts and springs (arrowed)

Intermediate pipe and silencer

8 Slacken the clamping ring bolts and disengage the clamps from the front and rear flange joints. Note that there may be an earth strap attached to one of the clamp bolts **(see illustration)**.
9 Unhook the intermediate pipe and silencer from its mounting rubber and remove it from underneath the vehicle.

17.8 Earth strap attachment at the exhaust intermediate pipe clamp

Tailpipe and silencer

10 Slacken the clamping ring bolt and disengage the clamp from the flange joint.
11 Unhook the tailpipe and silencer from its mounting rubbers and remove it from the car.

Heat shield(s)

12 The heat shields are secured to the underbody by various nuts and bolts. Each shield can be removed once the relevant exhaust section has been removed. If a shield is being removed to gain access to a component located behind it, it may prove sufficient in some cases to remove the retaining nuts and/or bolts, and simply lower the shield, without disturbing the exhaust system.

Refitting

13 Each section is refitted by reversing the removal sequence, noting the following:
a) *Ensure that all traces of corrosion have been removed from the flanges.*
b) *Inspect the rubber mountings for damage or deterioration, and renew as necessary.*
c) *Prior to assembling the spring-loaded joint, a smear of high-temperature grease should be applied to the joint mating surfaces.*
d) *Prior to tightening the exhaust system fasteners, ensure that all rubber mountings are correctly located, and that there is adequate clearance between the exhaust system and vehicle underbody.*

4.8a Undo the internal bolts (arrowed) securing the battery box and metal base to the mounting bracket . . .

4.8b . . . and the single outer bolt securing the box to the air cleaner mounting bracket

4.9 Lift the battery box out of the engine compartment

8 Undo the internal bolts securing the battery box and metal base to the mounting bracket, and the single outer bolt securing the box to the air cleaner mounting bracket **(see illustrations)**.

9 Carefully move aside all cables and hoses, then lift the battery box out of the engine compartment **(see illustration)**.

Refitting

10 Refitting is a reversal of removal, but smear petroleum jelly on the terminals when reconnecting the leads, and always reconnect the positive lead first, and the negative lead last.

11 With the battery reconnected, switch on the ignition and wait ten seconds before starting the engine. This will allow the vehicle electronic systems and control units to stabilise.

12 Enter the radio/cassette unit security codes with reference to the audio system documentation supplied with the vehicle.

5 Charging system - testing

Note: *Refer to the warnings given in "Safety first!" and in Section 1 of this Chapter before starting work.*

1 If the ignition warning light fails to illuminate when the ignition is switched on, first check the alternator wiring connections for security. If satisfactory, check that the warning light bulb has not blown, and that the bulbholder is secure in its location in the instrument panel. If the light still fails to illuminate, check the continuity of the warning light feed wire from the alternator to the bulbholder. If all is satisfactory, the alternator is at fault and should be renewed or taken to an auto-electrician for testing and repair.

2 If the ignition warning light illuminates when the engine is running, stop the engine and check that the drivebelt is correctly tensioned (see Chapter 1) and that the alternator connections are secure. If all is so far

satisfactory, have the alternator checked by an auto-electrician for testing and repair.

3 If the alternator output is suspect even though the warning light functions correctly, the regulated voltage may be checked as follows.

4 Connect a voltmeter across the battery terminals and start the engine.

5 Increase the engine speed until the voltmeter reading remains steady; the reading should be approximately 12 to 13 volts, and no more than 14 volts.

6 Switch on as many electrical accessories (eg, the headlights, heated rear window and heater blower) as possible, and check that the alternator maintains the regulated voltage at around 13 to 14 volts.

7 If the regulated voltage is not as stated, the fault may be due to worn brushes, weak brush springs, a faulty voltage regulator, a faulty diode, a severed phase winding or worn or damaged slip rings. The alternator should be renewed or taken to an auto-electrician for testing and repair.

6 Alternator drivebelt - removal, refitting and tensioning

Refer to the procedure given for the auxiliary drivebelt in Chapter 1.

7.3 Alternator wiring connections

7 Alternator - removal and refitting

Removal

1 Disconnect the battery negative lead.

2 Slacken the auxiliary drivebelt as described in Chapter 1 and disengage it from the alternator pulley.

3 Remove the rubber covers (where fitted) from the alternator terminals, then unscrew the retaining nuts and disconnect the wiring from the rear of the alternator **(see illustration)**.

4 On 2.1 litre diesel models, unbolt the power steering pump and move it to one side without disconnecting any hydraulic pipes or hoses (see Chapter 10).

5 Unscrew the nut/bolt securing the alternator to the upper mounting bracket **(see illustration)**. Unscrew the lower mounting bolt. Note that, where a long through-bolt is used to secure the alternator in position, the bolt does not need to be fully removed; the alternator can be disengaged from the bolt once it has been slackened sufficiently. On some models, it may be necessary to remove the drivebelt idler/tensioner pulley to gain access to the alternator mounting nuts and bolts (depending on specification).

6 Manoeuvre the alternator away from its mounting brackets and out from the engine compartment.

7.5 Alternator upper mounting bracket (2.0 litre petrol engine)

Refitting

7 Refitting is a reversal of removal, tensioning the auxiliary drivebelt as described in Chapter 1 on models with a manually adjusted tensioner, and ensuring that the alternator mountings are securely tightened.

8 Alternator - testing and overhaul

If the alternator is thought to be suspect, it should be removed from the vehicle and taken to an auto-electrician for testing. Most auto-electricians will be able to supply and fit brushes at a reasonable cost. However, check on the cost of repairs before proceeding as it may prove more economical to obtain a new or exchange alternator.

9 Starting system - testing

Note: *Refer to the precautions given in "Safety first!" and in Section 1 of this Chapter before starting work.*
1 If the starter motor fails to operate when the ignition key is turned to the appropriate position, the following possible causes may be to blame.
 a) *The coded anti-start system is engaged.*
 b) *The battery is faulty.*
 c) *The electrical connections between the switch, solenoid, battery and starter motor are somewhere failing to pass the necessary current from the battery through the starter to earth.*
 d) *The solenoid is faulty.*
 e) *The starter motor is mechanically or electrically defective.*
2 To check the battery, switch on the headlights. If they dim after a few seconds, this indicates that the battery is discharged - recharge (see Section 3) or renew the battery. If the headlights glow brightly, operate the ignition switch and observe the lights. If they dim, then this indicates that current is reaching the starter motor, therefore the fault must lie in the starter motor. If the lights continue to glow brightly (and no clicking sound can be heard from the starter motor solenoid), this indicates that there is a fault in the circuit or solenoid - see following paragraphs. If the starter motor turns slowly when operated, but the battery is in good condition, then this indicates that either the starter motor is faulty, or there is considerable resistance somewhere in the circuit.
3 If a fault in the circuit is suspected, disconnect the battery leads (including the earth connection to the body), the starter/solenoid wiring and the engine/transmission earth strap. Thoroughly clean the connections, and reconnect the leads and wiring, then use a

10.3 Remove the two retaining nuts (arrowed) and disconnect the wiring from the starter motor solenoid

voltmeter or test lamp to check that full battery voltage is available at the battery positive lead connection to the solenoid, and that the earth is sound. Smear petroleum jelly around the battery terminals to prevent corrosion - corroded connections are amongst the most frequent causes of electrical system faults.
4 If the battery and all connections are in good condition, check the circuit by disconnecting the wire from the solenoid blade terminal. Connect a voltmeter or test lamp between the wire end and a good earth (such as the battery negative terminal), and check that the wire is live when the ignition switch is turned to the `start' position. If it is, then the circuit is sound - if not the circuit wiring can be checked as described in Chapter 12.
5 The solenoid contacts can be checked by connecting a voltmeter or test lamp between the battery positive feed connection on the starter side of the solenoid, and earth. When the ignition switch is turned to the "start" position, there should be a reading or lighted bulb, as applicable. If there is no reading or lighted bulb, the solenoid is faulty and should be renewed.
6 If the circuit and solenoid are proved sound, the fault must lie in the starter motor. In this event, it may be possible to have the starter motor overhauled by a specialist, but check on the cost of spares before proceeding, as it may prove more economical to obtain a new or exchange motor.

10 Starter motor - removal and refitting

Removal

1 Disconnect the battery negative lead.
2 So that access to the motor can be gained both from above and below, chock the rear wheels then jack up the front of the vehicle and support it on axle stands. Where applicable, to improve access to the motor remove the air cleaner and ducting as necessary as described in the relevant Part of Chapter 4.
3 Slacken and remove the two retaining nuts and disconnect the wiring from the starter

10.4 Note the main engine earth strap connection on one of the starter motor mounting bolts (2.1 litre diesel engine)

motor solenoid. Recover the washers under the nuts **(see illustration)**.
4 Undo the three mounting bolts, supporting the motor as the bolts are withdrawn. Recover the washers from under the bolt heads and note the locations of any wiring or hose brackets secured by the bolts **(see illustration)**.
5 Manoeuvre the starter motor out from underneath the engine and recover the locating dowel(s) from the motor/transmission (as applicable).

Refitting

6 Refitting is a reversal of removal, ensuring that the locating dowel(s) are correctly positioned. Also make sure that any wiring or hose brackets are in place under the bolt heads as noted prior to removal.

11 Starter motor - testing and overhaul

If the starter motor is thought to be suspect, it should be removed from the vehicle and taken to an auto-electrician for testing. Most auto-electricians will be able to supply and fit brushes at a reasonable cost. However, check on the cost of repairs before proceeding as it may prove more economical to obtain a new or exchange motor.

12 Ignition switch - removal and refitting

The ignition switch is integral with the steering column lock, and can be removed as described in Chapter 10.

13 Oil pressure warning light switch - removal and refitting

Removal

1 The switch is located at the front of the cylinder block, above the oil filter mounting. Note that on some models access to the switch may be improved if the vehicle is jacked up and supported on axle stands so that the switch can be reached from underneath.

2 Disconnect the battery negative lead.

3 Remove the protective sleeve from the wiring plug (where applicable), then disconnect the wiring from the switch.

4 Unscrew the switch from the cylinder block, and recover the sealing washer. Be prepared for oil spillage, and if the switch is to be left removed from the engine for any length of time, plug the hole in the cylinder block.

Refitting

5 Examine the sealing washer for signs of damage or deterioration and if necessary renew.

6 Refit the switch, complete with washer, and tighten it securely. Reconnect the wiring connector.

7 Lower the vehicle to the ground then check and, if necessary, top-up the engine oil as described in Chapter 1.

14 Oil level sensor - removal and refitting

1 The sensor is located on the rear facing side of the cylinder block at the flywheel end.

2 The removal and refitting procedure is as described for the oil pressure switch in Section 13. Access is most easily obtained from underneath the vehicle **(see illustration)**.

14.2 Removing the oil level sensor from the cylinder block

Chapter 5 Part B:
Ignition system (petrol models)

Contents

Degrees of difficulty

Easy, suitable for novice with little experience	**Fairly easy,** suitable for beginner with some experience	**Fairly difficult,** suitable for competent DIY mechanic	**Difficult,** suitable for experienced DIY mechanic	**Very difficult,** suitable for expert DIY or professional

Specifications

System type	Static (distributorless) ignition system controlled by engine management ECU
Firing order	1-3-4-2 (number 1 cylinder at flywheel end of engine)
Ignition timing	Controlled by engine management ECU - see text

1 Ignition system - general information

On all models, the ignition system is integrated with the fuel injection system to form a combined engine management system under the control of one ECU (See the relevant Part of Chapter 4 for further information).

On 1.6 litre models, the ignition side of the system is of the static (distributorless) type, consisting only of a four output ignition coil. The ignition coil actually consists of two separate HT coils which supply two cylinders each (one coil supplies cylinders 1 and 4, and the other cylinders 2 and 3). Under the control of the ECU, the ignition coil operates on the "wasted spark" principle, ie. each spark plug sparks twice for every cycle of the engine, once on the compression stroke and once on the exhaust stroke. The ECU uses its inputs from the various sensors to calculate the required ignition advance setting and coil charging time.

On 1.8 and 2.0 litre models, the ignition side of the system is also of the static (distributorless) type and consists primarily of four ignition coils located in an ignition coil unit fitted to the centre of the cylinder head cover. The coils are integral with the spark plug caps and are pushed directly onto the spark plugs, one for each plug. This removes the need for any HT leads connecting the coils to the plugs. The ECU uses the inputs from the various sensors to calculate the required ignition advance setting and calculate the coil charging time.

2 Ignition system - testing

> ⚠️ **Warning: Voltages produced by an electronic ignition system are considerably higher than those produced by conventional ignition systems. Extreme care must be taken when working on the system with the ignition switched on. Persons with surgically-implanted cardiac pacemaker devices should keep well clear of the ignition circuits, components and test equipment.**

1 If a fault appears in the engine management (fuel injection/ignition) system first ensure that the fault is not due to a poor electrical connection or poor maintenance; ie, check that the air cleaner filter element is clean, the spark plugs are in good condition and correctly gapped, that the engine breather hoses are clear and undamaged, referring to Chapter 1 for further information. Also check that the accelerator cable is correctly adjusted as described in the relevant part of Chapter 4. If the engine is running very roughly, check the compression pressures and the valve clearances as described in Chapter 2A.

2 If these checks fail to reveal the cause of the problem, the car should be taken to a Peugeot dealer for testing. A wiring block connector is incorporated in the engine management circuit into which a special electronic diagnostic tester can be plugged. The tester will locate the fault quickly and simply, alleviating the need to test all the system components individually, an operation that carries a high risk of damaging the ECU.

3 The only ignition system checks which can be carried out by the home mechanic are those described in Chapter 1, relating to the spark plugs. If necessary, the system wiring and wiring connectors can be checked as described in Chapter 12 ensuring that the ECU wiring connector(s) have first been disconnected.

3 Ignition HT coil(s) - removal and refitting

Removal

1.6 litre models

1 Disconnect the battery negative terminal. The ignition HT coil is mounted on the left-hand end of the cylinder head.

2 Depress the retaining clip and disconnect the wiring connector from the HT coil **(see illustration)**.

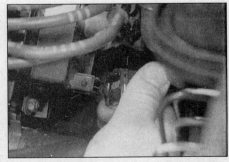

3.2 Disconnect the wiring connector from the ignition coil

3 Make a note of the correct fitted positions of the HT leads then disconnect them from the coil terminals.

4 Undo the four retaining screws securing the coil to its mounting bracket and remove it from the engine compartment.

1.8 and 2.0 litre models

5 Disconnect the battery negative terminal. There are four separate ignition HT coils, one on the top of each spark plug.

6 To gain access to the coils, disconnect the wiring connectors at the left-hand end of the coil unit, then undo the six retaining bolts and lift the coil unit upwards, off the spark plugs and from its location in the cylinder head cover. The individual coils can now be removed as required.

Refitting

7 Refitting is a reversal of the relevant removal procedure ensuring that the wiring connectors are securely reconnected and, where necessary, the HT leads are correctly connected.

4 Ignition timing -
checking and adjustment

1 On all models, there are no timing marks on the flywheel or crankshaft pulley. The timing is constantly being monitored and adjusted by the engine management ECU, and nominal values cannot be given. Therefore, it is not possible for the home mechanic to check the ignition timing.

2 The only way in which the ignition timing can be checked is using special electronic test equipment, connected to the engine management system diagnostic connector (refer to the relevant Part of Chapter 4 for further information).

Chapter 5 Part C:
Preheating system (diesel models)

Contents

Degrees of difficulty

Easy, suitable for novice with little experience	**Fairly easy,** suitable for beginner with some experience	**Fairly difficult,** suitable for competent DIY mechanic	**Difficult,** suitable for experienced DIY mechanic	**Very difficult,** suitable for expert DIY or professional

Specifications

Glow plugs .... Bosch 0 250 201 039

Torque wrench setting	Nm	lbf ft
Glow plugs	22	16

1 Preheating system - description and testing

Description

1 Each swirl chamber has a heater plug (commonly called a glow plug) screwed into it. The plugs are electrically-operated before and during start-up when the engine is cold. Electrical feed to the glow plugs is controlled by a relay/timer unit, in conjunction with the diesel injection system electronic control unit (ECU).

2 On certain models, the glow plugs provide a "post-heating" function, whereby the glow plugs remain switched on for a period after the engine has started. Once the starter has been switched off, the glow plugs begin a timed 3-minute "post-heating" cycle. The operation of the plugs cannot be cancelled for the first 15 seconds, but after the first 15 seconds, the supply to the plugs will be interrupted by:
 a) *Operation of the accelerator pedal beyond a travel of 11 mm for a duration of more than 2.5 seconds.*
 b) *A coolant temperature of more than 60°C.*

3 A warning light in the instrument panel tells the driver that preheating is taking place. When the light goes out, the engine is ready to be started. The voltage supply to the glow plugs continues for several seconds after the light goes out. If no attempt is made to start, the timer then cuts off the supply, in order to avoid draining the battery and overheating the glow plugs.

Testing

4 If the system malfunctions, testing is ultimately by substitution of known good units, but some preliminary checks may be made as follows.

5 Connect a voltmeter or 12-volt test lamp between the glow plug supply cable and earth (engine or vehicle metal). Make sure that the live connection is kept clear of the engine and bodywork.

6 Have an assistant switch on the ignition, and check that voltage is applied to the glow plugs. Note the time for which the warning light is lit, and the total time for which voltage is applied before the system cuts out. Switch off the ignition.

7 At an under-bonnet temperature of 20°C, typical times noted should be 5 or 6 seconds for warning light operation, followed by a further 10 seconds supply after the light goes out. Warning light time will increase with lower temperatures and decrease with higher temperatures.

8 If there is no supply at all, the relay or associated wiring is at fault.

9 To locate a defective glow plug, remove the air intake ducting (Chapter 4B) and, where necessary, disconnect the breather hose from the engine oil filler tube. Disconnect the main supply cable and the interconnecting wire or strap from the top of the glow plugs. Be careful not to drop the nuts and washers.

10 Use a continuity tester, or a 12-volt test lamp connected to the battery positive terminal, to check for continuity between each glow plug terminal and earth. The resistance of a glow plug in good condition is very low (less than 1 ohm), so if the test lamp does not light or the continuity tester shows a high resistance, the glow plug is certainly defective.

11 As a final check, the glow plugs can be removed and inspected as described in the following Section.

2 Glow plugs - removal, inspection and refitting

Removal

Caution: *If the preheating system has just been energised, or if the engine has been running, the glow plugs will be very hot.*

1 Disconnect the battery negative lead. To improve access, remove the air intake ducting (Chapter 4B) and, where necessary, disconnect the breather hose from the engine oil filler tube.

2 Unscrew the nut from the relevant glow plug terminal(s), and recover the washer(s). Note the main supply cable connection (usually to Number 2 cylinder glow plug) and the interconnecting wire fitted between the four plugs **(see illustration)**.

3 Where applicable, carefully move any obstructing pipes or wires to one side to enable access to the relevant glow plug(s).

4 Unscrew the glow plug(s) and remove from the cylinder head **(see illustration)**.

2.2 Unscrew the nut (arrowed) and disconnect the glow plug connecting wire

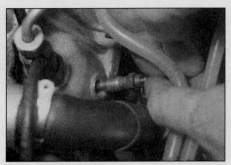

2.4 Unscrew the glow plug and remove it from the cylinder head

3.1 Preheating system control unit location on 1.9 litre models

3.4 Disconnect the wiring connector from the preheating system control unit then unscrew the two retaining nuts and free the main feed and supply wires (2.1 litre model shown)

Inspection

5 Inspect each glow plug for physical damage. Burnt or eroded glow plug tips can be caused by a bad injector spray pattern. Have the injectors checked if this sort of damage is found.

6 If the glow plugs are in good physical condition, check them electrically using a 12 volt test lamp or continuity tester as described in the previous Section.

7 The glow plugs can be energised by applying 12 volts to them to verify that they heat up evenly and in the required time. Observe the following precautions.

  a) *Support the glow plug by clamping it carefully in a vice or self-locking pliers. Remember it will become red-hot.*

  b) *Make sure that the power supply or test lead incorporates a fuse or overload trip to protect against damage from a short-circuit.*

  c) *After testing, allow the glow plug to cool for several minutes before attempting to handle it.*

8 A glow plug in good condition will start to glow red at the tip after drawing current for 5 seconds or so. Any plug which takes much longer to start glowing, or which starts glowing in the middle instead of at the tip, is defective.

Refitting

9 Refit by reversing the removal operations. Apply a smear of copper-based anti-seize compound to the plug threads and tighten the glow plugs to the specified torque. Do not overtighten, as this can damage the glow plug element.

---

3   Preheating system control unit - removal and refitting

Removal

1 The unit is located on the left-hand side of the engine compartment, on the side of the fusebox on 1.9 litre models, and on a bracket beneath the accelerator pedal position sensor on 2.1 litre models **(see illustration)**.

2 Disconnect the battery negative lead.

3 On 2.1 litre models, remove the air cleaner assembly and intake ducting as described in Chapter 4B.

4 Disconnect the wiring connector from the base of the unit then unscrew the two retaining nuts and free the main feed and supply wires from the unit **(see illustration)**.

5 Unscrew the retaining nut(s) and remove the unit from the engine compartment.

Refitting

6 Refitting is a reversal of removal, ensuring that the wiring connectors are correctly connected.

Chapter 6
Clutch

Contents

Degrees of difficulty

Easy, suitable for novice with little experience	**Fairly easy,** suitable for beginner with some experience	**Fairly difficult,** suitable for competent DIY mechanic	**Difficult,** suitable for experienced DIY mechanic	**Very difficult,** suitable for expert DIY or professional

Specifications

Type . . . . Single dry plate with diaphragm spring, cable or hydraulic operation

Friction plate diameter
Petrol models:
   1.6 and 1.8 litre models . . . . 200 mm
   2.0 litre models . . . . 215 mm
Diesel models . . . . 215 mm

Torque wrench setting	**Nm**	**lbf ft**
Pressure plate retaining bolts	20	15

1 General information

The clutch consists of a friction plate, a pressure plate assembly, a release bearing and the release mechanism; all of these components are contained in the large cast-aluminium alloy bellhousing, sandwiched between the engine and the transmission. The release mechanism is mechanical, and is operated by a self-adjusting cable on all models except the 2.1 litre diesel versions. On 2.1 litre diesel models the release mechanism is operated hydraulically by means of a master and slave cylinder and interconnecting hydraulic pipework.

The friction plate is fitted between the engine flywheel and the clutch pressure plate, and is allowed to slide on the transmission input shaft splines.

The pressure plate assembly is bolted to the engine flywheel. When the engine is running, drive is transmitted from the crankshaft, via the flywheel, to the friction plate (these components being clamped securely together by the pressure plate assembly) and from the friction plate to the transmission input shaft.

To interrupt the drive, the spring pressure must be relaxed. On the models covered in this manual, two different types of clutch release mechanism are used. The first is a conventional "push-type" mechanism, where an independent clutch release bearing, fitted concentrically around the transmission input shaft, is pushed onto the pressure plate assembly; this type is fitted to 1.6 and 1.8 litre petrol models. The second is a "pull-type" mechanism, where the clutch release bearing is an integral part of the pressure plate assembly, and is lifted away from the friction plate; this type is fitted to 2.0 litre petrol models and all diesel models.

On models with the conventional "push-type" mechanism, at the transmission end of the clutch cable, the outer cable is retained by a fixed mounting bracket, and the inner cable is attached to the release fork lever. Depressing the clutch pedal pulls the control cable inner wire, and this rotates the release fork by acting on the lever at the fork's upper end. The release fork then presses the release bearing against the pressure plate spring fingers. This causes the springs to deform and releases the clamping force on the pressure plate.

On 2.0 litre petrol and 1.9 litre diesel models with the "pull-type" mechanism, at the transmission end of the clutch cable the inner cable is attached to a fixed mounting bracket, and the outer cable acts against the release fork lever. Depressing the clutch pedal rotates the release fork. The release fork then lifts the release bearing, which is attached to the pressure plate springs, away from the friction plate, and releases the clamping force exerted at the pressure plate periphery.

On 2.1 litre diesel models with the "pull-type" mechanism, the clutch pedal is connected to the clutch master cylinder by a pushrod. The master cylinder is mounted on the engine compartment bulkhead with the slave cylinder mounted on the side of the transmission. A hydraulic fluid reservoir is also remotely mounted on the bulkhead and connected to the master cylinder by means of a fluid hose **(see illustration)**. Depressing the

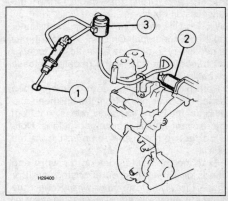

1.7 Hydraulic clutch components as fitted to 2.1 litre diesel models

  1 Master cylinder   3 Fluid reservoir
  2 Slave cylinder

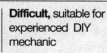

clutch pedal moves the piston in the master cylinder forwards, so forcing hydraulic fluid through the clutch hydraulic pipe to the slave cylinder. The piston in the slave cylinder moves forward under hydraulic pressure and actuates the release fork by means of a short pushrod. The release fork then lifts the release bearing, which is attached to the pressure plate springs, away from the friction plate, and releases the clamping force exerted at the pressure plate periphery.

The clutch master cylinder, fluid reservoir, slave cylinder, and interconnecting fluid pipework are all part of a maintenance-free, sealed assembly. The fluid reservoir cannot be opened and the fluid level does not require topping-up. In the event of fluid leakage or any malfunction of the hydraulic system, all the components must be renewed as a complete assembly.

On all models, adjustment of the clutch to compensate for wear of the friction plate linings is automatically taken up by the hydraulic clutch components, or by the self-adjusting mechanism incorporated in the cable.

2 Clutch cable - removal and refitting

Removal

1 Disconnect the battery negative terminal.
2 Open up the engine immobiliser key pad, then rotate the fastener through 90° and lower the fusebox cover. Disconnect the wiring connector from the key pad then slacken and remove the retaining screws and remove the driver's side lower panel from the facia.
3 Remove the air cleaner housing and intake duct components as described in the relevant Part of Chapter 4.
4 Working in the engine compartment, release the inner cable and outer cable fittings from the clutch release lever and mounting bracket and free the cable from the transmission housing.
5 Working inside the vehicle, release the inner cable from the pedal. On some models it may be necessary to depress a plastic clip located just beneath the top of the pedal to release the cable.
6 Return to the engine compartment, then release the cable guide from the bulkhead and withdraw the cable forwards, releasing it from any relevant retaining clips and guides. Note its correct routing, and remove it from the vehicle.
7 Examine the cable, looking for worn end fittings or a damaged outer casing, and for signs of fraying of the inner wire. Renew the cable if it shows signs of excessive wear or any damage.

Refitting

8 Apply a thin smear of multi-purpose grease

to the cable end fittings, then pass the cable through the engine compartment bulkhead.
9 Hold the clutch pedal in its raised position by wedging a suitable tool beneath it.
10 Guide the end of the cable into the pedal end (or plastic clip) making sure that it is fully engaged.
11 In the engine compartment refit the cable to the transmission housing and release lever. Re-secure the cable with any relevant retaining clips and guides.
12 Depress and release the clutch pedal several times to operate the self-adjusting mechanism and check that the clutch pedal operates correctly.
13 Refit the lower panel to the facia then refit the air cleaner components and reconnect the battery.

3 Clutch pedal - removal and refitting

Removal

1 Disconnect the battery negative terminal.
2 Open up the engine immobiliser key pad, then rotate the fastener through 90° and lower the fusebox cover. Disconnect the wiring connector from the key pad then slacken and remove the retaining screws and remove the driver's side lower panel from the facia.
3 On models with a cable-operated clutch, release the inner cable from the pedal. On some models it may be necessary to depress a plastic clip located just beneath the top of the pedal to release the cable. Carefully release the pedal-assist spring assembly from the pedal.
4 On models with a hydraulically-operated clutch, release the master cylinder pushrod balljoint from the pedal and allow the pedal to rise until it reaches its stop.
5 Slacken and remove the pivot bolt and nut, and remove the clutch pedal from the vehicle. Slide the spacer out from the pedal pivot. Examine all components for signs of wear or damage, renewing them as necessary.

Refitting

6 Apply a smear of multi-purpose grease to the spacer, and insert it into the pedal pivot bore.
7 Manoeuvre the pedal into position, and insert the pivot bolt. Refit the nut to the pivot bolt and tighten it securely.
8 Reconnect the clutch cable or master cylinder pushrod to the pedal. On cable-operated versions, refit the pedal assist spring assembly.
9 Depress and release the clutch pedal several times and check for correct operation.
10 Refit the lower panel to the facia and reconnect the battery.

4 Clutch hydraulic system components - removal and refitting

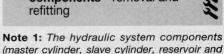

Note 1: *The hydraulic system components (master cylinder, slave cylinder, reservoir and pipework) are a sealed assembly and cannot be separated or dismantled.*
Note 2: *Access to the master cylinder is extremely limited and Peugeot recommend the use of a special slotted socket (tool 0216J) for this purpose. A suitable alternative can be fabricated from a box spanner with a slot cut in the side to accommodate the hydraulic hose.*

Removal

1 Disconnect the battery negative terminal.
2 Remove the air cleaner housing and intake duct components as described in the relevant Part of Chapter 4.
3 Open up the engine immobiliser key pad, then rotate the fastener through 90° and lower the fusebox cover. Disconnect the wiring connector from the key pad then slacken and remove the retaining screws and remove the driver's side lower panel from the facia.
4 Release the master cylinder pushrod balljoint from the pedal and allow the pedal to rise until it reaches its stop.
5 Working in the engine compartment, unclip the master cylinder fluid reservoir from the bulkhead.
6 Engage the Peugeot special tool, or the home-made alternative over the master cylinder and turn the cylinder 90° clockwise to release it from the bulkhead attachment.
7 Release the slave cylinder from the transmission by pushing it in by hand and at the same time turning it 90° anti-clockwise (see illustration).
8 Release the hydraulic pipework from the retaining clips and attachments in the engine compartment and remove the complete assembly from the vehicle.

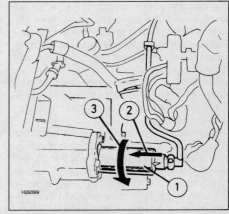

4.7 Release the slave cylinder (1) from the transmission by pushing it in (2) and turning it 90° anti-clockwise (3)

Refitting

Note: *On a new assembly, the slave cylinder pushrod is retained in the cylinder by a plastic collar which will automatically break off when the clutch pedal is depressed for the first time. Do not attempt to release this collar manually prior to fitting or the pushrod may be ejected.*

9 Push the clutch pedal to the floor by hand and retain it in this position.

10 Locate the master cylinder in position, aligning the white mark on the cylinder with the corresponding white mark on the bulkhead. Using the tool, push and turn the cylinder 90° anti-clockwise to secure.

11 Clip the master cylinder fluid reservoir into place on the bulkhead. Ensure that the fluid hoses are correctly routed and not chafing.

12 Lubricate the end of the slave cylinder pushrod with molybdenum disulphide grease then locate the slave cylinder in the transmission. Push it in by hand and at the same time turn it 90° clockwise to secure.

13 Reconnect the hydraulic pipework to the retaining clips and attachments in the engine compartment

14 Lubricate the master cylinder pushrod balljoint, then lift the clutch pedal and connect the pushrod.

15 With the assembly installed, slowly depress the clutch pedal to the floor, then slowly lift it again by hand. Wait for ten seconds and repeat this procedure. Depress the pedal again, release it and check that it rises correctly after being released.

16 Refit the lower panel to the facia then refit the air cleaner components and reconnect the battery.

---

 5 Clutch assembly - removal, inspection and refitting

 Warning: Dust created by clutch wear and deposited on the clutch components may contain asbestos, which is a health hazard. DO NOT blow it out with compressed air, or inhale any of it. DO NOT use petrol or petroleum-based solvents to clean off the dust. Brake system cleaner or methylated spirit should be used to flush the dust into a suitable receptacle. After the clutch components are wiped clean with rags, dispose of the contaminated rags and cleaner in a sealed, marked container.

Note: *Although some friction materials may no longer contain asbestos, it is safest to assume that they do, and to take precautions accordingly.*

Removal

1 Unless the complete engine/transmission is to be removed from the car and separated for major overhaul (see Chapter 2C), the clutch can be reached by removing the transmission as described in Chapter 7A.

2 Before disturbing the clutch, mark the relationship of the pressure plate assembly to the flywheel, using a marker pen or similar.

3 Working in a diagonal sequence, slacken the pressure plate bolts by half a turn at a time, until spring pressure is released and the bolts can be unscrewed by hand.

4 Prise the pressure plate assembly off its locating dowels, and collect the friction plate, noting which way round the friction plate is fitted.

Inspection

Note: *Due to the amount of work necessary to remove and refit clutch components, it is usually considered good practice to renew the clutch friction plate, pressure plate assembly and release bearing as a matched set, even if only one of these is actually worn enough to require renewal. It is also worth considering the renewal of the clutch components on a preventative basis if the engine and/or transmission have been removed for some other reason.*

5 Separate the pressure plate and friction plate and place them on the bench.

6 When cleaning clutch components, read first the warning at the beginning of this Section; remove dust using a clean, dry cloth, and working in a well-ventilated atmosphere.

7 Check the friction plate facings for signs of wear, damage or oil contamination. If the friction material is cracked, burnt, scored or damaged, or if it is contaminated with oil or grease (shown by shiny black patches), the friction plate must be renewed.

8 If the friction material is still serviceable, check that the centre boss splines are unworn, that the torsion springs are in good condition and securely fastened, and that all the rivets are tight. If any wear or damage is found, the friction plate must be renewed.

9 If the friction material is fouled with oil, this must be due to an oil leak from the crankshaft left-hand oil seal, from the sump-to-cylinder block joint, or from the transmission input shaft. Renew the seal or repair the joint, as appropriate, as described in Chapter 2 or 7, before installing the new friction plate.

10 Check the pressure plate assembly for obvious signs of wear or damage; shake it to check for loose rivets or worn or damaged fulcrum rings, and check that the drive straps securing the pressure plate to the cover do

not show signs (such as a deep yellow or blue discoloration) of overheating. If the diaphragm spring is worn or damaged, or if its pressure is in any way suspect, the pressure plate assembly should be renewed.

11 Examine the machined bearing surfaces of the pressure plate and of the flywheel; they should be clean, completely flat, and free from scratches or scoring. If either is discoloured from excessive heat, or shows signs of cracks, it should be renewed - although minor damage of this nature can sometimes be polished away using emery paper.

12 Check that the release bearing contact surface rotates smoothly and easily, with no sign of noise or roughness. Also check that the surface itself is smooth and unworn, with no signs of cracks, pitting or scoring. If there is any doubt about its condition, the bearing must be renewed. On clutches with a "pull-type" release mechanism, this means that the complete pressure plate assembly must also be renewed.

Refitting

13 On reassembly, ensure that the bearing surfaces of the flywheel and pressure plate are completely clean, smooth, and free from oil or grease. Use solvent to remove any protective grease from new components.

14 Fit the friction plate so its spring hub faces away from the flywheel; there may also be a marking to show which way round the plate is to be refitted **(see illustration)**.

15 Refit the pressure plate assembly, aligning the marks made on dismantling (if the original pressure plate is re-used), and locating the pressure plate on its locating dowels. Fit the pressure plate bolts, but tighten them only finger-tight, so that the friction plate can still be moved.

16 The friction plate must now be centralised, so that when the transmission is refitted, its input shaft will pass through the splines at the centre of the friction plate.

17 Centralisation can be achieved by passing a screwdriver or other long bar through the friction plate and into the hole in the crankshaft; the friction plate can then be moved around until it is centred on the crankshaft hole. Alternatively, a clutch-aligning tool can be used to eliminate the guesswork; these can be obtained from most accessory shops **(see illustration)**. A home-made aligning tool can

5.14 Ensure the friction plate is fitted the correct way round then install the pressure plate

5.17 Using a clutch-aligning tool to centralise the friction plate

be fabricated from a length of metal rod or wooden dowel which fits closely inside the crankshaft hole, and has insulating tape wound around it to match the diameter of the friction plate splined hole.

18 When the friction plate is centralised, tighten the pressure plate bolts evenly and in a diagonal sequence to the specified torque setting.

19 Refit the transmission as described in Chapter 7A.

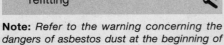

6 Clutch release mechanism - removal, inspection and refitting

Note: *Refer to the warning concerning the dangers of asbestos dust at the beginning of Section 5.*

Removal

1 Unless the complete engine/transmission is to be removed from the car and separated for major overhaul (see Chapter 2C), the clutch release mechanism can be reached by removing the transmission only, as described in Chapter 7A.

2 On models with a conventional "push-type" release mechanism, unhook the release bearing from the fork, and slide it off the input shaft **(see illustration)**. Drive out the roll pin, and remove the release lever from the top of the release fork shaft. Discard the roll pin - a new one must be used on refitting.

3 On both types of clutch, depress the retaining tabs, then slide the upper bush off the end of the release fork shaft. Disengage the shaft from its lower bush, and manoeuvre it out from the transmission. Depress the retaining tabs, and remove the lower pivot bush from the transmission housing **(see illustrations)**.

Inspection

4 Check the release mechanism, renewing any component which is worn or damaged.

6.2 Clutch release bearing (arrowed) and release fork and shaft

6.3b . . . release fork shaft . . .

Carefully check all bearing surfaces and points of contact.

5 When checking the release bearing itself, note that it is often considered worthwhile to renew it as a matter of course. Check that the contact surface rotates smoothly and easily, with no sign of noise or roughness, and that the surface itself is smooth and unworn, with no signs of cracks, pitting or scoring. If there is any doubt about its condition, the bearing must be renewed. On models with a "pull-type" release mechanism, this means that the complete pressure plate assembly must be renewed, as described in Section 5.

Refitting

6 Apply a smear of molybdenum disulphide

6.3a Removing the upper bush . . .

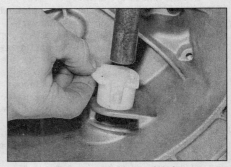

6.3c . . . and lower bush

grease to the shaft pivot bushes and the contact surfaces of the release fork.

7 Locate the lower pivot bush in the transmission, ensuring that it is securely retained by its locating tangs, and refit the release fork. Slide the upper bush down the shaft, and clip it into position in the transmission housing.

8 On models with a conventional "push-type" release mechanism, refit the release lever to the shaft. Align the lever with the shaft hole, and secure it in position by tapping a new roll pin fully into position. Slide the release bearing onto the input shaft, and engage it with the release fork.

9 Refit the transmission as described in Chapter 7A.

Chapter 7 Part A:
Manual transmission

Contents

Degrees of difficulty

| Easy, suitable for novice with little experience | | Fairly easy, suitable for beginner with some experience | | Fairly difficult, suitable for competent DIY mechanic | | Difficult, suitable for experienced DIY mechanic | | Very difficult, suitable for expert DIY or professional | |

Specifications

General

Type . . . . Manual, five forward speeds and reverse. Synchromesh on all forward speeds

Designation:
All models except 2.1 litre diesel BE3
2.1 litre diesel models ML5T

Lubrication

Recommended oil . . . . See "Lubricants, fluids and tyre pressures"
Capacity:
BE3 . . . . 2.0 litres
ML5T . . . . 1.9 litres

Torque wrench settings

	Nm	lbf ft
BE3 transmission:		
Gearchange selector rod to lever pivot bolt	15	11
Gearchange linkage bellcrank pivot bolt	28	21
Oil filler/level plug	20	15
Oil drain plug	30	22
Clutch release bearing guide sleeve bolts	12	9
Reversing light switch	25	18
Right-hand driveshaft intermediate bearing retaining bolt nuts	10	7
Engine movement limiter-to- driveshaft intermediate bearing housing	50	37
Engine movement limiter-to- subframe	85	62
Left-hand engine/transmission mounting:		
Rubber mounting-to- bracket bolts	30	22
Mounting stud to transmission	60	44
Mounting stud bracket-to-transmission	60	44
Centre nut	65	48
Engine-to-transmission fixing bolts	45	33
Clutch cable bracket retaining bolts ("pull-type" clutch only)	18	13
Roadwheel bolts	90	66

Torque wrench settings (continued)

	Nm	lbf ft
ML5T transmission:		
Oil filler/level plug	20	15
Oil drain plug	30	22
Gearchange lever housing bolts	7	5
Clutch release bearing guide sleeve bolts	12	9
Reversing light switch	25	18
Right-hand driveshaft intermediate bearing retaining bolt nuts	10	7
Engine movement limiter-to-driveshaft intermediate bearing housing	50	37
Engine movement limiter-to-subframe	85	62
Left-hand engine/transmission mounting:		
Mounting to bracket	30	22
Mounting bracket-to-transmission	30	22
Centre nut	65	48
Engine-to-transmission fixing bolts	60	44
Roadwheel bolts	90	66

1 General information

The transmission is contained in a cast-aluminium alloy casing bolted to the engine's left-hand end, and consists of the gearbox and final drive differential. Two transmission types are fitted; all models except the 2.1 litre diesel utilise the BE3 transmission, whereas the 2.1 litre diesel is fitted with the ML5T unit. Both transmission types are similar and operate as follows.

Drive is transmitted from the crankshaft via the clutch to the input shaft, which has a splined extension to accept the clutch friction plate, and rotates in sealed ball-bearings. From the input shaft, drive is transmitted to the output shaft, which rotates in a roller bearing at its right-hand end, and a sealed ball-bearing at its left-hand end. From the output shaft, the drive is transmitted to the differential crownwheel, which rotates with the differential case and planetary gears, thus driving the sun gears and driveshafts. The rotation of the planetary gears on their shaft allows the inner roadwheel to rotate at a slower speed than the outer roadwheel when the car is cornering.

The input and output shafts are arranged side by side, parallel to the crankshaft and driveshafts, so that their gear pinion teeth are in constant mesh. In the neutral position, the relevant input shaft and output shaft gear pinions rotate freely, so that drive cannot be transmitted to the output shaft and crownwheel.

Gear selection is via a floor-mounted lever actuating a selector rod mechanism on BE3 transmissions, or a selector cable mechanism on the ML5T units. The selector rod/cables cause the appropriate selector fork to move its respective synchro-sleeve along the shaft, to lock the gear pinion to the synchro-hub. Since the synchro-hubs are splined to the input and output shafts, this locks the pinion to the shaft, so that drive can be transmitted.

To ensure that gear-changing can be made quickly and quietly, a synchro-mesh system is fitted to all forward gears, consisting of baulk rings and spring-loaded fingers, as well as the gear pinions and synchro-hubs. The synchro-mesh cones are formed on the mating faces of the baulk rings and gear pinions.

2 Manual transmission - draining and refilling

Note: *A suitable square section wrench may be required to undo the transmission filler/level and drain plugs on some models. These wrenches can be obtained from most motor factors or your Peugeot dealer.*

1 This operation is much quicker and more efficient if the car is first taken on a journey of sufficient length to warm the engine/transmission up to operating temperature.

2 Park the car on level ground, switch off the ignition and apply the handbrake firmly. To ensure that the car remains level when refilling, jack up the front and rear of the car and support it securely on axle stands.

3 On models equipped with the BE3 transmission, remove the left-hand front roadwheel then release the screws and clips and remove the wheel arch liner from under the wing for access to the filler/level plug. On all models, remove the splash guard from under the engine.

4 Wipe clean the area around the filler/level plug. On the BE3 transmission, the filler/level plug is the largest bolt among those securing the end cover to the transmission; on the ML5T transmission, the filler/level plug is located on the rear face of the differential housing. Unscrew the filler/level plug from the transmission and recover the sealing washer.

5 Position a suitable container under the drain plug (situated on the final drive casing at the rear of the transmission) and unscrew the plug **(see illustration)**.

6 Allow the oil to drain completely into the container. If the oil is hot, take precautions against scalding. Clean both the filler/level and the drain plugs, being especially careful to wipe any metallic particles off the magnetic inserts. Discard the original sealing washers; they should be renewed whenever they are disturbed.

7 When the oil has finished draining, clean the drain plug threads and those of the transmission casing, fit a new sealing washer and refit the drain plug, tightening it to the specified torque wrench setting.

8 Refilling the transmission is an extremely awkward operation. Above all, allow plenty of time for the oil level to settle properly before checking it. Note that the car must be level when checking the oil level.

9 Refill the transmission with the exact amount of the specified type of oil then check the oil level as described in the relevant Part of Chapter 1; if the correct amount was poured into the transmission and a large amount flows out on checking the level, refit the filler/level plug and take the car on a short journey so that the new oil is distributed fully around the transmission components, then check the level again on your return.

10 When the level is correct, fit a new sealing washer to the filler/level plug. Tighten the plug to the specified torque wrench setting. Wash off any spilt oil. Refit the wheel arch liner and splash guard, and secure with the retaining screws and clips. Refit the roadwheel (if removed) then lower the car to the ground.

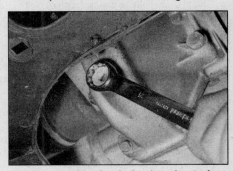

2.5 Unscrewing the drain plug situated on the final drive casing

3 Gearchange linkage (BE3 transmission) - removal and refitting

Removal

1 Remove the centre console (Chapter 11).

2 Chock the rear wheels, then jack up the front of the vehicle and support it on axle stands.

3 Refer to the relevant Part of Chapter 4 and remove the exhaust system and heat shields, as necessary for access to the gearchange linkage.

4 Slacken and remove the nut, and withdraw the pivot bolt securing the selector rod to the base of the gearchange lever.

5 Using a flat-bladed screwdriver, carefully lever the three link rods off their balljoints on the transmission (see illustration). Disengage the selector rod from the bellcrank pivot, and remove it from underneath the vehicle.

6 Carefully prise the plastic cap off the bolt securing the gearchange linkage bellcrank to the subframe.

7 Slacken and remove the bellcrank pivot bolt and washer, then manoeuvre the bellcrank and link rod out from under the vehicle, and recover the spacer and pivot bushes from the centre of the bellcrank.

8 Inspect all the linkage components for signs of wear or damage, paying particular attention to the pivot bushes and link rod balljoints, and renew worn components as necessary. If necessary, the gearchange lever can be removed and inspected as follows.

9 Slacken and remove the selector lever retaining nuts and lift off the retaining plate then lower the lever out from underneath the vehicle.

10 Peel back the lower gaiter from the base of the gearchange lever, then disengage the lever mounting plate, and slide the upper gaiter up the lever to gain access to the gearchange lever pivot ball. Examine the lever components for signs of wear or damage, paying particular attention to the rubber gaiters, and renew components as necessary. The lever can be separated from its baseplate after the retaining ring has been unclipped.

Refitting

11 Refitting is a reversal of the removal procedure, noting the following points:

a) Apply a smear of molybdenum disulphide grease to the gearchange lever pivot ball, the link rod balljoints and the bellcrank ball and pivot bushes.

b) Ensure that the gearchange lever rubber gaiters are correctly seated before refitting the lever assembly to the vehicle.

c) Ensure that the link rods are securely pressed onto their balljoints.

d) Refit the heat shields and exhaust components (Chapter 4) and the centre console (Chapter 11).

4 Gearchange cables (ML5T transmission) - removal and refitting

Removal

1 Remove the air cleaner assembly as described in Chapter 4B.

2 Remove the centre console as described in Chapter 11.

3 Working in the engine compartment, carefully prise the two gearchange cable balljoints from the selector levers on the transmission (see illustration).

4 Extract the two horseshoe shaped clips securing the cables to the mounting bracket on the transmission.

5 Chock the rear wheels, then jack up the front of the vehicle and support it on axle stands.

6 Refer to Chapter 4B and remove the exhaust system and heat shields, as necessary for access to the cables and gearchange lever housing.

7 From inside the car, remove the sound-proofing shim then unscrew the bolts securing the lever housing to the floor. Release any clips or ties securing the gearchange cables, then remove the lever housing and gearchange cables as an assembly from under the car.

Refitting

8 Refitting is a reversal of the removal procedure, noting the following points:

a) Ensure that the sound-proofing shim is correctly positioned when refitting the lever housing.

b) Ensure that the cables are fitted to the correct selector levers on the transmission - the 13.0 mm diameter balljoint connects to the upper lever and the 10.0 mm diameter balljoint connects to the side lever.

c) Refit the heat shields, exhaust components and air cleaner assembly (Chapter 4B) and the centre console (Chapter 11).

5 Oil seals - renewal

Driveshaft oil seals

Note: A new suspension lower balljoint nut will be required on refitting.

1 Chock the rear wheels, then jack up the front of the car and support it on axle stands. Remove the appropriate front roadwheel, and remove the splash guard from under the engine.

2 Drain the transmission oil as described in Section 2.

3 On models equipped with ABS, remove the wheel sensor as described in Chapter 9.

4 Slacken and remove the nut securing the front suspension lower balljoint to the swivel hub, and free the balljoint from the lower arm (see Chapter 10). Discard the nut and remove the protector plate (if loose).

Right-hand seal

5 Loosen the two intermediate bearing retaining bolt nuts, then rotate the bolts through 90° so that their offset heads are clear of the bearing outer race.

6 Carefully pull the swivel hub assembly outwards, and pull on the inner end of the driveshaft to free the intermediate bearing from its mounting bracket.

7 Once the driveshaft end is free from the transmission, slide the dust seal off the inner end of the shaft, noting which way around it is fitted, and support the inner end of the driveshaft to avoid damaging the constant velocity joints or gaiters.

8 Carefully prise the oil seal out of the transmission, using a large flat-bladed screwdriver (see illustration).

9 Remove all traces of dirt from the area around the oil seal aperture, then fill the space between the lips of the new oil seal with grease. Fit the new seal into its aperture, and drive it squarely into position using a suitable tubular drift (such as a socket) which bears only on the hard outer edge of the seal, until it abuts its locating shoulder. If the seal was supplied with a plastic protector sleeve, leave

3.5 Disconnect the three gearchange linkage link rods (arrowed) from their transmission balljoints

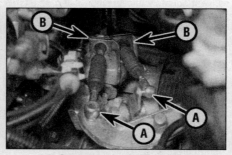

4.3 Gearchange cable balljoint attachments (A) and horseshoe shaped clips (B) securing the cables to the mounting bracket

5.8 Use a large flat-bladed screwdriver to prise the driveshaft oil seals out of position

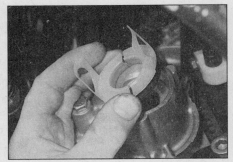

5.9a Fit the new seal to the transmission, noting the plastic seal protector . . .

5.9b . . . and tap it into position using a tubular drift

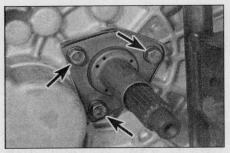

5.23a Clutch release bearing guide sleeve retaining bolts (arrowed) on the BE3 transmission . . .

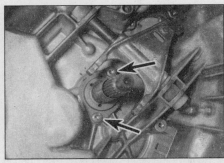

5.23b . . . and on the ML5T transmission (arrowed)

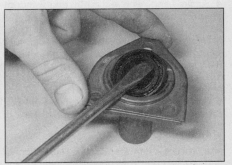

5.24 Removing the input shaft seal from the guide sleeve

this in position until the driveshaft has been refitted **(see illustrations)**.

10 Thoroughly clean the driveshaft splines, then apply a thin film of grease to the oil seal lips and to the driveshaft inner end splines.

11 Slide the dust seal into position on the end of the shaft, ensuring that its flat surface is facing the transmission.

12 Carefully locate the inner driveshaft splines with those of the differential sun gear, taking care not to damage the oil seal, then align the intermediate bearing with its mounting bracket, and push the driveshaft fully into position. If necessary, use a soft-faced mallet to tap the outer race of the bearing into position in the mounting bracket.

13 Ensure that the intermediate bearing is correctly seated, then rotate its retaining bolts back through 90° so that their offset heads are resting against the bearing outer race, and tighten the retaining nuts to the specified torque. Remove the plastic seal protector (where supplied), and slide the dust seal tight up against the oil seal.

14 Refit the protector plate (where removed) to the lower balljoint, then align the balljoint with the lower arm. Fit the new balljoint nut and tighten it to the specified torque setting (see Chapter 10).

15 Where necessary, refit the ABS wheel sensor as described in Chapter 9.

16 Refit the roadwheel and the engine splash guard, then lower the vehicle to the ground and tighten the roadwheel bolts to the specified torque.

17 Refill the transmission with the specified type and amount of fluid/oil, and check the level using the information given in Chapter 1.

Left-hand seal

18 Pull the swivel hub assembly outwards and withdraw the driveshaft inner constant velocity joint from the transmission, taking care not to damage the driveshaft oil seal. Support the driveshaft, to avoid damaging the constant velocity joints or gaiters.

19 On the BE3 transmission, renew the oil seal as described in paragraphs 8 to 10. On ML5T transmissions, unbolt the differential bearing stop plate, and prise or drift the oil seal out of the stop plate. Also remove the sealing O-ring. Thoroughly clean the stop plate, then fill the space between the lips of the new oil seal with grease. Fit the new seal into its aperture, and drive it squarely into position using a suitable tubular drift (such as a socket) which bears only on the hard outer edge of the seal, until it is fully seated. Locate a new O-ring in position then refit the stop plate to the transmission.

20 Carefully locate the inner constant velocity joint splines with those of the differential sun gear, taking care not to damage the oil seal, and push the driveshaft fully into position. Where fitted, remove the plastic protector from the oil seal.

21 Carry out the operations described above in paragraphs 14 to 17.

Input shaft oil seal

22 Remove the transmission as described in Section 8 or 9 as applicable.

23 Undo the three bolts (BE3 transmission) or two bolts (ML5T transmission) securing the clutch release bearing guide sleeve in position, and slide the guide off the input shaft, along with its O-ring or gasket **(see illustrations)**. Recover any shims or thrustwashers which have stuck to the rear of the guide sleeve, and refit them to the input shaft.

24 Carefully lever the oil seal out of the guide using a suitable flat-bladed screwdriver **(see illustration)**.

25 Before fitting a new seal, check the input shaft's seal rubbing surface for signs of burrs, scratches or other damage, which may have caused the seal to fail in the first place. It may be possible to polish away minor faults of this sort using fine abrasive paper; however, more serious defects will require the renewal of the input shaft. Ensure the input shaft is clean and greased, to protect the seal lips on refitting.

26 Dip the new seal in clean oil, and fit it to the guide sleeve.

27 Fit a new O-ring or gasket (as applicable) to the rear of the guide sleeve, then carefully slide the sleeve into position over the input shaft **(see illustration)**. Refit the retaining bolts and tighten them to the specified torque.

28 Take the opportunity to inspect the clutch components if not already done (Chapter 6). Finally, refit the transmission (Section 8 or 9).

Selector shaft oil seal (BE3 transmission)

29 Park the car on level ground, chock the rear wheels, then jack up the front of the

always use the recommended type, and ensure that it comes from a freshly-opened sealed container.

General

1 The correct operation of any hydraulic system is only possible after removing all air from the components and circuit; this is achieved by bleeding the system.

2 During the bleeding procedure, add only clean, unused hydraulic fluid of the recommended type; never re-use fluid that has already been bled from the system. Ensure that sufficient fluid is available before starting work.

3 If there is any possibility of incorrect fluid being already in the system, the brake components and circuit must be flushed completely with uncontaminated, correct fluid, and new seals should be fitted to the various components.

4 If hydraulic fluid has been lost from the system, or air has entered because of a leak, ensure that the fault is cured before proceeding further.

5 Park the vehicle on level ground, switch off the engine and select first or reverse gear, then chock the wheels and release the handbrake.

6 Check that all pipes and hoses are secure, unions tight and bleed screws closed. Clean any dirt from around the bleed screws.

7 Unscrew the master cylinder reservoir cap, and top the master cylinder reservoir up to the "MAX" level line; refit the cap loosely, and remember to maintain the fluid level at least above the "MIN" level line throughout the procedure, or there is a risk of further air entering the system.

8 There are a number of one-man, do-it-yourself brake bleeding kits currently available from motor accessory shops. It is recommended that one of these kits is used whenever possible, as they greatly simplify the bleeding operation, and also reduce the risk of expelled air and fluid being drawn back into the system. If such a kit is not available, the basic (two-man) method must be used, which is described in detail below.

9 If a kit is to be used, prepare the vehicle as described previously, and follow the kit manufacturer's instructions, as the procedure may vary slightly according to the type being used; generally, they are as outlined below in the relevant sub-section.

10 Whichever method is used, the same sequence must be followed (paragraphs 11 and 12) to ensure that the removal of all air from the system.

Bleeding sequence

11 If the system has been only partially disconnected, and suitable precautions were taken to minimise fluid loss, it should be necessary only to bleed thatof the system (ie the primary or secondary circuit).

12 If the complete system is to be bled, then it should be done working in the following sequence:

   a) Right-hand front brake.
   b) Left-hand front brake.
   c) Right-hand rear brake.
   d) Left-hand rear brake.

Bleeding - basic (two-man) method

13 Collect a clean glass jar, a suitable length of plastic or rubber tubing which is a tight fit over the bleed screw, and a ring spanner to fit the screw. The help of an assistant will also be required.

14 Remove the dust cap from the first screw in the sequence. Fit the spanner and tube to the screw, place the other end of the tube in the jar, and pour in sufficient fluid to cover the end of the tube.

15 Ensure that the master cylinder reservoir fluid level is maintained at least above the "MIN" level line throughout the procedure.

16 Have the assistant fully depress the brake pedal several times to build up pressure, then maintain it on the final downstroke.

17 While pedal pressure is maintained, unscrew the bleed screw (approximately one turn) and allow the compressed fluid and air to flow into the jar. The assistant should maintain pedal pressure, following it down to the floor if necessary, and should not release it until instructed to do so. When the flow stops, tighten the bleed screw again, have the assistant release the pedal slowly, and recheck the reservoir fluid level.

18 Repeat the steps given in paragraphs 16 and 17 until the fluid emerging from the bleed screw is free from air bubbles. If the master cylinder has been drained and refilled, and air is being bled from the first screw in the sequence, allow approximately five seconds between cycles for the master cylinder passages to refill.

19 When no more air bubbles appear, tighten the bleed screw securely, remove the tube and spanner, and refit the dust cap. Do not overtighten the bleed screw.

20 Repeat the procedure on the remaining screws in the sequence, until all air is removed from the system and the brake pedal feels firm again.

Bleeding - using a one-way valve kit

21 As their name implies, these kits consist of a length of tubing with a one-way valve fitted, to prevent expelled air and fluid being drawn back into the system; some kits include a translucent container, which can be positioned so that the air bubbles can be more easily seen flowing from the end of the tube.

22 The kit is connected to the bleed screw, which is then opened **(see illustration)**. The user returns to the driver's seat, depresses the brake pedal with a smooth, steady stroke, and slowly releases it; this is repeated until the expelled fluid is clear of air bubbles.

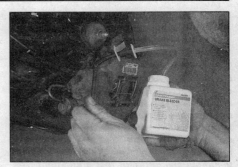

2.22 Bleeding a rear brake caliper

23 Note that these kits simplify work so much that it is easy to forget the master cylinder reservoir fluid level; ensure that this is maintained at least above the "MIN" level line at all times.

Bleeding - using a pressure-bleeding kit

24 These kits are usually operated by the reservoir of pressurised air contained in the spare tyre. However, note that it will probably be necessary to reduce the pressure to a lower level than normal; refer to the instructions supplied with the kit.

25 By connecting a pressurised, fluid-filled container to the master cylinder reservoir, bleeding can be carried out simply by opening each screw in turn (in the specified sequence), and allowing the fluid to flow out until no more air bubbles can be seen in the expelled fluid.

26 This method has the advantage that the large reservoir of fluid provides an additional safeguard against air being drawn into the system during bleeding.

27 Pressure-bleeding is particularly effective when bleeding "difficult" systems, or when bleeding the complete system at the time of routine fluid renewal.

All methods

28 When bleeding is complete, and firm pedal feel is restored, wash off any spilt fluid, tighten the bleed screws securely, and refit their dust caps.

29 Check the hydraulic fluid level in the master cylinder reservoir, and top-up if necessary (see *"Weekly checks"*).

30 Discard any hydraulic fluid that has been bled from the system; it will not be fit for re-use.

31 Check the feel of the brake pedal. If it feels at all spongy, air must still be present in the system, and further bleeding is required. Failure to bleed satisfactorily after a reasonable repetition of the bleeding procedure may be due to worn master cylinder seals.

Note: *If difficulty is experienced in bleeding the braking circuit on models with ABS, this maybe due to air being trapped in the ABS regulator unit. If this is the case then the vehicle should be taken to a Peugeot dealer so that the system can be bled using special electronic test equipment.*

3 Hydraulic pipes and hoses - renewal

Caution: On models equipped with ABS, disconnect the battery before disconnecting any braking system hydraulic union and do not reconnect the battery until after the hydraulic system has been bled. Failure to do this could lead to air entering the regulator unit requiring the unit to be bled using special Peugeot test equipment (see Section 2).

Note: *Before starting work, refer to the note at the beginning of Section 2 concerning the dangers of hydraulic fluid.*

1 If any pipe or hose is to be renewed, minimise fluid loss by first removing the master cylinder reservoir cap, then tightening it down onto a piece of polythene to obtain an airtight seal. Alternatively, flexible hoses can be sealed, if required, using a proprietary brake hose clamp; metal brake pipe unions can be plugged (if care is taken not to allow dirt into the system) or capped immediately they are disconnected. Place a wad of rag under any union that is to be disconnected, to catch any spilt fluid.

2 If a flexible hose is to be disconnected, unscrew the brake pipe union nut before removing the spring clip which secures the hose to its mounting bracket.

3 To unscrew the union nuts, it is preferable to obtain a brake pipe spanner of the correct size; these are available from most large motor accessory shops (see illustration). Failing this, a close-fitting open-ended spanner will be required, though if the nuts are tight or corroded, their flats may be rounded-off if the spanner slips. In such a case, a self-locking wrench is often the only way to unscrew a stubborn union, but it follows that the pipe and the damaged nuts must be renewed on reassembly. Always clean a union and surrounding area before disconnecting it. If disconnecting a component with more than one union, make a careful note of the connections before disturbing any of them.

4 If a brake pipe is to be renewed, it can be obtained, cut to length and with the union nuts and end flares in place, from Peugeot dealers. All that is then necessary is to bend it to shape, following the line of the original, before fitting it to the car. Alternatively, most motor accessory shops can make up brake pipes from kits, but this requires very careful measurement of the original, to ensure that the replacement is of the correct length. The safest answer is usually to take the original to the shop as a pattern.

5 On refitting, do not overtighten the union nuts. It is not necessary to exercise brute force to obtain a sound joint.

6 Ensure that the pipes and hoses are correctly routed, with no kinks, and that they are secured in the clips or brackets provided. After fitting, remove the polythene from the

3.3 Using a brake pipe spanner to slacken a union nut

reservoir, and bleed the hydraulic system as described in Section 2. Wash off any spilt fluid, and check carefully for fluid leaks.

4 Front brake pads - renewal

 Warning: Renew both sets of front brake pads at the same time - never renew the pads on only one wheel, as uneven braking may result. Note that the dust created by wear of the pads may contain asbestos, which is a health hazard. Never blow it out with compressed air, and don't inhale any of it. An approved filtering mask should be worn when working on the brakes. DO NOT use petrol or petroleum-based solvents to clean brake parts; use brake cleaner or methylated spirit only.

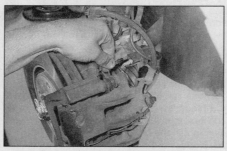

4.2 Disconnect the pad wear sensor wiring connectors and release the wiring from its retaining clips

4.5 . . . then pivot the caliper upwards and away from the brake pads and tie it to the suspension strut . . .

Note: *New guide pin bolts must be used on refitting.*

1 Apply the handbrake, then jack up the front of the vehicle and support it on axle stands. Remove the front roadwheels.

2 Trace the brake pad wear sensor wiring back from the pads, and disconnect it from the wiring connector. Note the routing of the wiring, and free it from any relevant retaining clips (see illustration).

3 Push the piston into its bore by pulling the caliper outwards.

4 Slacken and remove the caliper lower guide pin bolt, using a slim open-ended spanner to prevent the guide pin itself from rotating (see illustration). Discard the guide pin bolt - a new one must be used on refitting.

5 With the lower guide pin bolt removed, pivot the caliper away from the brake pads and mounting bracket, and tie it to the suspension strut using a suitable piece of wire (see illustration).

6 Withdraw the two brake pads from the caliper mounting bracket; the shims (where fitted) should be bonded to the pad, but may have come unstuck in use (see illustration).

7 First measure the thickness of each brake pad's friction material (see illustration). If either pad is worn at any point to the specified minimum thickness or less, all four pads must be renewed. Also, the pads should be renewed if any are fouled with oil or grease; there is no satisfactory way of degreasing friction material, once contaminated. If any of the brake pads are worn unevenly, or are fouled with oil or grease, trace and rectify the cause before reassembly.

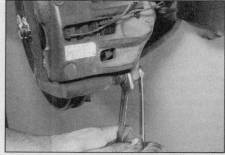

4.4 Slacken and remove the caliper lower guide pin bolt . . .

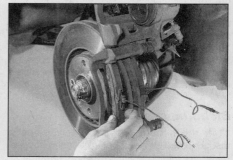

4.6 . . . the brake pads can then be removed from the mounting bracket

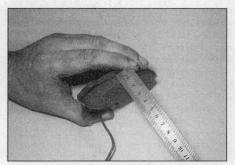

4.7 Measuring brake pad friction material thickness

4.9 Examine the guide pin gaiters for signs of damage and renew if necessary

4.12a Pivot the caliper back into position, passing the pad wear sensor wiring through the aperture . . .

4.12b . . . then fit the new guide pin bolt and tighten it to the specified torque

14 Depress the brake pedal repeatedly, until the pads are pressed into firm contact with the brake disc, and normal (non-assisted) pedal pressure is restored.

15 Repeat the above procedure on the remaining front brake caliper.

16 Refit the roadwheels, then lower the vehicle to the ground and tighten the roadwheel bolts to the specified torque.

17 Check the hydraulic fluid level as described in "Weekly checks".

> **HAYNES HiNT**
> *New pads will not give full braking efficiency until they have bedded in. Be prepared for this, and avoid hard braking as far as possible for the first hundred miles or so after pad renewal.*

5 Rear brake pads - renewal

⚠ *Warning: Renew both sets of rear brake pads at the same time - never renew the pads on only one wheel, as uneven braking may result. Note that the dust created by wear of the pads may contain asbestos, which is a health hazard. Never blow it out with compressed air, and don't inhale any of it. An approved filtering mask should be worn when working on the brakes. DO NOT use petrol or petroleum-based solvents to clean brake parts; use brake cleaner or methylated spirit only.*

1 Chock the front wheels, then jack up the rear of the vehicle and support it on axle stands. Remove the rear wheels.

2 Extract the small spring clip from the each pad retaining pin then slide the retaining pins out from the caliper, noting the correct fitted location of the pad anti-rattle spring **(see illustrations)**. Remove the anti-rattle spring noting which way around it is fitted.

3 Using pliers if necessary, withdraw both the inner and outer pads from the caliper; the shims (where fitted) should be bonded to the pad, but may have come unstuck during use **(see illustration)**.

8 If the brake pads are still serviceable, carefully clean them using a clean, fine wire brush or similar, paying particular attention to the sides and back of the metal backing. Clean out the grooves in the friction material, and pick out any large embedded particles of dirt or debris. Carefully clean the pad locations in the caliper mounting bracket.

9 Prior to fitting the pads, check that the guide pins are free to slide easily in the caliper mounting bracket, and check that the rubber guide pin gaiters are undamaged **(see illustration)**. Brush the dust and dirt from the caliper and piston, but **do not** inhale it, as it is a health hazard. Inspect the dust seal around the piston for damage, and the piston for evidence of fluid leaks, corrosion or damage. If attention to any of these components is necessary, refer to Section 10.

10 If new brake pads are to be fitted, the caliper piston must be pushed back into the cylinder to make room for them. Either use a G-clamp or similar tool, or use suitable pieces of wood as levers. Provided that the master cylinder reservoir has not been overfilled with hydraulic fluid, there should be no spillage, but keep a careful watch on the fluid level while retracting the piston. If the fluid level rises above the "MAX" level line at any time, the surplus should be siphoned off or ejected via a plastic tube connected to the bleed screw (see Section 2). **Note:** *Do not syphon the fluid by mouth, as it is poisonous; use a syringe or an old poultry baster.*

11 Ensuring that the friction material of each pad is against the brake disc, fit the pads to the caliper mounting bracket. If the shims (where fitted) have become detached, ensure that they are correctly positioned on each pads backing plate.

12 Pivot the caliper down into position over the pads, passing the pad warning sensor wiring through the caliper aperture. If the threads of the new guide pin bolt are not already pre-coated with locking compound, apply a suitable thread-locking compound to them (Peugeot recommend Loctite Frenetanch - available from your Peugeot dealer). Press the caliper into position, then install the guide pin bolt, tightening it to the specified torque setting while retaining the guide pin with an open-ended spanner **(see illustrations)**.

13 Reconnect the brake pad wear sensor wiring connectors, ensuring that the wiring is correctly routed through the loop of the caliper bleed screw cap.

5.2a Remove the spring clips (arrowed) . . .

5.2b . . . then withdraw the retaining pins and recover the anti-rattle spring, noting which way around it is fitted

5.3 Removing the rear brake pads from the caliper

4 First measure the thickness of the friction material of each brake pad. If either pad is worn at any point to the specified minimum thickness or less, all four pads must be renewed. Also, the pads should be renewed if any are fouled with oil or grease; there is no satisfactory way of degreasing friction material, once contaminated. If any of the brake pads are worn unevenly, or fouled with oil or grease, trace and rectify the cause before reassembly. Examine the retaining pins for signs of wear and renew if necessary. New brake pads and retaining pin kits are available from Peugeot dealers.

5 If the brake pads are still serviceable, carefully clean them using a clean, fine wire brush or similar, paying particular attention to the sides and back of the metal backing. Clean out the grooves in the friction material, and pick out any large embedded particles of dirt or debris. Carefully clean the pad locations in the caliper body/mounting bracket.

6 Prior to fitting the pads, check that the guide sleeves are free to slide easily in the caliper body, and check that the rubber guide sleeve gaiters are undamaged. Brush the dust and dirt from the caliper and piston, but **do not** inhale it, as it is a health hazard. Inspect the dust seal around the piston for damage, and the piston for evidence of fluid leaks, corrosion or damage. If attention to any of these components is necessary, refer to Section 11.

7 If new brake pads are to be fitted, the caliper piston must be pushed back into the cylinder to make room for them. Either use a G-clamp or similar tool, or use suitable pieces of wood as levers. Provided that the master cylinder reservoir has not been overfilled with hydraulic fluid, there should be no spillage, but keep a careful watch on the fluid level while retracting the piston. If the fluid level rises above the "MAX" level line at any time, the surplus should be siphoned off or ejected via a plastic tube connected to the bleed screw (see Section 2). **Note:** *Do not syphon the fluid by mouth, as it is poisonous; use a syringe or an old poultry baster.*

8 Slide the brake pads into position in the caliper, ensuring each pad's friction material is facing the brake disc. If the shims (where fitted) have become detached, ensure that

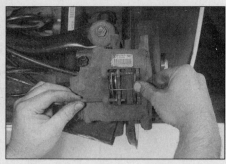

5.9 On refitting ensure the upper retaining pin passes through the centre of the anti-rattle spring and ensure the spring ends are located behind the lower pin

they are correctly positioned on each pad's backing plate

9 Fit the anti-rattle spring to the top of the pads, making sure it is fitted the correct way up. Slide the first pad retaining pin into position, ensuring it passes through the holes in both pad backing plates and the centre of the anti-rattle spring. Slide the second pad retaining pin into position, ensuring that the anti-rattle spring ends are correctly located behind the pin **(see illustration)**. Ensure that the anti-rattle spring and pads are correctly engaged with the retaining pins, then secure the pins in position with the spring clips.

10 Depress the brake pedal repeatedly until the pads are pressed into firm contact with the brake disc, and normal (non-assisted) pedal pressure is restored. Check that the inner pad lug is correctly engaged with one of the caliper piston slots.

11 Repeat the above procedure on the remaining rear brake caliper.

12 Refit the roadwheels, then lower the vehicle to the ground and tighten the roadwheel bolts to the specified torque setting.

13 Check the hydraulic fluid level as described in *"Weekly checks"*.

HAYNES HiNT *New pads will not give full braking efficiency until they have bedded in. Be prepared for this, and avoid hard braking as far as possible for the first hundred miles or so after pad renewal.*

---

6 Rear brake shoes - renewal

⚠ *Warning: Brake shoes must be renewed on both rear wheels at the same time - never renew the shoes on only one wheel, as uneven braking may result. Also, the dust created by wear of the shoes may contain asbestos, which is a health hazard. Never blow it out with compressed air, and don't*

inhale any of it. An approved filtering mask should be worn when working on the brakes. DO NOT use petrol or petroleum-based solvents to clean brake parts; use brake cleaner or methylated spirit only.

1 Remove the brake drum as described in Section 9.

2 Working carefully, and taking the necessary precautions, remove all traces of brake dust from the brake drum, backplate and shoes.

3 Measure the thickness of the friction material of each brake shoe at several points; if either shoe is worn at any point to the specified minimum thickness or less, all four shoes must be renewed as a set. The shoes should also be renewed if any are fouled with oil or grease; there is no satisfactory way of degreasing friction material, once contaminated.

4 If any of the brake shoes are worn unevenly, or fouled with oil or grease, trace and rectify the cause before reassembly.

5 To renew the brake shoes, proceed as follows. If all the components are in good condition, refit the brake drum as described in Section 9.

6 Note the correct fitted location of all components then, using a pair of pliers, remove the shoe retainer spring cups by depressing and turning them through 90°. With the cups removed, lift off the springs and withdraw the retainer pins **(see illustration)**.

7 Ease the shoes out one at a time from the lower pivot point, to release the tension of the return spring, then disconnect the lower return spring from both shoes.

8 Ease the upper end of both shoes out from their wheel cylinder locations, taking care not to damage the wheel cylinder seals, and disconnect the handbrake cable from the trailing shoe. The brake shoe and adjuster strut assembly can then be manoeuvred out of position and away from the backplate. Do not depress the brake pedal until the brakes are reassembled; wrap a strong elastic band around the wheel cylinder pistons to retain them.

9 With the shoe and adjuster strut assembly on a bench, make a note of the correct fitted positions of the springs and adjuster strut, to use as a guide on reassembly **(see illustration)**. Release the handbrake lever stop-peg (if not already done), then carefully

6.6 Removing a shoe retainer spring cup

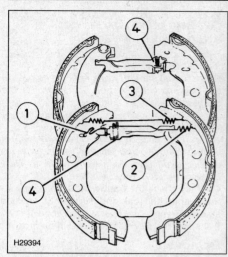

6.9 Correct fitted locations of the brake shoe adjuster strut and associated components

1 Adjuster strut bolt retaining spring
2 Adjuster strut spring
3 Upper return spring
4 Adjuster strut assembly

detach the adjuster strut bolt retaining spring from the leading shoe. Disconnect the upper return spring, then detach the leading shoe and return spring from the trailing shoe and strut assembly. Unhook the spring securing the adjuster strut to the trailing shoe, and separate the two.

10 Depending on the type of brake shoes being installed, it may be necessary to remove the handbrake lever from the original trailing shoe, and install it on the new shoe. Secure the lever in position with a new retaining clip. All return springs should be renewed, regardless of their apparent condition; spring kits are available from Peugeot dealers.

11 Withdraw the adjuster bolt from the strut, and carefully examine the assembly for signs of wear or damage. Pay particular attention to the threads of the adjuster bolt and the knurled adjuster wheel, and renew if necessary. Note that left-hand and right-hand struts are not interchangeable - they are marked "G" (gauche/left) and "D" (droit/right) respectively. Also note that the strut adjuster bolts are not interchangeable; the left-hand strut bolt has a left-handed thread (unscrews **clockwise**), and the right-hand bolt a right-handed thread.

12 Ensure that the components on the end of the strut are correctly positioned, then apply a little high-melting-point grease to the threads of the adjuster bolt. Screw the adjuster wheel onto the bolt until only a small gap exists between the wheel and the head of the bolt, then install the bolt in the strut.

13 Fit the adjuster strut retaining spring to the trailing shoe, ensuring that the shorter hook of the spring is engaged with the shoe. Attach the adjuster strut to the spring end, then ease the strut into position in its slot in the trailing shoe.

6.16 Apply a little high-melting point grease to the shoe contact points on the backplate

14 Engage the upper return spring with the trailing shoe, then hook the leading shoe onto the other end of the spring, and lever the leading shoe down until the adjuster bolt head is correctly located in its groove. Once the bolt is correctly located, hook its retaining spring into the slot on the leading shoe.

15 Peel back the rubber protective caps, and check the wheel cylinder for fluid leaks or other damage; check that both cylinder pistons are free to move easily. Refer to Section 12, if necessary, for information on wheel cylinder renewal.

16 Prior to installation, clean the backplate, and apply a thin smear of high-temperature brake grease or anti-seize compound (eg Duckhams Copper 10) to all those surfaces of the backplate which bear on the shoes, particularly the wheel cylinder pistons and lower pivot point **(see illustration)**. Do not allow the lubricant to foul the friction material.

17 Ensure that the handbrake lever stop-peg is correctly located against the edge of the trailing shoe, and remove the elastic band fitted to the wheel cylinder.

18 Manoeuvre the shoe and strut assembly into position on the vehicle, and locate the upper end of both shoes with the wheel cylinder pistons. Attach the handbrake cable to the trailing shoe lever. Fit the lower return spring to both shoes, and ease the shoes into position on the lower pivot point.

19 Tap the shoes to centralise them with the backplate, then refit the shoe retainer pins and springs, and secure them in position with the spring cups.

20 Using a screwdriver, turn the strut adjuster wheel to expand the shoes until the brake drum just slides over the shoes.

21 Refit the brake drum as described in Section 9.

22 Repeat the above procedure on the remaining rear brake.

23 Once both sets of rear shoes have been renewed, adjust the lining-to-drum clearance by repeatedly depressing the brake pedal. Whilst depressing the pedal, have an assistant listen to the rear drums, to check that the adjuster strut is functioning correctly; if so, a clicking sound will be emitted by the strut as the pedal is depressed.

24 Check and, if necessary, adjust the handbrake as described in Section 17.

25 On completion, check the hydraulic fluid level as described in "Weekly checks".

HAYNES HiNT *New shoes will not give full braking efficiency until they have bedded in. Be prepared for this, and avoid hard braking as far as possible for the first hundred miles or so after shoe renewal.*

7 Front brake disc - inspection, removal and refitting

Note: *Before starting work, refer to the note at the beginning of Section 4 concerning the dangers of asbestos dust.*

Inspection

Note: *If either disc requires renewal, BOTH should be renewed at the same time, to ensure even and consistent braking. New brake pads should also be fitted.*

1 Apply the handbrake, then jack up the front of the car and support it on axle stands. Remove the appropriate front roadwheel.

2 Slowly rotate the brake disc so that the full area of both sides can be checked; remove the brake pads if better access is required to the inboard surface. Light scoring is normal in the area swept by the brake pads, but if heavy scoring or cracks are found, the disc must be renewed.

3 It is normal to find a lip of rust and brake dust around the disc's perimeter; this can be scraped off if required. If, however, a lip has formed due to excessive wear of the brake pad swept area, then the disc's thickness must be measured using a micrometer. Take measurements at several places around the disc, at the inside and outside of the pad swept area; if the disc has worn at any point to the specified minimum thickness or less, the disc must be renewed **(see illustration)**.

4 If the disc is thought to be warped, it can be checked for run-out. Either use a dial gauge mounted on any convenient fixed point, while the disc is slowly rotated, or use feeler blades

7.3 Measuring brake disc thickness using a micrometer

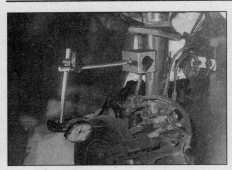

7.4 Using a dial gauge to check brake disc runout

to measure (at several points all around the disc) the clearance between the disc and a fixed point, such as the caliper mounting bracket **(see illustration)**. If the measurements obtained are at the specified maximum or beyond, the disc is excessively warped, and must be renewed; however, it is worth checking first that the hub bearing is in good condition (Chapters 1 and/or 10). Also try the effect of removing the disc and turning it through 180°, to reposition it on the hub; if the run-out is still excessive, the disc must be renewed.

5 Check the disc for cracks, especially around the wheel bolt holes, and any other wear or damage, and renew if necessary.

Removal

6 Slacken and remove the two bolts securing the brake caliper mounting bracket to the swivel hub. Slide the caliper assembly off the

disc and tie the assembly to the front coil spring, using a piece of wire or string, to avoid placing any strain on the hydraulic brake hose.
7 Use chalk or paint to mark the relationship of the disc to the hub, then remove the screws securing the brake disc to the hub, and remove the disc. If it is tight, lightly tap its rear face with a hide or plastic mallet.

Refitting

8 Refitting is the reverse of the removal procedure, noting the following points:
a) Ensure that the mating surfaces of the disc and hub are clean and flat.
b) Align (if applicable) the marks made on removal, and tighten the disc retaining screws to the specified torque setting.
c) If a new disc has been fitted, use a suitable solvent to wipe any preservative coating from the disc, before refitting the caliper.
d) Prior to installation, clean the threads of the caliper bracket mounting bolts and coat them with thread-locking compound (Peugeot recommend Loctite Frenetanch - available from your Peugeot dealer). Slide the caliper into position, making sure the pads pass either side of the disc, and tighten the caliper bracket bolts to the specified torque setting.
e) Refit the roadwheel then lower the vehicle to the ground and tighten the wheel bolts to the specified torque. Apply the footbrake several times to force the pads back into contact with the disc before driving the vehicle.

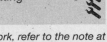

8 Rear brake disc - inspection, removal and refitting

Note: *Before starting work, refer to the note at the beginning of Section 5 concerning the dangers of asbestos dust.*

Inspection

Note: *If either disc requires renewal, BOTH should be renewed at the same time, to ensure even and consistent braking. New brake pads should also be fitted.*

1 Firmly chock the front wheels, then jack up the rear of the car and support it on axle stands. Remove the relevant rear roadwheel.
2 Inspect the disc as described in Section 7.

Removal

3 Slide out the retaining clip and release the brake pipe from its clip on the front of the hub assembly **(see illustration)**.
4 Slacken and remove the caliper mounting bolt then remove the protective cap from the guide bush and slacken and remove the guide pin bolt. Slide the caliper assembly off the disc and tie the assembly to the coil spring, using a piece of wire or string, to avoid placing any strain on the hydraulic brake pipe **(see illustrations)**.
5 Use chalk or paint to mark the relationship of the disc to the hub, then remove the screws securing the brake disc to the hub. Ensure that the handbrake is fully released then remove the disc from the vehicle, if necessary

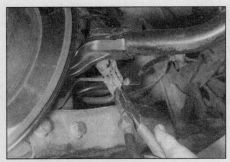

8.3 Slide out the retaining clip and free the brake pipe from the hub assembly

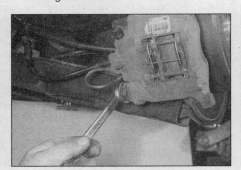

8.4a Siacken and remove the mounting bolt . . .

8.4b . . . then remove the cap from the guide bush . . .

8.4c . . . and unscrew the guide pin bolt

8.4d Slide the caliper assembly off the disc and tie it to the rear suspension to avoid straining the brake pipe

8.5a Undo the retaining screws (arrowed) . . .

8.5b . . . and remove the rear brake disc from the vehicle

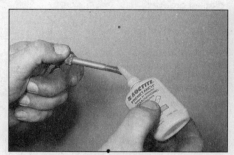

8.6a Apply locking compound to the threads of the caliper mounting and guide pin bolts . . .

8.6b . . . and tighten them to the specified torque settings

gently tap the disc to free it from the hub. If the disc is still tight on the handbrake shoes even with the brake fully released, back off the adjuster as described in Section 17 **(see illustrations)**.

Refitting

6 Refitting is the reverse of the removal procedure, noting the following points:

a) Ensure that the mating surfaces of the disc and hub are clean and flat.
b) Align (if applicable) the marks made on removal, and tighten the disc retaining screws to the specified torque.
c) If a new disc has been fitted, use a suitable solvent to wipe any preservative coating from the disc, before refitting the caliper.
d) Clean the threads of the caliper mounting and guide pin bolts and coat them with thread-locking compound. Slide the caliper into position, making sure the pads pass either side of the disc, then refit the bolts tightening them to the specified torque settings **(see illustrations)**. Refit the cap to the guide bush.
e) Prior to refitting the roadwheel, adjust the handbrake shoes (refer to Section 17).
f) Refit the roadwheel, then lower the vehicle to the ground and tighten the roadwheel bolts to the specified torque. Depress the brake pedal several times to force the pads back into contact with the disc.

9 Rear brake drum - removal, inspection and refitting

Note: Before starting work, refer to the note at the beginning of Section 6 concerning the dangers of asbestos dust.

Removal

1 Chock the front wheels, then jack up the rear of the vehicle and support it on axle stands. Remove the appropriate rear wheel.
2 Slacken and remove the screws securing the brake drum to the hub.
3 Ensure that the handbrake is fully released and remove the brake drum from the vehicle. It may be difficult to remove the drum due to the drum being corroded onto the hub, or the brake shoes binding on the inner circumference of the drum. If the drum is tight, tap the periphery of the drum using a hide or plastic mallet. If the brake shoes are binding, first check that the handbrake is fully released, then proceed as follows.
4 Referring to Section 17, fully slacken the handbrake cable adjuster to obtain maximum freeplay in the cable. Remove the access plug from the rear of the brake backplate (the plug is usually coloured blue) then, using a screwdriver or punch, push the handbrake lever outwards until the stop-peg slips behind the brake shoe web **(see illustration)**. This will retract the brake shoes fully and so allow the brake drum to be withdrawn easily. Once the drum is removed, refit the access plug to the backplate.

Inspection

Note: If either drum requires renewal, BOTH should be renewed at the same time, to ensure even and consistent braking. New brake shoes should also be fitted.
5 Working carefully, remove all traces of brake dust from the drum, but avoid inhaling the dust, as it is a health hazard.
6 Clean the outside of the drum, and check it for obvious signs of wear or damage, such as cracks around the roadwheel bolt holes; renew the drum if necessary.
7 Examine carefully the inside of the drum. Light scoring of the friction surface is normal, but if heavy scoring is found, the drum must be renewed. It is usual to find a lip on the drum's inboard edge which consists of a mixture of rust and brake dust; this should be scraped away, to leave a smooth surface which can be polished with fine (120- to 150-grade) emery paper. If, however, the lip is due to the friction surface being recessed by excessive wear, then the drum must be renewed.
8 If the drum is thought to be excessively worn, or oval, its internal diameter must be measured at several points using an internal micrometer. Take measurements in pairs, the second at right-angles to the first, and compare the two, to check for signs of ovality. Provided that it does not enlarge the drum to beyond the specified maximum diameter, it may be possible to have the drum refinished by skimming or grinding; if this is not possible, the drums on both sides must be renewed. Note that if the drum is to be skimmed, BOTH drums must be refinished, to maintain a consistent internal diameter on both sides.

Refitting

9 If a new brake drum is to be installed, use a suitable solvent to remove any preservative coating that may have been applied to its interior. Note that it may also be necessary to shorten the adjuster strut length, by rotating the strut wheel, to allow the drum to pass over the brake shoes.

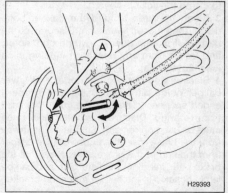

9.4 To fully release the handbrake lever, remove the access plug and use a screwdriver or punch (A) to push the lever outwards

10 Ensure that the handbrake lever stop-peg is correctly repositioned against the edge of the brake shoe web and that the mating surfaces of the drum and hub are clean and dry.

11 Manoeuvre the drum into position and tighten its retaining screws to the specified torque setting.

12 Depress the footbrake several times to operate the self-adjusting mechanism.

13 Repeat the above procedure on the remaining rear brake assembly (where necessary), then check and, if necessary, adjust the handbrake cable (see Section 17).

14 On completion, refit the roadwheel(s), then lower the car to the ground and tighten the wheel bolts to the specified torque.

10 Front brake caliper - removal, overhaul and refitting

Caution: On models equipped with ABS, disconnect the battery before disconnecting any braking system hydraulic union and do not reconnect the battery until after the hydraulic system has been bled. Failure to do this could lead to air entering the regulator unit requiring the unit to be bled using special Peugeot test equipment (see Section 2).
Note: Before starting work, refer to the note at the beginning of Section 2 concerning the dangers of hydraulic fluid, and to the warning at the beginning of Section 4 concerning the dangers of asbestos dust.

Removal

Note: New guide pin bolts will be required on refitting.

1 Apply the handbrake, then jack up the front of the vehicle and support it on axle stands. Remove the appropriate roadwheel.

2 Minimise fluid loss by first removing the master cylinder reservoir cap, and then tightening it down onto a piece of polythene, to obtain an airtight seal. Alternatively, use a brake hose clamp, a G-clamp or a similar tool to clamp the flexible hose.

3 Clean the area around the caliper hose union, then loosen the union. Disconnect the pad wear warning sensor wiring connector, and free it from any relevant retaining clips **(see illustration)**.

4 Slacken and remove the upper and lower caliper guide pin bolts, using a slim open-ended spanner to prevent the guide pin itself from rotating. Discard the bolts, new ones must be used on refitting. Lift the caliper away from the brake disc, then unscrew the caliper from the end of the brake hose. Note that the brake pads need not be disturbed, and can be left in position in the caliper mounting bracket.

Overhaul

5 With the caliper on the bench, wipe away all traces of dust and dirt, but *avoid inhaling the dust, as it is a health hazard.*

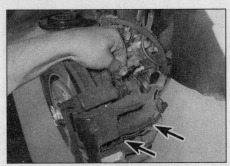

10.3 Disconnect the pad wear sensor wiring and free it from its retaining clips (arrowed)

6 Withdraw the partially ejected piston from the caliper body, and remove the dust seal.

> **HAYNES HINT** *If the piston cannot be withdrawn by hand, it can be pushed out by applying compressed air to the brake hose union hole. Only low pressure should be required, such as is generated by a foot pump. As the piston is expelled, take great care not to trap your fingers between the piston and caliper.*

7 Using a small screwdriver, extract the piston hydraulic seal, taking great care not to damage the caliper bore.

8 Thoroughly clean all components, using only methylated spirit, isopropyl alcohol or clean hydraulic fluid as a cleaning medium. Never use mineral-based solvents such as petrol or paraffin, as they will attack the hydraulic system's rubber components. Dry the components immediately, using compressed air or a clean, lint-free cloth. Use compressed air to blow clear the fluid passages.

9 Check all components, and renew any that are worn or damaged. Check particularly the cylinder bore and piston; these should be renewed (note that this means the renewal of the complete body assembly) if they are scratched, worn or corroded in any way. Similarly check the condition of the guide pins and their gaiters; both pins should be undamaged and (when cleaned) a reasonably tight sliding fit in the caliper bracket. If there is any doubt about the condition of any component, renew it.

10 If the assembly is fit for further use, obtain the appropriate repair kit; the components are available from Peugeot dealers in various combinations. All rubber seals should be renewed as a matter of course; these should never be re-used.

11 On reassembly, ensure that all components are clean and dry.

12 Soak the piston and the new piston (fluid) seal in clean hydraulic fluid. Smear clean fluid on the cylinder bore surface.

13 Fit the new piston (fluid) seal, using only your fingers (no tools) to manipulate it into the cylinder bore groove.

14 Fit the new dust seal to the rear of the piston and seat the outer lip of the seal in the caliper body groove. Carefully ease the piston squarely into the cylinder bore using a twisting motion. Press the piston fully into position, and seat the inner lip of the dust seal in the piston groove.

15 If the guide pins are being renewed, lubricate the pin shafts with the special grease supplied in the repair kit, and fit the gaiters to the pin grooves. Insert the pins into the caliper bracket and seat the gaiters correctly in the bracket grooves.

Refitting

16 Screw the caliper body fully onto the flexible hose union.

17 Ensure that the brake pads are still correctly fitted in the caliper mounting bracket and refit the caliper, passing the pad warning sensor wiring through the caliper aperture.

18 If the threads of the new guide pin bolts are not already pre-coated with locking compound, apply a suitable locking compound to them (Peugeot recommend Loctite Frenetanch - available from your Peugeot dealer). Fit the new lower guide pin bolt, then press the caliper into position and fit the new upper guide pin bolt. Tighten both guide pin bolts to the specified torque while retaining the guide pin with an open-ended spanner.

19 Reconnect the brake pad wear sensor wiring connectors, ensuring that the wiring is correctly routed through the loop of the caliper bleed screw cap.

20 Tighten the brake hose union nut to the specified torque, then remove the brake hose clamp or polythene (where fitted).

21 Bleed the hydraulic system as described in Section 2. Note that, providing the precautions described were taken to minimise brake fluid loss, it should only be necessary to bleed the relevant front brake.

22 Refit the roadwheel, then lower the vehicle to the ground and tighten the roadwheel bolts to the specified torque.

11 Rear brake caliper - removal, overhaul and refitting

Caution: On models equipped with ABS, disconnect the battery before disconnecting any braking system hydraulic union and do not reconnect the battery until after the hydraulic system has been bled. Failure to do this could lead to air entering the regulator unit requiring the unit to be bled using special Peugeot test equipment (see Section 2).
Note: Before starting work, refer to the note at the beginning of Section 2 concerning the dangers of hydraulic fluid, and to the warning

11.8a Apply locking compound to the guide pin and mounting bolt threads . . .

11.8b . . . and tighten them to the specified torque

at the beginning of Section 5 concerning the dangers of asbestos dust.

Removal

1 Chock the front wheels, then jack up the rear of the vehicle and support on axle stands. Remove the relevant rear wheel.

2 Remove the brake pads as described in Section 5.

3 Minimise fluid loss by first removing the master cylinder reservoir cap, and then tightening it down onto a piece of polythene, to obtain an airtight seal. Alternatively, use a brake hose clamp, a G-clamp or a similar tool to clamp the flexible hose at the nearest convenient point to the brake caliper.

4 Wipe away all traces of dirt around the brake hose union on the caliper. Unscrew the union nut and disconnect the brake pipe from the caliper. Plug the pipe and caliper unions to minimise fluid loss and prevent dirt entry.

5 Slacken and remove the caliper mounting bolt then remove the protective cap from the guide bush and slacken and remove the guide pin bolt. Remove the caliper from the vehicle.

Overhaul

6 The caliper can be overhauled as described in Section 10. The only notable difference between the front and rear caliper is in the guide pin/bush arrangement. If either the guide bush or spacer show signs of wear or damage they must be renewed; both components are available in repair kits from Peugeot dealers.

Refitting

7 Clean the threads of the caliper mounting and guide pin bolts and coat them with thread-locking compound (Peugeot recommend Loctite Frenetanch - available from your Peugeot dealer).

8 Refit the caliper and insert the mounting and guide pin bolts, tightening them to the specified torque settings **(see illustrations)**. Refit the protective cap to the guide bush.

9 Reconnect the brake pipe to the caliper, and tighten the brake hose union nut to the specified torque. Remove the brake hose clamp or polythene (where fitted).

10 Refit the brake pads as described in Section 5.

11 Bleed the hydraulic system as described in Section 2. Note that, providing the precautions described were taken to minimise brake fluid loss, it should only be necessary to bleed the relevant front brake.

12 Refit the roadwheel, then lower the vehicle to the ground and tighten the roadwheel bolts to the specified torque.

---

12 Rear wheel cylinder - removal and refitting

Caution: On models equipped with ABS, disconnect the battery before disconnecting any braking system hydraulic union and do not reconnect the battery until after the hydraulic system has been bled. Failure to do this could lead to air entering the regulator unit requiring the unit to be bled using special Peugeot test equipment (see Section 2).

Note: *Before starting work, refer to the note at the beginning of Section 2 concerning the dangers of hydraulic fluid, and to the warning at the beginning of Section 6 concerning the dangers of asbestos dust.*

Removal

1 Remove the brake drum as described in Section 9.

2 Minimise fluid loss by first removing the master cylinder reservoir cap, and then tightening it down onto a piece of polythene, to obtain an airtight seal. Alternatively, use a

brake hose clamp, a G-clamp or a similar tool to clamp the flexible hose at the nearest convenient point to the wheel cylinder **(see illustration)**.

3 Using pliers, carefully unhook the upper brake shoe return spring, and remove it from both brake shoes. Pull the upper ends of the shoes away from the wheel cylinder to disengage them from the pistons.

4 Wipe away all traces of dirt around the brake pipe union at the rear of the wheel cylinder, and unscrew the union nut **(see illustration)**. Carefully ease the pipe out of the wheel cylinder, and plug or tape over its end to prevent dirt entry. Wipe off any spilt fluid immediately.

5 Unscrew the two wheel cylinder retaining bolts from the rear of the backplate, and remove the cylinder, taking great care not to allow surplus hydraulic fluid to contaminate the brake shoe linings.

6 Note that it is not possible to overhaul the cylinder, since no components are available separately. If faulty, the complete wheel cylinder assembly must be renewed.

Refitting

7 Ensure that the backplate and wheel cylinder mating surfaces are clean, then spread the brake shoes and manoeuvre the wheel cylinder into position.

8 Engage the brake pipe, and screw in the union nut two or three turns to ensure that the thread has started.

9 Insert the two wheel cylinder retaining bolts, tightening them to the specified torque, then tighten the brake pipe union nut to the specified torque.

10 Remove the clamp from the flexible brake hose, or the polythene from the master cylinder reservoir (as applicable).

11 Ensure that the brake shoes are correctly located in the cylinder pistons, then carefully refit the brake shoe upper return spring, using a screwdriver to stretch the spring into position.

12 Refit the brake drum as described in Section 9.

13 Bleed the brake hydraulic system as described in Section 2. Providing suitable precautions were taken to minimise loss of fluid, it should only be necessary to bleed the relevant rear brake.

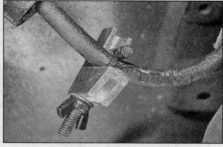

12.2 To minimise fluid loss, clamp the brake hose at the nearest convenient point to the wheel cylinder

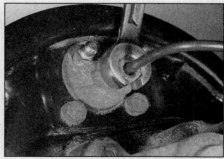

12.4 Using a brake pipe spanner to unscrew the wheel cylinder union nut

13 Master cylinder - removal, overhaul and refitting

Caution: *On models equipped with ABS, disconnect the battery before disconnecting any braking system hydraulic union and do not reconnect the battery until after the hydraulic system has been bled. Failure to do this could lead to air entering the regulator unit requiring the unit to be bled using special Peugeot test equipment (see Section 2).*
Note: *Before starting work, refer to the warning at the beginning of Section 2 concerning the dangers of hydraulic fluid.*

Removal

1 To provide improved access on some models it will be necessary to remove the air cleaner housing duct (see Chapter 4).
2 Remove the master cylinder reservoir cap and filter, and syphon the hydraulic fluid from the reservoir. **Note:** *Do not syphon the fluid by mouth, as it is poisonous; use a syringe or an old poultry baster.* Alternatively, open any convenient bleed screw in the system, and gently pump the brake pedal to expel the fluid through a plastic tube connected to the screw (see Section 2). Disconnect the wiring connector from the brake fluid level sender unit.
3 Remove the retaining clip then slide out the fluid reservoir retaining pin. Lift the reservoir upwards and away from the master cylinder body, and recover the mounting seals from the cylinder ports. If the mounting seals show signs of wear or deterioration, they must be renewed.
4 Wipe clean the area around the brake pipe unions on the side of the master cylinder, and place absorbent rags beneath the pipe unions to catch any surplus fluid. Make a note of the correct fitted positions of the unions, then unscrew the union nuts and carefully withdraw the pipes. Plug or tape over the pipe ends and master cylinder orifices, to minimise the loss of brake fluid, and to prevent the entry of dirt into the system. Wash off any spilt fluid immediately with cold water.
5 Slacken and remove the two nuts securing the master cylinder to the vacuum servo unit, then withdraw the unit from the engine compartment. If the sealing ring fitted to the rear of the master cylinder shows signs of damage or deterioration, it must be renewed.

Overhaul

6 The master cylinder can be overhauled after obtaining the relevant repair kit from a Peugeot dealer. Ensure that the correct repair kit is obtained for the master cylinder being worked on. Note the locations of all components to ensure correct refitting, and lubricate the new seals using clean brake fluid. Follow the assembly instructions supplied with the repair kit.

Refitting

7 Prior to refitting, measure the distance from the end of the vacuum servo unit pushrod to the servo master cylinder mating surface. This should be 22.3 ± 0.1 mm; if not seek the advice of a Peugeot dealer before refitting the master cylinder.
8 Remove all traces of dirt from the master cylinder and servo unit mating surfaces and ensure that the sealing ring is correctly fitted to the rear of the master cylinder.
9 Fit the master cylinder to the servo unit, ensuring that the servo unit pushrod enters the master cylinder bore centrally. Refit the master cylinder mounting nuts, and tighten them to the specified torque.
10 Wipe clean the brake pipe unions and refit them to the master cylinder ports, tightening them to the specified torque.
11 Press the mounting seals fully into the master cylinder ports then carefully ease the fluid reservoir into position. Slide the reservoir retaining pin into position and secure it in position, making sure the retaining clip is correctly located in the pin groove.
12 Refit any components removed to improve access then refill the master cylinder reservoir with new fluid. Bleed the complete hydraulic system as described in Section 2.

14 Brake pedal - removal and refitting

Removal

1 Disconnect the battery negative terminal.
2 Open up the engine immobiliser key pad, then rotate the fastener through 90° and lower the fusebox cover. Disconnect the wiring connector from the key pad then slacken and remove the retaining screws and remove the driver's side lower panel from the facia.
3 Slide off the retaining clip(s) and withdraw the clevis pin securing the pedal crossover linkage/servo unit pushrod to the pedal.
4 Slacken and remove the pivot bolt and nut, and remove the brake pedal from the vehicle. Slide the spacer out from the pedal pivot. Examine all components for signs of wear or damage, renewing them as necessary.

Refitting

5 Apply a smear of multi-purpose grease to the spacer, and insert it into the pedal pivot bore.
6 Manoeuvre the pedal into position, making sure it is correctly engaged with the pushrod, and insert the pivot bolt. Refit the nut to the pivot bolt and tighten it to the specified torque.
7 Align the pedal with the pushrod and insert the clevis pin, securing it in position with the retaining clip(s).
8 Refit the lower panel to the facia and reconnect the battery.

15 Vacuum servo unit - testing, removal and refitting

Testing

1 To test the operation of the servo unit, depress the footbrake several times to exhaust the vacuum, then start the engine whilst keeping the pedal firmly depressed. As the engine starts, there should be a noticeable "give" in the brake pedal as the vacuum builds up. Allow the engine to run for at least two minutes, then switch it off. If the brake pedal is now depressed it should feel normal, but further applications should result in the pedal feeling firmer, with the pedal stroke decreasing with each application.
2 If the servo does not operate as described, first inspect the servo unit check valve as described in Section 16. On diesel engine models, also check the operation of the vacuum pump as described in Section 26.
3 If the servo unit still fails to operate satisfactorily, the fault lies within the unit itself. Repairs to the unit are not possible - if faulty, the servo unit must be renewed.

Removal

4 Remove the master cylinder as described in Section 13.
5 Slacken the retaining clip (where fitted) and disconnect the vacuum hose from the servo unit check valve. Proceed as described under the relevant sub-heading.

Right-hand drive models

Note: *Access to the servo unit and crossover linkage is exceptionally poor (especially on diesel models) but can only be improved by removing the cylinder head (where possible) or the engine!.*
6 Undo the retaining screws and remove the cover from the right-hand end of the pedal crossover linkage housing.
7 Slacken and remove the pivot bolt and nut securing the crossover linkage rod to the pedal end pivot, then unscrew the two bolts securing the linkage housing to the pedal end bracket.
8 Unclip the cover from the servo end of the crossover linkage housing then slacken and remove the four nuts securing the housing to the bulkhead.
9 Ease the housing away from the bulkhead, then slacken and remove the servo unit retaining nuts. Remove the retaining clip, then slide out the clevis pin securing the servo unit to the linkage pivot.
10 Manoeuvre the servo unit out of position, along with its gasket which is fitted between the servo and housing. Renew the gasket if it shows signs of damage.

Left-hand drive models

11 Disconnect the servo unit pushrod from the brake pedal as described in paragraphs 2 and 3 of Section 14.

12 Slacken and remove the nuts securing the servo unit to the bulkhead, and manoeuvre the unit out of position. Recover the seal which is fitted between the servo and bulkhead.

Refitting

Right-hand drive models

13 Refitting is the reverse of removal, noting the following points.
  a) *Prior to refitting, measure the distance from the end of the vacuum servo unit pushrod to the servo master cylinder mating surface. This should be 22.3 ± 0.1 mm; if not seek the advice of a Peugeot dealer before refitting the master cylinder.*
  b) *Lubricate all crossover linkage pivot points with multi-purpose grease.*
  c) *Tighten the servo unit and mounting bracket nuts and bolts to their specified torque settings.*
  d) *Refit the master cylinder as described in Section 13 and bleed the complete hydraulic system as described in Section 2.*

Left-hand drive models

14 Prior to refitting, measure the distance from the end of the vacuum servo unit pushrod to the servo master cylinder mating surface. This should be 22.3 ± 0.1 mm; if not seek the advice of a Peugeot dealer before refitting the master cylinder.
15 Ensure that the gasket is correctly fitted to the rear of the servo unit, then manoeuvre the unit into position.
16 Make sure the pushrod is correctly engaged with the pedal, then refit the servo unit mounting nuts and tighten them to the specified torque.
17 Align the pedal with the pushrod and insert the clevis pin, securing it in position with the retaining clip(s). Refit the lower panel to the facia.
18 Connect the vacuum hose to the check valve and securely tighten its retaining clip.
19 Refit the master cylinder as described in Section 13, and bleed the complete hydraulic system as described in Section 2.

16 Vacuum servo unit check valve - removal, testing and refitting

Removal

1 Slacken the retaining clip (where fitted), and disconnect the vacuum hose from the servo unit check valve.
2 Withdraw the valve from its rubber sealing grommet, using a pulling and twisting motion. Remove the grommet from the servo.

Testing

3 Examine the check valve for signs of damage, and renew if necessary. The valve may be tested by blowing through it in both directions. Air should flow through the valve in one direction only - when blown through from the servo unit end of the valve. Renew the valve if this is not the case.
4 Examine the rubber sealing grommet and flexible vacuum hose for signs of damage or deterioration, and renew as necessary.

Refitting

5 Fit the sealing grommet into position in the servo unit.
6 Carefully ease the check valve into position, taking great care not to displace or damage the grommet. Reconnect the vacuum hose to the valve and, where necessary, securely tighten its retaining clip.
7 On completion, start the engine and check for air leaks from the check valve-to-servo unit connection.

17 Handbrake - adjustment

Rear drum brake models

1 To check the handbrake adjustment, fully release the handbrake then apply the footbrake firmly several times to establish correct shoe-to-drum clearance, then apply and release the handbrake several times to ensure that the self-adjust mechanism is fully adjusted. Applying normal moderate pressure, pull the handbrake lever to the fully-applied position, counting the number of clicks emitted from the handbrake ratchet mechanism. If adjustment is correct, there should be between 10 and 11 clicks before the handbrake is fully applied. If this is not the case, adjust as follows.
2 Chock the front wheels, then jack up the rear of the vehicle and support it on axle stands.
3 To gain access to the handbrake adjuster, unscrew the retaining nuts/bolts and remove the exhaust system rear heatshield.
4 With the handbrake lever fully released, slacken the locknut and rotate the adjuster on the left-hand side of the relay mechanism. Screw the adjuster in or out (as applicable) until there is approximately 0.5 to 1.0 mm of freeplay between the front cable and the right-hand rear cable **(see illustrations)**. Once the adjuster is correctly positioned, securely tighten the locknut.
5 Check the handbrake adjustment by applying the handbrake fully, counting the clicks emitted from the handbrake ratchet and, if necessary, re-adjust.
6 Refit the heatshield then lower the vehicle to the ground.

Rear disc brake models

7 To check the handbrake adjustment, applying normal moderate pressure, pull the handbrake lever to the fully-applied position, counting the number of clicks emitted from the handbrake ratchet mechanism. If adjustment is correct, there should be between 6 and 7 clicks before the handbrake is fully applied. If this is not the case, adjust as follows noting that it should only be necessary to adjust the cable if the handbrake shoes have not been disturbed.

Adjusting the handbrake shoes

8 Chock the front wheels, then jack up the rear of the vehicle and support it on axle stands. Remove both rear roadwheels.
9 Working on the first disc, using a pair of pointed nose pliers, remove the adjuster access plug from the front of the brake disc **(see illustration)**.

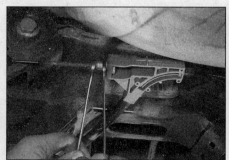

17.4a Slacken the lock nut and rotate the adjuster nut . . .

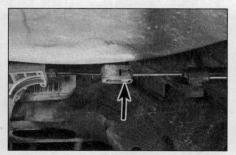

17.4b . . . to obtain the correct amount of free play at the point (arrowed) between the right-hand cable and front cable end fittings

17.9 On models with rear disc brakes, remove the access plug from brake disc

17.11a Using a flat-bladed screwdriver inserted through the access hole . . .

10 Rotate the disc and position the access hole directly opposite the brake caliper so that access can be gained to the handbrake shoe adjuster knurled ring.

11 Make sure the handbrake is fully released, then insert a screwdriver in through the access hole and fully expand the handbrake shoes by rotating the adjuster knurled ring (see illustrations). When the disc can no longer be turned, back the knurled ring off by 5 or 6 teeth (catches) so that the wheel is free to rotate easily.

12 Refit the access plug to the brake disc. Ensure that the plug is positioned correctly so that its slot is at right-angles to the centre line from the hub to the plug hole.

13 Repeat paragraphs 9 to 12 on the opposite disc.

14 Refit the roadwheels then adjust the cable as follows. On completion lower the vehicle to the ground and tighten the wheelbolts to the specified torque setting.

Adjusting the handbrake cable

15 The handbrake cable is adjusted as described in paragraphs 2 to 6.

18 Handbrake lever -
removal and refitting

Removal

1 Chock the front wheels then jack up the rear of the vehicle and support it on axle stands.

2 Referring to Section 17, release the handbrake lever and back off the adjuster to obtain maximum freeplay in the cable.

3 Remove the centre console as described in Chapter 11.

4 Peel back the gaiter (where necessary) and disconnect the wiring connector from the handbrake warning light switch.

5 Detach the handbrake cable from the lever then slacken and remove the lever retaining nuts, and remove the lever from the vehicle.

Refitting

6 Refitting is a reversal of removal. Tighten the lever retaining nuts to the specified torque, and adjust the handbrake (see Section 17).

17.11b . . . rotate the adjuster knurled ring (shown with disc removed) as described in text to correctly set the handbrake shoe-to-drum clearance

19 Handbrake cables -
removal and refitting

Removal

1 The handbrake cable consists of three sections, a front section which incorporates the adjuster mechanism and right- and left-hand rear sections which connect the rear brakes to the adjuster mechanism on the front cable. Each section can be removed individually.

2 Firmly chock the front wheels, then jack up the rear of the vehicle and support it on axle stands.

3 Referring to Section 17, remove the heatshield and slacken the adjuster to obtain maximum freeplay in the cable. Proceed as described under the relevant sub-heading.

19.12a Tap the handbrake outer cable out from the backplate . . .

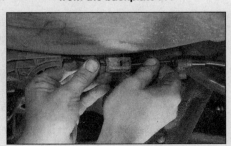

19.12c The right-hand cable end fitting simply unhooks from the front cable . . .

Front cable

4 Remove the centre console (Chapter 11).

5 Fully release the handbrake then detach the cable from the handbrake lever, and release the cable from its retaining clips and ties.

6 From underneath the vehicle, detach the right-hand rear cable from the front cable adjuster, then unscrew the adjuster and detach the left-hand rear cable.

7 Free the front cable from its retaining clips and ties, and withdraw the cable from underneath the vehicle.

Rear cable - drum brake models

8 Remove the relevant rear brake drum as described in Section 9.

9 Detach the end of the inner cable from the brake shoe lever, and tap the outer cable out of the rear of the backplate.

10 Work back along the length of the cable, freeing it from any relevant retaining clips and ties. Free the cable from the adjuster mechanism (the right-hand cable is clipped in position and the left-hand cable screwed in) and remove it from underneath the vehicle.

Rear cable - disc brake models

11 Remove the relevant set of handbrake shoes as described in Section 20, and detach the expander mechanism from the end of the cable.

12 Tap the outer cable out of the backplate then work back along the length of the cable, freeing it from any relevant retaining clips and ties. Free the cable from the adjuster mechanism (the right-hand cable is clipped in position and the left-hand cable screwed in) and remove it from underneath the vehicle (see illustrations).

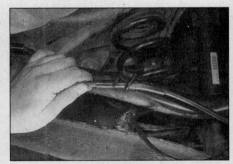

19.12b . . . and free the cable from its retaining clips

19.12d . . . whereas the left-hand cable needs to be unscrewed

20.2 Rotate the handbrake upper shoe retaining spring through 90° and remove it from the vehicle

20.3a Unhook the upper return spring . . .

20.3b . . . and remove the adjuster from between the handbrake shoes

20.4 Disengage the upper shoe from the expander then remove the shoe and lower return spring

20.5a Remove the retaining spring and lower shoe . . .

20.5b . . . and detach the expander mechanism from the end of the cable, noting its fitted arrangement and taking care not to lose the pivot pin (arrowed)

Refitting

13 Refitting is a reversal of the removal procedure, adjusting the handbrake as described in Section 17.

20 Handbrake shoes (rear disc brake models) - removal and refitting

Removal

1 Remove the brake disc as described in Section 8, and make a note of the correct fitted position of all components.
2 Using an Allen key, compress the upper shoe retaining spring, then rotate it through 90° and remove it from the backplate **(see illustration)**.
3 Carefully unhook and remove the handbrake shoe upper return spring then free the adjuster, noting which way around it is fitted, and remove it from between the shoes **(see illustrations)**.
4 Free the upper shoe from the expander mechanism, then carefully unhook the lower return spring and remove both components **(see illustration)**.
5 Remove the lower shoe retaining spring (see paragraph 2) and remove the handbrake shoe, taking great care not to drop the expander. Note the correct fitted orientation of the expander assembly, then detach it from the end of the handbrake cable **(see illustrations)**.
6 Inspect the handbrake shoes for signs of

wear or contamination, and renew if necessary. It is recommended that the return springs are renewed as a matter of course. Peugeot do not state any wear limit for the shoe friction material thickness, but anything less than 1 mm is not ideal.
7 Whilst the shoes are removed, clean and inspect the condition of the shoe adjuster and expander mechanisms, renew them if they show signs of wear or damage **(see illustration)**. If all is well, apply a fresh coat of high-temperature grease to the threads of the adjuster and sliding surfaces of the expander mechanism. Do allow the grease to contact the shoe friction material.

Refitting

8 Prior to installation, clean the backplate, and apply a thin smear of high-temperature brake grease or anti-seize compound to all

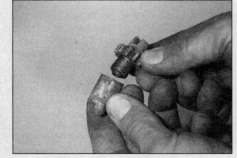

20.7 Examine the adjuster mechanism for signs of wear or damage

those surfaces of the backplate which bear on the shoes. Do not allow the lubricant to foul the friction material.
9 Ensure that the expander mechanism is correctly assembled, then engage it with the end of the handbrake cable **(see illustration)**.
10 Ensure that the expander legs are correctly positioned against the back plate stops, then fit the lower handbrake shoe. Ensure that the shoe is correctly engaged with the expander and secure it in position retaining spring **(see illustration)**.
11 Offer up the upper shoe and lower return spring. Hook the spring into position on both shoes, then manoeuvre the upper shoe into position on the backplate. Ensure that the upper shoe is correctly engaged with the expander, then secure it in position with the retaining spring.
12 Fully retract the adjuster assembly and

20.9 Ensure the expander mechanism is correctly engaged with the cable . . .

20.10 . . . then fit the lower handbrake shoe and secure it in position with the retaining spring

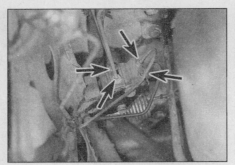

21.6 Load-sensitive pressure regulating valve pipe unions (arrowed)

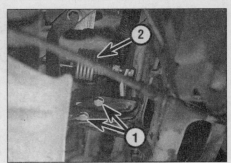

21.8 Undo the retaining bolts (1) then detach the spring (2) and remove the valve from underneath the vehicle

manoeuvre it into position between the shoes. Using pliers, hook the upper return spring onto the lower shoe, then stretch it into position in the upper shoe.

13 Check all components are correctly fitted, and centralise the handbrake shoes.

14 Refit the brake disc (see Section 8). Prior to refitting the roadwheel, adjust the handbrake shoes and cable (see Section 17).

21 Rear brake pressure-regulating valve - testing, removal and refitting

Caution: On models equipped with ABS, disconnect the battery before disconnecting any braking system hydraulic union, and do not reconnect the battery until after the hydraulic system has been bled. Failure to do this could lead to air entering the regulator unit, requiring the unit to be bled using special Peugeot test equipment (see Section 2).

Testing

1 On some models, a load-sensitive pressure regulating valve is fitted into the hydraulic circuit to the rear brakes. The valve is mounted onto the underside of the rear of the vehicle, and is attached to the rear suspension anti-roll bar by a spring. The valve measures the load on the rear axle, via the movement of the anti-roll bar, and regulates the hydraulic pressure being applied to the rear brakes to help prevent rear wheels locking up under hard braking.

2 On some smaller-capacity models with rear drum brakes, the valves are incorporated into the wheel cylinders; on these models, the valves are pressure-sensitive only, and are not affected by the load being carried.

3 Specialist equipment is required to check the performance of the valve(s), so if the valve is thought to be faulty, the car should be taken to a suitably-equipped Peugeot dealer for testing. Repairs are not possible and, if faulty, the valve must be renewed; on models with a load-sensitive valve, adjustment is possible, but again specialist equipment is needed to carry out this procedure.

Removal

Note: *Before starting work, refer to the warning at the beginning of Section 2 concerning the dangers of hydraulic fluid.*

Load-sensitive valve

4 Firmly chock the front wheels, then jack up the rear of the vehicle and support it on axle stands.

5 Minimise fluid loss by first removing the master cylinder reservoir cap, and then tightening it down onto a piece of polythene, to obtain an airtight seal.

6 Wipe clean the area around the brake pipe unions on the valve, and place absorbent rags beneath the pipe unions to catch any surplus fluid **(see illustration)**. To avoid confusion on refitting, make alignment marks between the pipes and valve assembly.

7 Slacken the union nuts and disconnect the brake pipes from the valve. Plug or tape over the pipe ends and valve orifices, to minimise the loss of brake fluid, and to prevent the entry of dirt into the system. Wash off any spilt fluid immediately with cold water.

8 Slacken and remove the valve retaining bolts, then unhook the valve spring from its bracket and remove the valve assembly from underneath the vehicle **(see illustration)**.

Pressure-sensitive valve

9 The valve is an integral part of the rear wheel cylinder. Refer to Section 12 for removal and refitting details.

Refitting

Load-sensitive valve

10 Prior to refitting, thoroughly clean the valve retaining bolt threads and apply a few drops of thread-locking compound (Peugeot recommend Loctite Frenetanch - available from your Peugeot dealer) to each one.

11 Manoeuvre the valve assembly into position, and hook the spring into the bracket on the anti-roll bar. Align the valve with its mounting bracket, and refit the retaining bolts, tightening them to the specified torque setting.

12 Refit the brake pipes to their specific unions on the valve, and tighten the union nuts to the specified torque setting.

13 Remove the polythene from the master cylinder reservoir, and bleed the complete hydraulic system as described in Section 2. If a new valve assembly has been fitted, it is recommended that the vehicle is taken to a Peugeot dealer so that the valve operation can be checked and, if necessary, adjusted using their special test equipment.

Pressure-sensitive valve

14 Refit the wheel cylinder (see Section 12).

22 Stop-light switch - removal, refitting and adjustment

Note: *On some models it will be necessary to remove the steering column to gain access to the switch.*

1 The stop-light switch is located on the pedal bracket behind the facia. On models with automatic transmission or cruise control there are two switches fitted to the bracket – the stop-light switch is the left-hand of the two.

Removal

2 Open up the engine immobiliser key pad, then rotate the fastener through 90° and lower the fusebox cover. Disconnect the wiring connector from the key pad, then slacken and remove the retaining screws and remove the driver's side lower panel from the facia. Access to the switch is very poor, and can only be improved by removing the steering column (see Chapter 10) **(see illustration)**.

22.2 Stop-light switch (arrowed) viewed with the steering column removed

3 Disconnect the wiring, then unscrew the switch and remove it from the bracket.

Refitting and adjustment

4 Screw the switch back into position in the mounting bracket, until the gap between the end of the main body of the switch and the lug on the brake pedal is around 2 to 3 mm.
5 Once the stop-light switch is correctly positioned, reconnect the wiring connector, and check the operation of the stop-lights. The stop-lights should illuminate after the brake pedal has travelled about 5 mm. Adjust the switch as necessary, then refit the steering column (where removed) lower facia panel.

23 Anti-lock braking system (ABS) - general information

ABS is fitted to some larger-capacity models as standard and was available as an option on all others. The system comprises a hydraulic regulator unit and the four roadwheel sensors. The regulator unit contains the electronic control unit (ECU), the eight hydraulic solenoid valves (two for each brake - one inlet and one outlet) and the electrically-driven return pump. The purpose of the system is to prevent the wheel(s) locking during heavy braking. This is achieved by automatic release of the brake on the relevant wheel, followed by re-application of the brake. In the case of the rear wheels both brakes are applied at the same time.

The solenoid valves are controlled by the ECU, which itself receives signals from the four wheel sensors (front sensors are fitted to the hubs, and the rear sensors are fitted to the caliper mounting brackets), which monitor the speed of rotation of each wheel. By comparing these signals, the ECU can determine the speed at which the vehicle is travelling. It can then use this speed to determine when a wheel is decelerating at an abnormal rate, compared to the speed of the vehicle, and therefore predicts when a wheel is about to lock. During normal operation, the system functions in the same way as a non-ABS braking system.

If the ECU senses that a wheel is about to lock, it closes the relevant outlet solenoid valves in the hydraulic unit, which then isolates the relevant brake(s) on the wheel(s) which is/are about to lock from the master cylinder, effectively sealing-in the hydraulic pressure.

If the speed of rotation of the wheel continues to decrease at an abnormal rate, the ECU opens the inlet solenoid valves on the relevant brake(s), and operates the electrically-driven return pump which pumps the hydraulic fluid back into the master cylinder, releasing the brake. Once the speed of rotation of the wheel returns to an acceptable rate, the pump stops; the solenoid valves switch again, allowing the hydraulic master cylinder pressure to return to the caliper, which then re-applies the brake. This cycle can be carried out many times a second.

The action of the solenoid valves and return pump creates pulses in the hydraulic circuit. When the ABS system is functioning, these pulses can be felt through the brake pedal.

The operation of the ABS system is entirely dependent on electrical signals. To prevent the system responding to any inaccurate signals, a built-in safety circuit monitors all signals received by the ECU. If an inaccurate signal or low battery voltage is detected, the ABS system is automatically shut down, and the warning light on the instrument panel is illuminated, to inform the driver that the ABS system is not operational. Normal braking should still be available, however.

If a fault does develop in the ABS system, the vehicle must be taken to a Peugeot dealer for fault diagnosis and repair.

24 Anti-lock braking system (ABS) components - removal and refitting

Regulator assembly

Caution: Disconnect the battery before disconnecting the regulator hydraulic unions, and do not reconnect the battery until after the hydraulic system has been bled. Also ensure that the unit is stored upright (in the same position as it is fitted to the vehicle) and is not tipped onto its side or upside down. Failure to do this could lead to air entering the regulator unit, requiring the unit to be bled using special Peugeot test equipment on refitting (see Section 2).
Note: *Before starting work, refer to the warning at the beginning of Section 2 concerning the dangers of hydraulic fluid.*

Removal

1 Disconnect the battery negative lead.
2 Release the retaining clip and disconnect the main wiring connector from the regulator assembly. Unscrew the retaining nut and disconnect the earth lead from the regulator.
3 Mark the locations of the hydraulic fluid pipes to ensure correct refitting, then unscrew the union nuts, and disconnect the pipes from the regulator assembly. Be prepared for fluid spillage, and plug the open ends of the pipes and the regulator, to prevent dirt ingress and further fluid loss.

24.16a Slacken and remove the retaining bolt and nut (arrowed) . . .

4 Slacken and remove the regulator mounting nuts and remove the assembly from the engine compartment. If necessary, the mounting bracket can then be unbolted and removed from the vehicle. Renew the regulator mountings if they show signs of wear or damage.

Refitting

5 Manoeuvre the regulator into position and locate it in the mounting bracket. Refit the mounting nuts and tighten them to the specified torque setting.
6 Reconnect the hydraulic pipes to the correct unions on the regulator and tighten the union nuts to the specified torque.
7 Reconnect the wiring connector to the regulator and connect the earth lead, tightening its retaining nut securely.
8 Bleed the complete hydraulic system as described in Section 2. Once the system is correctly bled, reconnect the battery.

Electronic control unit (ECU)

Removal

9 The ECU can be removed with the regulator unit in position on the vehicle. To gain access to the ECU, remove the battery and battery tray (see Chapter 5).
10 Release the retaining clip and disconnect the wiring connector from the ECU.
11 Slacken and remove the retaining bolts, and carefully ease the ECU squarely away from the regulator.

Refitting

12 Align the ECU with the regulator connectors, and ease the unit into position. Refit the retaining bolts and tighten them to the specified torque setting.
13 Reconnect the wiring connector and refit the battery.

Front wheel sensor

Removal

14 Disconnect the battery negative lead.
15 Apply the handbrake, then jack up the front of the vehicle and support securely on axle stands. To improve access, remove the roadwheel.
16 Slacken and remove the retaining nut and screw, and remove the protective shield from the sensor **(see illustrations)**.

24.16b . . . and remove the protective shield

24.18a Slacken and remove the retaining bolt . . .

24.18b . . . and withdraw the front wheel sensor from the hub

24.25a Free the rear wheel sensor wiring
from its retaining clips . . .

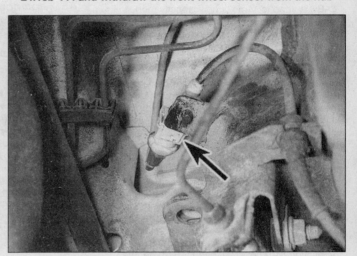

24.25b . . . and disconnect the sensor
wiring connector (arrowed) . . .

17 Trace the wiring back from the sensor, releasing it from all the relevant clips and ties whilst noting its correct routing, and disconnect the wiring connector.

18 Slacken and remove the retaining bolt and withdraw the sensor from the swivel hub (see illustrations).

Refitting

19 Ensure that the mating faces of the sensor and the swivel hub are clean, and apply a little grease to the swivel hub bore before refitting.

20 Make sure the sensor tip is clean and ease it into position in the swivel hub.

21 Clean the threads of the sensor bolt and apply a few drops of thread-locking compound (Peugeot recommend Loctite Frenetanch - available from your Peugeot dealer). Refit the retaining bolt and tighten it to the specified torque.

22 Work along the sensor wiring, making sure it is correctly routed, securing it in

position with all the relevant clips and ties. Reconnect the wiring connector.

23 Refit the protective shield to the sensor and securely tighten its retaining nut and screw. Lower the vehicle and (where necessary) tighten the wheel bolts to the specified torque.

Rear wheel sensor

Removal

24 Chock the front wheels, then jack up the rear of the vehicle and support it on axle stands. To improve access, remove the appropriate roadwheel.

25 Trace the wiring back from the sensor, releasing it from all the relevant clips and ties whilst noting its correct routing, and disconnect the wiring connector (see illustrations).

26 Slacken and remove the retaining bolt and withdraw the sensor (see illustration).

Refitting

27 Ensure that the mating faces of the sensor and the hub are clean, and apply a little grease to the hub bore before refitting.

28 Make sure the sensor tip is clean and ease it into position in the swivel hub.

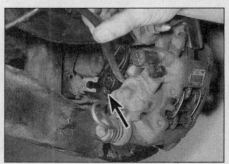

24.26 . . . then remove the retaining bolt
(arrowed) and remove sensor

25.4a On 1.9 litre diesel engines, fit new sealing rings (arrowed) to the pump recesses . . .

25.4b . . . then refit the pump, ensuring the drive dog is correctly aligned with the camshaft slot (arrowed)

29 Clean the threads of the sensor bolt and apply a few drops of thread-locking compound (Peugeot recommend Loctite Frenetanch - available from your Peugeot dealer). Refit the retaining bolt and tighten it to the specified torque.

30 Work along the sensor wiring, making sure it is correctly routed, securing it in position with all the relevant clips and ties. Reconnect the wiring connector, then lower the vehicle and (where necessary) tighten the wheel bolts to the specified torque.

25 Vacuum pump (diesel engine models) - removal and refitting

Removal

1 If necessary, to improve access to the vacuum pump, remove the air cleaner duct (see Chapter 4).

2 Release the retaining clip and disconnect the vacuum hose from the pump.
3 Slacken and remove the retaining bolts/nut (as applicable) securing the pump to the left-hand end of the cylinder head, then remove the pump. On 1.9 litre engines, the pump has two sealing rings (one large and one small); on 2.1 litre engines, there is only one. Discard the sealing rings - new ones must be used on refitting.

Refitting

4 Fit new sealing ring(s) to the pump recess(es), then align the drive dog with the slot in the end of the camshaft, and refit the pump to the cylinder head, ensuring that the sealing ring(s) remain correctly seated **(see illustrations)**.
5 Refit the pump mounting bolts/nut (as applicable) and tighten them securely.
6 Reconnect the vacuum hose to the pump, tightening its retaining clip securely, and (where necessary) refit the air cleaner duct.

26 Vacuum pump (diesel engine models) - testing

1 The operation of the braking system vacuum pump can be checked using a vacuum gauge.
2 Disconnect the vacuum pipe from the pump, and connect the gauge to the pump union using a suitable length of hose.
3 Start the engine and allow it to idle, then measure the vacuum created by the pump. As a guide, after one minute, a minimum of approximately 500 mm Hg should be recorded. If the vacuum registered is significantly less than this, it is likely that the pump is faulty. However, seek the advice of a Peugeot dealer before condemning the pump.
4 Overhaul of the vacuum pump is not possible, since no components are available separately for it. If faulty, the complete pump assembly must be renewed.

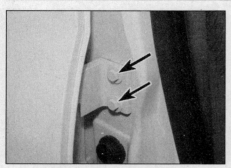

11.9 Unscrew the hinge retaining bolts (arrowed) and remove the rear door

11.14 On refitting, secure the wiring connector by rotating the locking ring until the index marks are aligned

9 Remove the door as described in paragraphs 4 to 7 **(see illustration)**.

Refitting

Front door

10 Manoeuvre the door into position and refit the hinge retaining bolts. Align the hinges with the marks made prior to removal, then tighten them to the securely.
11 Refit the rubber cover onto the check link, then align the link with the pillar and securely tighten its retaining bolts.
12 Where necessary, feed the wiring back into the door, and seat the rubber grommet in position. Ensure that the wiring is correctly routed and securely reconnected, then secure it in position with the necessary clips and ties. Seat the insulation panel back in position, and refit the trim panel as described in Section 12.
13 Check the door alignment and, if necessary, adjust. If the paintwork around the hinges has been damaged, paint the affected area with a suitable touch-in brush to prevent corrosion.

Rear door

14 Carry out the operations described in paragraphs 10, 11 and 13. Reconnect the wiring connector and secure it in position by rotating the locking ring until the index marks align **(see illustration)**.

Adjustment

15 Close the door and check the door alignment with surrounding body panels. If necessary, slight adjustment of the door position can be made by slackening the hinge retaining bolts and repositioning the hinge/ door as necessary. Once the door is correctly positioned, securely tighten the hinge bolts.

12 Door inner trim panel - removed and refitting

(icon)

Removal

Note: *Door trim panel design varies according to the equipment level of the vehicle, and therefore some trim panel fastener locations*

on your vehicle might be different to those shown in the accompanying illustrations.
1 Disconnect the battery negative terminal and proceed as described under the relevant sub-heading.

Front door

2 Carefully unclip the exterior mirror inner trim panel from the front of the door **(see illustration)**. On models with manually-adjusted mirrors, remove the rubber gaiter from the adjustment handle prior to unclipping the trim panel.
3 On models with manually-operated windows, pull the window regulator handle off its spindle and remove the spacer.
4 Working as described in Chapter 12, remove the switch(es) from the door armrest and also remove the loudspeaker from the door.
5 Lift the door lock inner handle and carefully prise out the handle surround **(see illustration)**.
6 Prise out the trim retaining screw cover from the lower rear corner of the trim panel, and slacken and remove the retaining screw **(see illustrations)**.
7 Remove the trim retaining screw cover(s), then slacken and remove the screw(s) securing the underside of the armrest to the door.
8 Where necessary, remove the trim retaining screw cover from the base of the armrest pocket, then slacken and remove the retaining screw and lift the pocket out of position. Also slacken and remove the screw (where fitted) securing the switch panel section of the trim panel in position **(see illustrations)**.

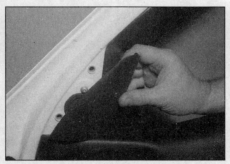

12.2 Removing the mirror inner trim panel from the door

12.5 Removing the inner handle surround

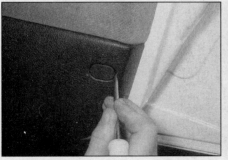

12.6a Prise out the trim cover . . .

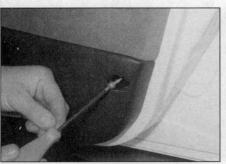

12.6b . . . then slacken and remove the trim panel retaining screw

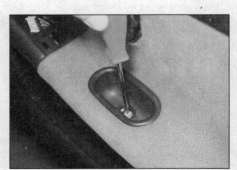

12.8a Remove the trim cover then undo the retaining screw . . .

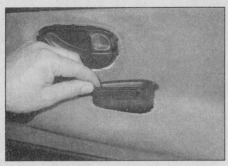

12.8b . . . and remove the armrest pocket from the trim panel

12.8c Where necessary, undo the screw securing the switch panel section of the trim panel in position

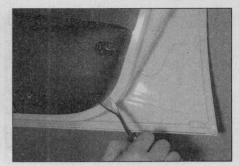

12.9a Unclip the trim panel . . .

12.9b . . . and move it upwards and away from the door

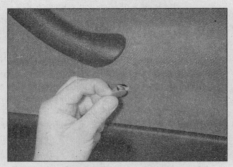

12.10a On the rear door, remove the trim covers . . .

12.10b . . . and undo the retaining screws (arrowed)

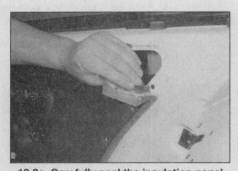

13.2a Carefully peel the insulation panel away from the door . . .

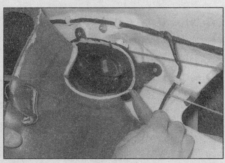

13.2b . . . and inner handle to gain access to the lock components

13.2c If the insulation panel is to be removed completely it will be necessary to drill out the rivets and remove the trim panel mounting brackets

9 Make a final check that all the retaining screws have been removed, then carefully unclip the base of the trim panel from the door and manoeuvre it upwards and out of position **(see illustrations)**. As the panel is removed, free the wiring harness noting its correct routing.

Rear door

10 Remove the trim panel as described in paragraphs 3 to 9 **(see illustrations)**.

Refitting

11 Refitting of the trim panel is the reverse of removal. Prior to clipping the panel in position, ensuring all the wiring (where necessary) is correctly routed and passed through the relevant apertures. On completion check the operation of all switches.

13 Door handle and lock components - removal and refitting

Removal

1 Remove the inner trim panel as described in Section 12.
2 To gain access to the handle and lock components, it is necessary to peel/cut the foam insulation panel away from the door. **Note:** *This is likely to result in the panel being damaged, necessitating its renewal. If the panel needs to be renewed, it will be necessary to drill out the rivets (see paragraph 4) and remove the armrest/trim panel brackets; new pop rivets will be required on refitting to secure the brackets in position* **(see illustrations)**.

Door lock inner handle

Note: *A pop rivet gun and suitable rivets will be required on refitting.*
3 Peel/cut the insulation panel sufficiently away from the door to gain access to the handle (see paragraph 2).
4 Carefully drill the heads off the rivets securing the handle to the door, whilst taking great care not to damage the handle itself. Recover the remains of the rivets from inside the door.
5 Free the handle from the door, then disconnect the link rods and remove the handle assembly **(see illustration)**.

Front door lock cylinder

6 Peel/cut the insulation panel sufficiently away from the door to gain access to the lock assembly (see paragraph 2).

13.5 Drill out the rivets then detach the inner handle from the link rods and remove it from the door

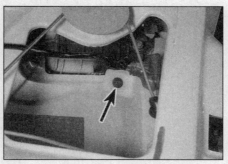

13.7a Undo the upper retaining screws (arrowed) . . .

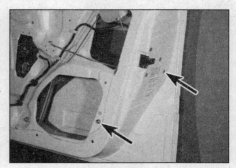

13.7b . . . and the lower nut and outer screw (arrowed) . . .

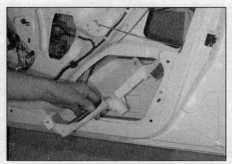

13.7c . . . and manoeuvre the lock protective cover from the front door

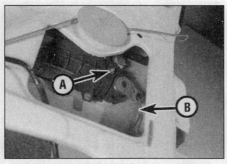

13.9a Undo the retaining nut (A) then detach the link rod (B) . . .

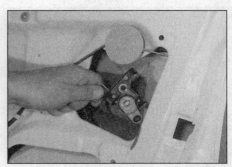

13.9b . . . and remove the lock cylinder mounting plate from the door

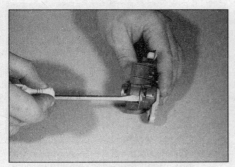

13.10a Slide out the retaining clip . . .

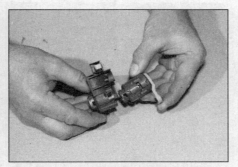

13.10b . . . then separate the lock cylinder housing and mounting plate

13.10c Insert the key and withdraw the lock cylinder from its housing

7 Slacken and remove the lower retaining nut and the upper retaining screws, and manoeuvre the lock protective cover out from inside the door assembly **(see illustrations)**.

8 To improve access to the lock cylinder, release the retaining clip and disconnect the wiring connector from the lock assembly.

9 Slacken and remove the rear retaining nut from the exterior handle, then manoeuvre the lock cylinder mounting plate assembly out of position, disconnecting it from the link rod **(see illustrations)**.

10 To remove the lock cylinder, prise out the retaining clip then separate the lock cylinder, housing and mounting plate. Insert the key into the lock cylinder and withdraw it from the housing **(see illustrations)**.

Front door exterior handle

11 Remove the lock cylinder assembly as described in paragraphs 6 to 9.

12 Undo the front retaining nut then detach the link rod from the handle and manoeuvre the handle out from the door, along with its rubber seal **(see illustrations)**.

Front door lock assembly

13 Peel/cut the insulation panel sufficiently away from the door to gain access to the lock and handle components (see paragraph 2).

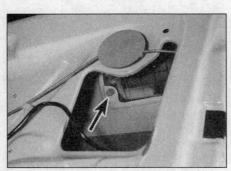

13.12a Undo the retaining nut (arrowed) . . .

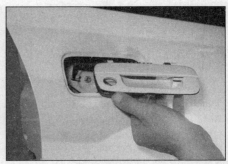

13.12b . . . and remove the handle and seal from the door

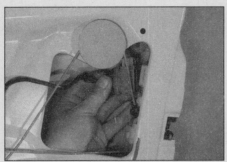

13.16 Lift the clip and disconnect the wiring connector from the lock assembly

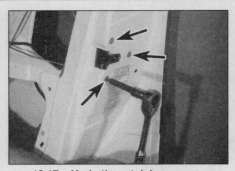

13.17a Undo the retaining screws (arrowed) . . .

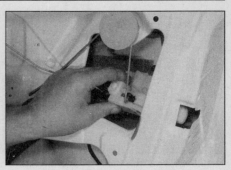

13.17b . . . and manoeuvre the lock assembly out of position

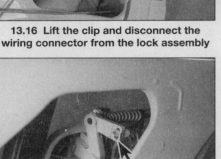

13.20a Detach the link rod (arrowed) . . .

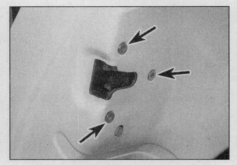

13.20b . . . then undo the lock retaining screws (arrowed)

13.21a Detach the link rods from the lock . . .

14 Slacken and remove the lower retaining nut and the upper retaining screws, and manoeuvre the lock protective cover out from inside the door assembly (see paragraph 7).
15 Remove the inner handle as described in paragraphs 4 and 5.
16 Release the retaining clip and disconnect the wiring connector from the lock assembly **(see illustration)**.
17 Slacken and remove the retaining screws, then unhook the link rods from the lock assembly and manoeuvre it out from the door **(see illustrations)**. Do not attempt to dismantle the lock assembly, if it is faulty the complete unit must be renewed.

Rear door lock assembly

18 Peel/cut the insulation panel sufficiently away from the door to gain access to the lock and handle components (see paragraph 2).
19 Remove the inner handle as described in paragraphs 4 and 5.
20 Unhook the link rod connecting the lock to the handle, then slacken and remove the lock retaining screws **(see illustrations)**.
21 Manoeuvre the lock assembly out of position and remove it from the door. Note that it may be necessary to unhook the inner handle link rods from the lock assembly, noting there correct fitted locations, in order to gain the clearance required **(see illustrations)**.

Rear door exterior handle

22 Peel/cut the insulation panel sufficiently away from the door to gain access to the lock and handle components (see paragraph 2).
23 Release the retaining clip and disconnect the wiring connector from the lock.

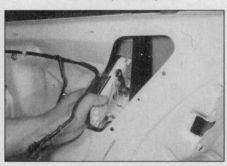

13.21b . . . and manoeuvre the lock out from the door

13.25b . . . then unscrew the front retaining nut . . .

24 Unhook the link rod from the door handle.
25 Remove the access plug from the rear of the door, then undo the retaining nuts and remove the handle and seal from the outside of the door **(see illustrations)**.

13.25a Remove the access plug from the rear of the door, then slacken and remove the handle rear retaining nut . . .

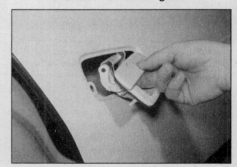

13.25c . . . and remove the handle and seal from the rear door

Refitting

26 Refitting is the reverse of removal, ensuring that all link rods are clipped securely in position. Prior to sticking the insulation

Chapter 12
Body electrical system

Contents

Degrees of difficulty

Easy, suitable for novice with little experience	Fairly easy, suitable for beginner with some experience	Fairly difficult, suitable for competent DIY mechanic	Difficult, suitable for experienced DIY mechanic	Very difficult, suitable for expert DIY or professional

Specifications

System type .... 12-volt negative earth

Bulbs
Wattage

Exterior lights
Headlight	55 (H7 type)
Front foglight	55 (H1 type)
Front sidelight	5
Direction indicator	21
Direction indicator side repeater	5
Stop/tail	21/5
Reversing light	21
Rear foglight	21
Number plate light	5

Interior light
Front courtesy lights	5
Rear courtesy lights	5
Luggage compartment light	5

Torque wrench setting	Nm	lbf ft
Airbag control unit nuts	8	6

1 General information and precautions

 Warning: Before carrying out any work on the electrical system, read through the precautions given in Safety First! at the beginning of this manual and Chapter 5.

The electrical system is of the 12 volt negative earth type. Power for the lights and all electrical accessories is supplied by a lead/acid type battery which is charged by the alternator.

This Chapter covers repair and service procedures for the various electrical components not associated with engine. Information on the battery, alternator and starter motor can be found in Chapter 5.

It should be noted that prior to working on any component in the electrical system, the battery negative terminal should first be disconnected, to prevent the possibility of electrical short circuits and/or fires.

2 Electrical fault finding - general information

Note: *Refer to the precautions given in 'Safety first!' and in Section 1 of this Chapter before starting work. The following tests relate to testing of the main electrical circuits, and should not be used to test delicate electronic circuits (such as anti-lock braking systems), particularly where an electronic control module (ECU) is used.*

General

1 A typical electrical circuit consists of an electrical component, any switches, relays, motors, fuses, fusible links or circuit breakers related to that component, and the wiring and connectors which link the component to both the battery and the chassis. To help to pinpoint a problem in an electrical circuit, wiring diagrams are included at the end of this Manual.

2 Before attempting to diagnose an electrical fault, first study the appropriate wiring diagram to obtain a complete understanding of the components included in the particular circuit concerned. The possible sources of a fault can be narrowed down by noting if other components related to the circuit are operating properly. If several components or circuits fail at one time, the problem is likely to be related to a shared fuse or earth connection.

3 Electrical problems usually stem from simple causes, such as loose or corroded connections, a faulty earth connection, a blown fuse, a melted fusible link, or a faulty relay (refer to Section 3 for details of testing relays). Visually inspect the condition of all fuses, wires and connections in a problem circuit before testing the components. Use the wiring diagrams to determine which terminal connections will need to be checked in order to pinpoint the trouble spot.

4 The basic tools required for electrical fault-finding include a circuit tester or voltmeter (a 12-volt bulb with a set of test leads can also be used for certain tests); a self-powered test light (sometimes known as a continuity tester); an ohmmeter (to measure resistance); a battery and set of test leads; and a jumper wire, preferably with a circuit breaker or fuse incorporated, which can be used to bypass suspect wires or electrical components. Before attempting to locate a problem with test instruments, use the wiring diagram to determine where to make the connections.

5 To find the source of an intermittent wiring fault (usually due to a poor or dirty connection, or damaged wiring insulation), a 'wiggle' test can be performed on the wiring. This involves wiggling the wiring by hand to see if the fault occurs as the wiring is moved. It should be possible to narrow down the source of the fault to a particular section of wiring. This method of testing can be used in conjunction with any of the tests described in the following sub-Sections.

6 Apart from problems due to poor connections, two basic types of fault can occur in an electrical circuit - open circuit, or short circuit.

7 Open circuit faults are caused by a break somewhere in the circuit, which prevents current from flowing. An open circuit fault will prevent a component from working, but will not cause the relevant circuit fuse to blow.

8 Short circuit faults are caused by a 'short' somewhere in the circuit, which allows the current flowing in the circuit to 'escape' along an alternative route, usually to earth. Short circuit faults are normally caused by a breakdown in wiring insulation, which allows a feed wire to touch either another wire, or an earthed component such as the bodyshell. A short circuit fault will normally cause the relevant circuit fuse to blow.

Finding an open circuit

9 To check for an open circuit, connect one lead of a circuit tester or voltmeter to either the negative battery terminal or a known good earth.

10 Connect the other lead to a connector in the circuit being tested, preferably nearest to the battery or fuse.

11 Switch on the circuit, bearing in mind that some circuits are live only when the ignition switch is moved to a particular position.

12 If voltage is present (indicated either by the tester bulb lighting or a voltmeter reading, as applicable), this means that the section of the circuit between the relevant connector and the battery is problem-free.

13 Continue to check the remainder of the circuit in the same fashion.

14 When a point is reached at which no voltage is present, the problem must lie between that point and the previous test point with voltage. Most problems can be traced to a broken, corroded or loose connection.

Finding a short circuit

15 To check for a short circuit, first disconnect the load(s) from the circuit (loads are the components which draw current from a circuit, such as bulbs, motors, heating elements, etc).

16 Remove the relevant fuse from the circuit, and connect a circuit tester or voltmeter to the fuse connections.

17 Switch on the circuit, bearing in mind that some circuits are live only when the ignition switch is moved to a particular position.

18 If voltage is present (indicated either by the tester bulb lighting or a voltmeter reading, as applicable), this means that there is a short circuit.

19 If no voltage is present, but the fuse still blows with the load(s) connected, this indicates an internal fault in the load(s).

Finding an earth fault

20 The battery negative terminal is connected to 'earth'- the metal of the engine/transmission and the car body - and most systems are wired so that they only receive a positive feed, the current returning through the metal of the car body. This means that the component mounting and the body form of that circuit. Loose or corroded mountings can therefore cause a range of electrical faults, ranging from total failure of a circuit, to a puzzling partial fault. In particular, lights may shine dimly (especially when another circuit sharing the same earth point is in operation), motors (eg. wiper motors or the radiator cooling fan motor) may run slowly, and the operation of one circuit may have an apparently unrelated effect on another. Note that on many vehicles, earth straps are used between certain components, such as the engine/transmission and the body, usually where there is no metal-to-metal contact between components due to flexible rubber mountings, etc.

21 To check whether a component is properly earthed, disconnect the battery and connect one lead of an ohmmeter to a known good earth point. Connect the other lead to the wire or earth connection being tested. The resistance reading should be zero; if not, check the connection as follows.

22 If an earth connection is thought to be faulty, dismantle the connection and clean back to bare metal both the bodyshell and the wire terminal or the component earth connection mating surface. Be careful to remove all traces of dirt and corrosion, then use a knife to trim away any paint, so that a clean metal-to-metal joint is made. On reassembly, tighten the joint fasteners securely; if a wire terminal is being refitted, use serrated washers between the terminal and the bodyshell to ensure a clean and secure connection. When the connection is

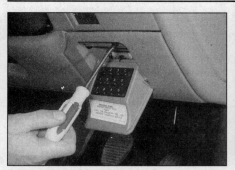

3.2a Open up the immobiliser keypad then rotate the fastener 90° and lower the fusebox cover . . .

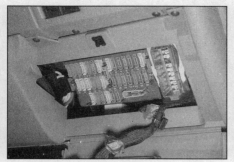

3.2b . . . to gain access to the main fusebox

3.2c Unclip the lid to gain access to the engine compartment fuses

remade, prevent the onset of corrosion in the future by applying a coat of petroleum jelly or silicone-based grease or by spraying on (at regular intervals) a proprietary ignition sealer or a water-dispersant lubricant.

3 Fuses and relays - general information

Fuses

1 The majority of fuses are located in the fusebox situated behind the driver's side lower facia panel. Additional fuses (including the larger, higher-rated fuses) are located in the fuse/relay box on the left-hand side of the engine compartment.
2 To gain access to the main fusebox, fold down the engine immobiliser keypad then rotate the fastener through 90° and lower the fusebox cover. To gain access to the fuses in the engine compartment, simply unclip the cover from the fuse/relay box; some of the higher-rated fuses are located in a separate box mounted in front of the main box **(see illustrations)**.
3 A list of the circuits each fuse protects is given on the fusebox cover.
4 To remove a fuse, first switch off the circuit concerned (or the ignition), then pull the fuse out of its terminals. The wire within the fuse should be visible; if the fuse is blown it will be broken or melted.
5 Always renew a fuse with one of an identical rating; never use a fuse with a different rating from the original, nor substitute anything else. Never renew a fuse more than once without tracing the source of the trouble. The fuse rating is stamped on top of the fuse; note that the fuses are also colour-coded for easy recognition.
6 If a new fuse blows immediately, find the cause before renewing it again; a short to earth as a result of faulty insulation is most likely. Where a fuse protects more than one circuit, try to isolate the defect by switching on each circuit in turn (if possible) until the fuse blows again. Always carry a supply of

spare fuses of each relevant rating on the vehicle, a spare of each rating should be clipped into the base of the fusebox.

Relays

7 The majority of relays are either located in the fuse/relay box in the engine compartment or behind the driver's side lower facia panel; the exceptions are as follows.
  a) *The sunroof relay - located behind the overhead console.*
  b) *Rear screen/tailgate wiper relay - fitted to the wiper motor bracket.*
  c) *Cooling fan relay(s) - located in the fan shroud or at the side of the radiator.*
8 If a circuit or system controlled by a relay develops a fault and the relay is suspect, operate the system; if the relay is functioning it should be possible to hear it click as it is energised. If this is the case, the fault lies with the components or wiring of the system. If the relay is not being energised, then either the relay is not receiving a main supply or a switching voltage or the relay itself is faulty. Testing is by the substitution of a known good unit, but be careful; while some relays are identical in appearance and in operation, others look similar but perform different functions.
9 To renew a relay, first ensure that the ignition switch is off. The relay can then simply be pulled out from the socket and the new relay pressed in.

4 Switches - removal and refitting

Note: *Disconnect the battery negative lead before removing any switch, and reconnect the lead after refitting the switch.*

Ignition switch/ steering column lock

1 Refer to Chapter 10.

Steering column combination switches

2 Undo the retaining screws securing the steering column lower shroud in position then unclip both the upper and lower shrouds from the column, disconnecting the cruise control and/or radio control switch wiring connector(s) (as applicable). Remove the lower shroud and position the upper shroud clear of the switches.
3 To remove an individual switch assembly, disconnect the wiring, then remove the retaining screws and slide the switch out of its mounting bracket **(see illustrations)**.
4 To remove the complete switch and mounting bracket assembly it will first be necessary to remove the steering wheel (see Chapter 10); on models with a driver's airbag, also remove the contact unit as described in Section 26. On all models, disconnect the wiring connectors from the switches, then

4.3a Slacken the retaining screws (arrowed) . . .

4.3b . . . then slide the combination switch out of position and disconnect its wiring (shown with steering wheel removed)

4.4 To remove the complete combination switch assembly, disconnect the wiring connectors then undo the screws (arrowed)

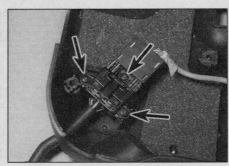

4.7 Undo the retaining screws (arrowed) and remove the radio switch from the steering column lower shroud

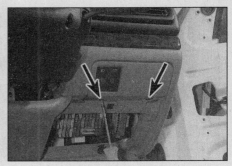

4.10 Undo the retaining screws (arrowed) . . .

4.11a . . . and remove the driver's side switch panel from the facia. Disconnect the wiring connector . . .

4.11b . . . and remove the relevant switch from the panel

4.14 Prise out the blanking plug to reveal the centre switch panel retaining screws

undo the retaining screws and remove the assembly from the top of the steering column (see illustration).

5 Refitting is the reverse of removal, ensuring all wiring connectors are securely reconnected.

Radio control/ cruise control switches

6 Undo the retaining screws securing the steering column lower shroud in position and remove the shroud, disconnecting the switch wiring connector(s).

7 Undo the retaining screws and remove the relevant switch assembly from the lower shroud (see illustration).

8 Refitting is the reverse of removal, ensuring that the switch wiring is correctly routed.

Driver's side facia switches

9 Open up the engine immobiliser keypad then rotate the fastener 90° and lower the fusebox cover.

10 Slacken and remove the screws from the base of the switch panel (see illustration).

11 Withdraw the switch panel from the facia and disconnect its wiring connectors. Each individual switch can then be unclipped and removed from the mounting panel (see illustrations).

12 Refitting is the reverse of removal noting that the correct fitted location of each switch is indicated by symbols on the switch panel.

Centre facia switches

13 Remove the multi-function display as described in Section 11. On models with no multi-function display unit, carefully prise out the storage compartment from the right-hand side of the switches.

14 Carefully prise out the blanking plug from the end of the switch panel to reveal the panel retaining screws; on some models, the alarm LED is fitted to the blanking plug (see illustration).

15 Slacken and remove the retaining screws then remove the switch panel from the facia, disconnecting the wiring connectors as they become accessible. Each individual switch

can then be unclipped and remove from the mounting panel (see illustrations).

16 Refitting is the reverse of removal.

Centre console switches

17 The switch panel can be pushed out of position once the centre console assembly has been unbolted from the floor. See Chapter 11 for centre console removal and refitting details. Each individual switch can then be unclipped and removed from the panel.

Door mounted switches

18 Carefully prise the switch panel cover out from the armrest (see illustration).

4.15a Undo the retaining screws (arrowed) and remove the switch panel assembly from the vehicle . . .

4.15b . . . each switch can then be pushed out of position

4.18 Carefully prise out the switch panel cover . . .

4.19a . . . then ease the relevant switch out of position . . .

4.19b . . . and disconnect it from the wiring

4.21 Unclip the cover from the overhead console . . .

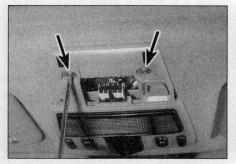

4.22a . . . and undo the retaining screws (arrowed) . . .

4.22b . . . then lower the console out and disconnect the wiring connectors

19 Each individual switch can then be carefully prised out of position and its wiring disconnected (see illustrations).
20 Refitting is the reverse of removal.

Overhead console switches

21 Unclip the cover from the rear of the overhead console (see illustration).
22 Undo the two retaining screws and free the console from the roof lining. Disconnect the wiring connectors and remove the console from the vehicle (see illustrations).
23 To remove the sunroof switch, slacken and remove the retaining screws and lift off

the printed circuit board; the switch can then be slid out of position (see illustrations). All the other switches are integral with the console and can only be renewed by replacing the complete console assembly.
24 Refitting is the reverse of removal ensuring that the wiring is correctly routed. Do not overtighten the circuit board screws, as the board is easily broken.

Seat switches

25 Carefully prise the switch out from the side of the seat, and disconnect it from the wiring connector(s).

26 Reconnect the wiring connector, and clip the switch back into position.

Stop-light switch

27 Refer to Chapter 9.

Handbrake warning light switch

28 Remove the centre console as described in Chapter 11.
29 Disconnect the wiring connector from the warning light switch, then unclip the switch and remove it from the handbrake lever.
30 Refitting in the reverse of removal.

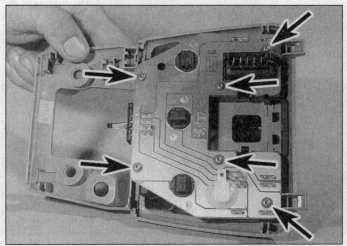

4.23a Undo the retaining screws and remove the printed circuit board . . .

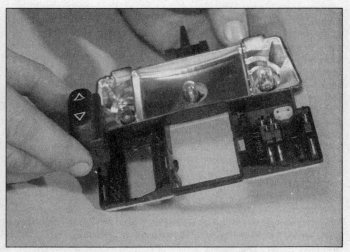

4.23b . . . the sunroof switch can then be slid out of position

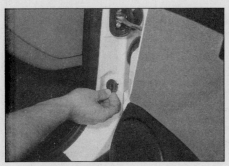

4.31a Remove the rubber cover . . .

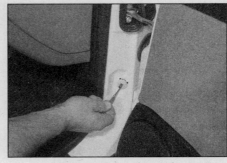

4.31b . . . then release the retaining clips . . .

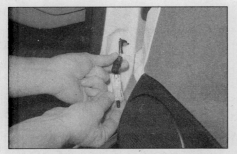

4.31c . . . and remove the courtesy light switch from the door pillar, disconnecting it from the wiring

4.35 Luggage compartment light switch - Saloon models

Courtesy light switch

31 Open the door and remove the rubber cover from the switch. Release the retaining clips and carefully ease the switch out from the pillar, disconnecting its wiring connector as it becomes accessible **(see illustrations)**. Tie a piece of string to the wiring to prevent it falling back into the door pillar.

32 Refitting is a reverse of the removal procedure. Refit the rubber cover to the switch prior to clipping it into the door pillar.

Luggage compartment light switch

33 On Saloon models, open up the boot lid then remove the retaining clips and lift off the inner trim panel to gain access to the switch.

34 On Estate models, open up the tailgate then undo the retaining screws and remove the inner handle. Unclip the surround from the lock inner button then prise out the trim clips and remove the inner trim panel from the tailgate.

35 Undo the retaining bolt and remove the switch, disconnecting it from the wiring connector **(see illustration)**.

36 Refitting is the reverse of removal.

Windscreen wiper rain sensor switch

37 Carefully unclip the rear view mirror housing from its mounting on the inside of the windscreen by pulling it gently downwards.

38 Disconnect the wiring connector then carefully release the side retaining clips and remove the rain sensor from the windscreen.

Caution: Do not touch the rain sensor lens or the windscreen glass in the area of the sensor. These areas must be kept spotlessly clean if the sensor is to function correctly.

39 Refitting is the reverse of removal, ensuring that the sensor and mirror are clipped securely in position.

---

5 Bulbs (exterior lights) - renewal

General

1 Whenever a bulb is renewed, note the following points.

a) *Disconnect the battery negative lead before starting work.*

5.2 Depress the retaining clip and remove the access cover from the rear of the headlight unit

b) *Remember that if the light has just been in use, the bulb may be extremely hot.*
c) *Always check the bulb contacts and holder, ensuring that there is clean metal-to-metal contact between the bulb and its live(s) and earth. Clean off any corrosion or dirt before fitting a new bulb.*
d) *Wherever bayonet-type bulbs are fitted (see Specifications) ensure that the live contact(s) bear firmly against the bulb contact.*
e) *Always ensure that the new bulb is of the correct rating and that it is completely clean before fitting it; this applies particularly to headlight/foglight bulbs (see below).*

Headlight

2 Release the retaining clips and remove the access cover from the rear of the headlight unit **(see illustration)**.

3 Disconnect the wiring connector from the rear of the bulb **(see illustration)**.

4 Unhook and release the ends of the bulb retaining clip and release it from the rear of the light unit. Withdraw the bulb.

5 When handling the new bulb, use a tissue or clean cloth to avoid touching the glass with the fingers; moisture and grease from the skin can cause blackening and rapid failure of this type of bulb. If the glass is accidentally touched, wipe it clean using methylated spirit.

6 Install the new bulb, ensuring that its locating tabs are correctly located in the light cut-outs, and secure it in position with the retaining clip.

7 Reconnect the wiring connector and refit the access cover, making sure it is securely refitted.

Front sidelight

8 Depress the retaining clip and remove the access cover from the rear of the headlight unit.

9 Rotate the sidelight bulbholder and release it from the headlight unit. The bulb is of the capless (push-fit) type, and can be removed by simply pulling it out of the bulbholder.

10 Refitting is the reverse of the removal procedure, making sure the access cover is securely refitted.

5.3 Disconnect the wiring connector then release the retaining clip and remove the bulb

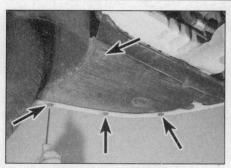

5.12 Undo the screws (arrowed) and remove the cover from beneath the foglight

5.13a Disconnect the wiring connector . . .

5.13b . . . then release the clip and remove the reflector assembly from the foglight

5.14 Unhook the spring clip (arrowed) and pivot the reflector away from the cover

5.15a Disconnect the wiring connector (arrowed) then release the retaining clip . . .

5.15b . . . and remove the foglight bulb

Front foglight

11 If necessary, to improve access, firmly apply the handbrake then jack up the front of the vehicle and support it on axle stands.

12 Undo the retaining screws and remove the plastic cover from beneath the foglight **(see illustration)**.

13 Disconnect the wiring connector then release the retaining clip and remove the rear cover assembly from the foglight **(see illustrations)**.

14 Disengage the spring clip and tilt the reflector assembly away from the cover **(see illustration)**.

15 Disconnect the wiring connector then unhook the bulb retaining clip and remove the bulb **(see illustrations)**.

16 When handling the new bulb, use a tissue or clean cloth to avoid touching the glass with the fingers; moisture and grease from the skin

can cause blackening and rapid failure of this type of bulb. If the glass is accidentally touched, wipe it clean using methylated spirit.

17 Install the new bulb, ensuring that its locating tabs are correctly located in the reflector cut-outs, and secure it in position with the retaining clip.

18 Reconnect the wiring connector and clip the reflector back into position on the cover.

19 Refit the cover assembly and secure it in position with the retaining clip.

20 Reconnect the wiring connector then refit the plastic cover, tightening its retaining screws securely. Where necessary, lower the vehicle to the ground.

Front direction indicator

21 To improve access on the left-hand side, remove the protective cover from the battery.

22 Rotate the bulbholder anti-clockwise and remove it from the rear of the light unit. The

bulb is a bayonet fit in the holder, and can be removed by pressing it and twisting in an anti-clockwise direction **(see illustration)**.

23 Refitting is a reverse of the removal procedure.

Front direction indicator side repeater

24 Carefully unclip the light unit and withdraw it from the wing **(see illustration)**.

25 Twist the bulbholder anti-clockwise and remove it from the light. The bulb is of the capless (push-fit) type, and can be removed by simply pulling it out of the bulbholder **(see illustration)**.

26 Refitting is a reversal of removal.

Rear light cluster - Saloon models

27 From inside the luggage compartment, slacken and remove the retaining screws and

5.22 Removing the front direction indicator bulb

5.24 Carefully prise the side repeater light out from the wing . . .

5.25 . . . then free the bulbholder and pull out the bulb

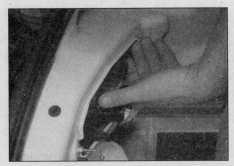

5.27a On Saloon models, undo the retaining screws and remove the rear trim panel from the luggage compartment

5.27b Remove the storage compartment (fastener location arrowed) . . .

5.27c . . . then release the rear retaining clips and peel back the side trim panel to gain access to the rear light cluster

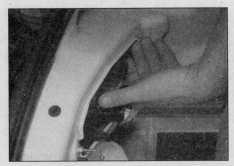

5.28 Depress the retaining clips and remove the bulbholder from the rear cluster . . .

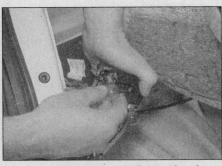

5.29 . . . the relevant bulb can then be removed by pressing it in and turning anti-clockwise

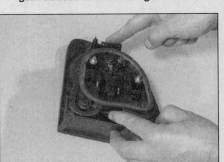

5.32 On Estate models, release the retaining clips and remove the bulbholder from the rear light unit . . .

remove the rear trim panel. Release the retaining clips (pull out the centre pins then prise out the complete clip) and peel back the trim panel to gain access to the rear of the light assembly, it may also prove necessary to undo the retaining screw and remove the tie-down hook. On some models, if work is being carried out on the left-hand side it will also be necessary to unscrew the fastener and remove the storage compartment to gain the necessary clearance required **(see illustrations)**.
28 Release the retaining clips and remove the bulbholder assembly from the rear of the light cluster **(see illustration)**.
29 All bulbs have bayonet fittings. The relevant bulb can be removed by pressing in and rotating anti-clockwise **(see illustration)**.

Note that the stop/taillight bulb has offset pins to ensure it is fitted the correct way around.
30 Refitting is the reverse of the removal sequence.

Rear light - Estate models

31 Remove the light unit (see Section 7).
32 Release the retaining clips and remove the bulbholder from the rear of the light unit **(see illustration)**.
33 All bulbs have bayonet fittings. The relevant bulb can be removed by pressing in and rotating anti-clockwise **(see illustration)**. Note that the stop/taillight bulb has offset pins to ensure it is fitted the correct way around.
34 Refitting is the reverse of the removal sequence.

Number plate light - Saloon models

35 Release the retaining clips and remove the lens from the light unit. The bulb is of the capless (push-fit) type, and can be removed by simply pulling it out of the light unit **(see illustrations)**.
36 Refitting is the reverse of removal, ensuring that the lens is clipped securely in position.

Number plate light - Estate models

37 Undo the retaining screw and remove the lens from the light unit. The bulb is of the capless (push-fit) type, and can be removed by simply pulling it out of the light unit **(see illustrations)**.

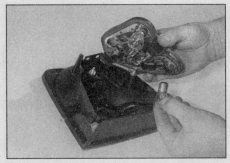

5.33 . . . remove the relevant bulb by pressing it in and turning anti-clockwise

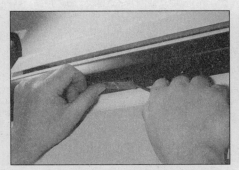

5.35a On Saloon models carefully prise out the number plate light lens . . .

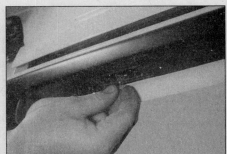

5.35b . . . and pull the bulb out from its holder

38 Refitting is the reverse of removal. Do not overtighten the screw, as the lens is easily cracked.

High-level stop-light

39 Remove the light unit as described in Section 7, then remove the bulb/holder from the rear of the light unit.
40 Refitting is the reverse of the removal.

---

6 Bulbs (interior lights) - renewal

General

1 Refer to Section 5, paragraph 1.

Front seat courtesy light and reading light

Models with an overhead console

2 Using a flat-bladed screwdriver, carefully unclip the lens from the overhead console (see illustration).
3 Each individual bulb can then be removed by simply pulling it out of its holder (see illustration).
4 Refitting is the reverse of removal.

Models without an overhead console

5 Using a small, flat-bladed screwdriver, carefully prise light unit assembly out of position (see illustration).
6 Twist the bulbholder anti-clockwise and remove it from the light. The bulb is of the capless (push-fit) type, and can be removed

5.37a On Estate models, undo the retaining screw and remove the lens from the number plate light . . .

5.37b . . . then pull out the bulb from the light unit

by simply pulling it out of the bulbholder (see illustrations).
7 Refitting is the reverse of removal.

Rear courtesy light

8 Refer to the information given above in paragraphs 5 to 7.

Luggage compartment light

9 Refer to the information given above in paragraphs 5 to 7.

Instrument panel illumination/warning lights

10 Remove the instrument panel as described in Section 9.
11 Twist the relevant bulbholder anti-clockwise and withdraw it from the rear of the panel (see illustration).
12 All bulbs are integral with their holders. Be very careful to ensure the new bulbs are of the correct rating, the same as those removed;

this is especially important in the case of the ignition/battery charging warning light.
13 Refit the bulbholder to the rear of the instrument panel then refit the instrument panel as described in Section 9.

Glovebox illumination light bulb

14 Open up the glovebox and renew the bulb as described in paragraphs 5 to 7.

Heater control panel illumination bulb

15 Remove the heater control panel from the facia as described in Chapter 3, noting that it is not necessary to detach the control cables (where fitted).
16 Twist the relevant bulbholder anti-clockwise and remove it from the control unit.
17 The bulb is of the capless (push-fit) type, and can be removed by simply pulling it out of the bulbholder.
18 Refitting is the reverse of removal.

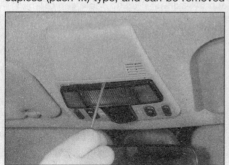
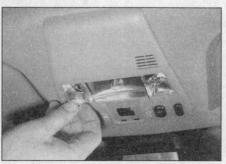

6.2 Carefully prise out the lens from the overhead console . . .

6.3 . . . then pull the relevant bulb out of position

6.5 Carefully prise the courtesy light unit out from the headlining . . .

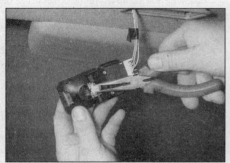
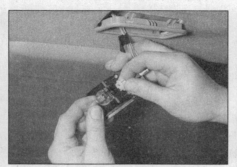
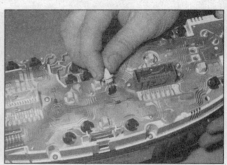

6.6a . . . then remove the bulbholder from the rear of the light . . .

6.6b . . . and pull out the bulb

6.11 Removing an instrument panel bulbholder

6.20 Removing the clock illumination bulb

6.23 Removing a multi-function display
illumination bulb

7.2a Undo the retaining nut and bolts . . .

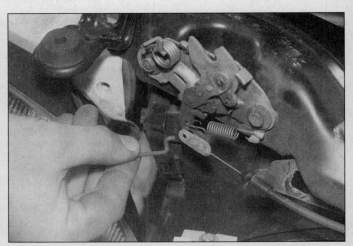

7.2b . . . then detach the bonnet release cable and remove
crossmember assembly from the vehicle

Clock illumination bulb

19 Remove the clock (see Section 13).
20 Using a pair of pliers, twist the bulbholder through 90° and remove it from the side of the clock **(see illustration)**.
21 Refitting is the reverse of removal.

Multi-function display bulb

22 Remove the multi-function display as described in Section 11.
23 Twist the relevant bulbholder through 90° and remove it from the display **(see illustration)**.
24 Refitting is the reverse of removal.

Switch illumination bulbs

25 All of the switches are fitted with illuminating bulbs; some are also fitted with a bulb to show when the circuit concerned is operating. On most switches, these bulbs are an integral part of the switch assembly, and cannot be obtained separately. Bulb replacement will therefore require the renewal of the complete switch assembly.

7 Exterior light units - removal and refitting

Note: *Disconnect the battery negative lead before removing any light unit, and reconnect the lead after refitting the light.*

Headlight

1 Remove the radiator grille, as described in Chapter 11, Section 31.
2 Slacken and remove the nuts securing the fan shroud to the bonnet lock crossmember, then undo the retaining bolts securing the crossmember in position. Unhook the bonnet release cable from the lock and remove the crossmember assembly **(see illustrations)**.
3 From underneath the wheelarch, prise out the small access cover from the liner to gain access to the headlight retaining spring. Using a pair of pointed-nose pliers or a piece of welding rod with a hooked end, unhook the spring from the body **(see illustrations)**. On some models it may be possible to access the spring from inside the engine compartment.

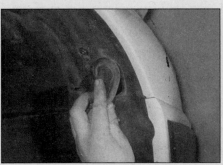

7.3a Remove the access cover from the wheelarch liner . . .

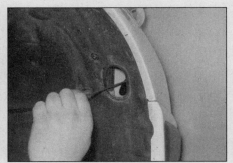

7.3b . . . and unhook the headlight retaining spring

7.4a Undo the headlight retaining bolts . . .

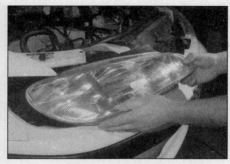

7.4b . . . then manoeuvre the headlight unit out of position . . .

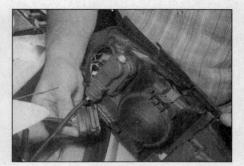

7.4c . . . and disconnect the wiring connectors

7.5a Twist the headlight levelling motor anti-clockwise to free it from the light . . .

7.5b . . . then unclip the motor balljoint from the reflector assembly

7.7 Undo the retaining screws and remove the plastic cover from beneath the foglight

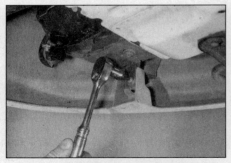

7.8a Unhook the upper retaining spring then undo the lower retaining screw . . .

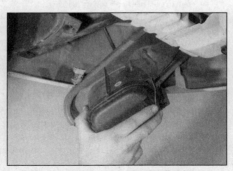

7.8b . . . and remove the foglight from underneath the bumper

7.9 The foglight can be adjusted via the cover access hole using an Allen key

4 Slacken and remove the headlight retaining bolts (there are three in total) then disconnect the wiring and manoeuvre the headlight unit out of position **(see illustrations)**.

5 On models equipped with a headlight levelling system, if necessary, remove the motor from the rear of the light unit by rotating it anti-clockwise and carefully unclipping its balljoint from the rear of the reflector assembly **(see illustrations)**.

6 Refitting is a direct reversal of the removal procedure. Lightly tighten the retaining bolts and check the alignment of the headlight with the bumper and bonnet. Once the light unit is correctly positioned, securely tighten the retaining bolts and check the headlight beam alignment using the information given in Section 8.

Front foglight

7 To improve access, firmly apply the handbrake then jack up the front of the vehicle and support it on axle stands. Undo the retaining screws and remove the plastic cover from beneath the foglight **(see illustration)**.

8 Disconnect the wiring connector then undo the lower retaining screw. Unhook the light unit upper retaining spring then manoeuvre the foglight out from underneath the front bumper **(see illustrations)**.

9 Refitting is the reverse of removal, ensuring that the upper retaining spring is correctly engaged with the light unit lug. If necessary, adjust the foglight aim using the adjuster on the rear of the light unit; the adjuster can be rotated using an Allen key once the access plug has been removed from the cover,

alternatively remove the cover completely and rotate the adjuster by hand **(see illustration)**.

Front direction indicator side repeater

10 Unclip the front of the light unit and withdraw it from the wing. Free the bulb holder by rotating it anti-clockwise, and remove the light unit from the vehicle. See Section 5 (bulb renewal) for illustrations.

11 Refitting is a reverse of the removal procedure.

Rear light cluster - Saloon models

12 From inside the luggage compartment, slacken and remove the retaining screws and remove the rear trim panel. Release the retaining clips (pull out the centre pins then

7.13 On Saloon models, disconnect the wiring connector(s) . . .

7.14a . . . then undo the retaining nuts . . .

7.14b . . . and remove the rear light unit

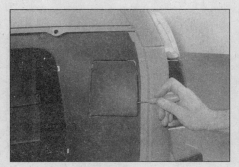

7.16 On Estate models, unclip the access cover . . .

7.17 . . . then disconnect the wiring connector. Unscrew the nut (arrowed) and remove the rear wing light unit

7.20a On Estate models, open up the access cover and disconnect the wiring connector, then undo the nuts (arrowed) . . .

prise out the complete clip) and peel back the trim panel to gain access to the rear of the light assembly, it may also prove necessary to undo the retaining screw and remove the tie-down hook. On some models, if work is being carried out on the left-hand side it will also be necessary to unscrew the fastener and remove the storage compartment to gain the necessary clearance required (see Section 5 for illustrations).

13 Depress the retaining clip(s) and disconnect the wiring connector(s) from the rear of the light cluster **(see illustration)**.

14 Slacken and remove the retaining nuts and remove the light unit from the vehicle **(see illustrations)**.

15 Refitting is the reverse of removal, ensuring that the retaining nuts are securely tightened.

Rear wing light - Estate models

16 Remove the storage compartment cover from the luggage compartment, and open up the access cover in the compartment to reveal the light unit **(see illustration)**.

17 Depress the retaining clip and disconnect the wiring connector, then undo the retaining nut and remove the light unit from the wing **(see illustration)**.

18 Refitting is the reverse of removal, tightening the retaining nut securely.

Tailgate light unit - Estate models

19 Open up the tailgate then release the retaining clips and open up the light unit access cover in the tailgate trim panel.

20 Depress the retaining clip and disconnect the wiring connector. Undo the retaining nuts then release the retaining clips and remove the light unit from the tailgate **(see illustrations)**.

21 Refitting is the reverse of removal, tightening the retaining nut securely.

High-level stop-light

Saloon models

22 Using hooked pieces of welding rod, insert the rods into the cut-outs on each end of the light unit and release the retaining clips by pulling them downwards **(see illustration)**.

23 Slide the light unit backwards to free it from its guides and remove it from the vehicle, disconnecting the wiring connector as it becomes accessible **(see illustration)**.

24 Refitting is the reverse of removal.

7.20b . . . and remove the rear light unit from the tailgate

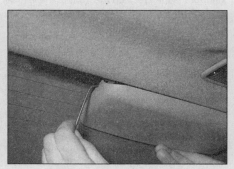

7.22 On Saloon models, using a hooked piece of welding rod, release the clips . . .

7.23 . . . then free the high-level stop-light from its guides and disconnect the wiring

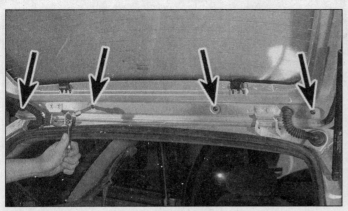

7.25 On Estate models undo the tailgate spoiler retaining screws (arrowed) . . .

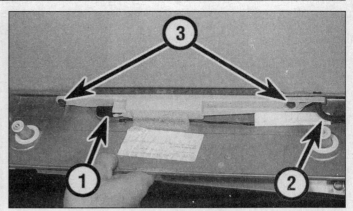

7.26 . . . then disconnect the wiring connector (1) and washer hose (2). Undo the retaining screws (3) and separate the high-level stop-light and spoiler

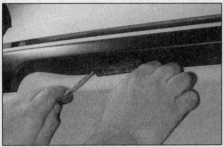

7.28a On Saloon models carefully prise out the number plate light from the bumper . . .

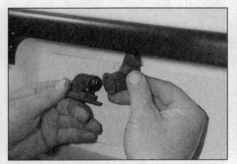

7.28b . . . and disconnect it from the wiring

7.30 On Estate models, remove the tailgate inner trim panel

Estate models

25 Open up the tailgate then slacken and remove the spoiler retaining screws from the top edge of the tailgate **(see illustration)**.
26 Release the spoiler then disconnect the wiring connector and washer hose and remove it from the tailgate. Undo the retaining screws and separate the stop-light and spoiler **(see illustration)**.
27 Refitting is the reverse of removal.

Number plate light

Saloon models

28 Carefully prise the light unit out from the bumper/tailgate, disconnecting its wiring connector as it becomes accessible **(see illustrations)**.

29 On refitting, reconnect the wiring connector and clip the light unit securely in position.

Estate models

30 Open up the tailgate then undo the retaining screws and remove the inner handle. Unclip the surround from the lock inner button, then prise out the trim clips and remove the trim panel from the tailgate **(see illustration)**.
31 Disconnect the wiring connector from the rear of the light unit and push the light out of position **(see illustration)**.
32 Refitting is the reverse of removal.

8 Headlight beam alignment - general information

Accurate adjustment of the headlight beam is only possible using optical beam setting equipment, and this work should therefore be carried out by a Peugeot dealer or suitably-equipped workshop.

For reference, the headlights can be adjusted by rotating the adjuster Allen screws on the rear of the headlight unit. The upper screw adjusts the headlight beam vertical aim, and the lower screw the headlight beam horizontal aim.

On models equipped with headlight levelling, ensure that the headlight beam

adjuster switch is set to position "0" before the headlights are adjusted. On models not equipped with headlight levelling, ensure that the manual adjuster on the rear of each light unit is set to position "0" before adjustment.

9 Instrument panel - removal and refitting

Removal

1 Disconnect the battery negative terminal.
2 Fully lower the steering column to improve access to the instrument panel.
3 Carefully prise out the access cover from the driver's end of the facia **(see illustration)**.

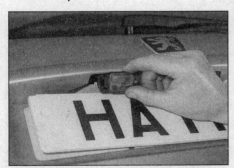

7.31 Push the number plate light out of position

9.3 Prise out the access cover from the driver's end of the facia

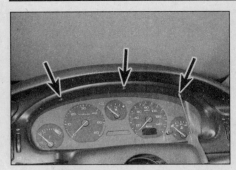

9.4a Undo the retaining screws (arrowed) . . .

9.4b . . . then unclip the base of the shroud from the facia . . .

9.4c . . . and remove it from the vehicle (steering wheel removed for clarity)

9.5a Undo the retaining screws (arrowed) . . .

9.5b . . . then release the clip and withdraw the instrument panel from the facia

9.6 Release the clips and disconnect the instrument panel wiring connectors

4 Slacken and remove the three retaining screws from the top of the instrument panel. Carefully unclip the shroud and remove it from the vehicle; the shroud can be pushed out from behind, via the facia aperture **(see illustrations)**.

5 Unscrew the four instrument panel retaining screws. Insert a screwdriver between the top of the panel and the facia, and carefully lever the instrument panel out of position **(see illustrations)**.

6 Withdraw the panel until the wiring connectors are accessible, then release the retaining clips and disconnect both connectors **(see illustration)**. The instrument panel can then be removed from the vehicle.

Refitting

7 Reconnect the wiring connectors, securing them in position with the retaining clips, and clip the instrument panel back into position in the facia. Refit the panel retaining screws and tighten securely.

8 Clip the shroud back into position and securely tighten its retaining screws. Refit the cover to the end of the facia.

9 Reconnect the battery and check the operation of the panel warning lights to ensure that they are functioning correctly.

10 Instrument panel components - *removal and refitting*

At the time of writing, it was unclear if any of the instrument panel components were

available separately. Refer to your Peugeot dealer for the latest parts information; they will be able to advise you on the best course of action should the instrument(s) develop a fault.

11 Multi-function display - *removal and refitting*

Removal

1 Taking great care not to damage either the unit or facia, carefully prise the multi-function display from the facia **(see illustration)**. If preferred, to avoid damage, remove the instrument panel shroud as described in paragraphs 1 to 4 of Section 10, then reach in behind the multi-function display and push it out of position.

11.1 Carefully prise the multi-function display out of position . . .

2 Disconnect the wiring connector and remove the unit from the facia **(see illustration)**.

Refitting

3 Refitting is the reverse of removal.

12 Cigarette lighter - *removal and refitting*

Removal

1 Disconnect the battery negative terminal.

Manual transmission models

2 Unclip the gearchange lever gaiter from the centre console.

3 Reach in behind the cigarette lighter, then disconnect the wiring connector(s) and push the cigarette lighter out of position.

11.2 . . . and disconnect the wiring

Automatic transmission models

4 Remove the centre console as described in Chapter 11. The cigarette lighter can then easily be pushed out of position.

Refitting

5 Refitting is a reversal of the removal procedure, ensuring all the wiring connectors are securely reconnected.

13 Clock - removal and refitting

Removal

1 Disconnect the battery negative terminal.
2 Taking great care not to damage the clock or facia, gently prise the clock out of position and disconnect it from the wiring connector **(see illustrations)**.

Refitting

3 Refitting is the reverse of removal.

14 Horn(s) - removal and refitting

Removal

Models fitted with an air horn

1 The air horn assembly (both the horn and compressor) are located behind the left-hand front wing.
2 To gain access to the assembly, firmly apply the handbrake then jack up the front of the vehicle and support it on axle stands.
3 Disconnect the wiring connector(s) then slacken and remove the horn and compressor mounting nuts and remove the assembly from the vehicle. The horn and compressor can then be separated.

Models fitted with conventional horns

4 Models not fitted with an air horn are fitted with twin conventional horns. The horns are located behind the front bumper, one is fitted on the right-hand side and the other on the left-hand side.
5 To gain access to the assembly, firmly apply the handbrake then jack up the front of the vehicle and support it on axle stands. Undo the retaining screws, and free the wheelarch liner/cover from the underside of the bumper and wheelarch (as applicable).
6 Disconnect the wiring connector(s) then slacken and remove the mounting nut(s) and remove the horn(s) from the vehicle.

Refitting

7 Refitting is the reverse of removal.

13.2a Carefully prise out the clock from the facia panel . . .

15.2 Unscrew the wiper arm retaining nut and remove the arm

15 Wiper arm - removal and refitting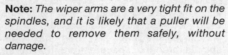

Note: *The wiper arms are a very tight fit on the spindles, and it is likely that a puller will be needed to remove them safely, without damage.*

Removal

1 Operate the wiper motor then switch it off so that the wiper arm returns to the at-rest position.
2 Prise off the wiper arm retaining nut cover (where fitted) then slacken and remove the nut **(see illustration)**.
3 Lift the blade off the glass and pull the wiper arm off the motor. Carefully lever the arm off the spindle using a large, flat-bladed screwdriver. If the arm is very tight, free it from the spindle using a suitable puller **(see illustration)**.

16.3a Unscrew the retaining nut . . .

13.2b . . . and disconnect its wiring connector

15.3 If the arm is a tight-fit, a puller will be required to free it from the spindle

Refitting

4 Ensure that the wiper and spindle are clean and dry, then refit the arm. Ensure that the arm is correctly positioned, then securely tighten the retaining nut. Where necessary, refit the spindle nut cover.

16 Windscreen wiper motor and linkage - removal and refitting

Removal

1 Disconnect the battery negative terminal.
2 Remove the wiper arms as described in the previous Section.
3 Unscrew the retaining nut, then unclip and remove the left- and right-hand plastic inlet vent covers from the base of the windscreen **(see illustrations)**.

16.3b . . . then unclip and remove the left- and right-hand inlet vent covers . . .

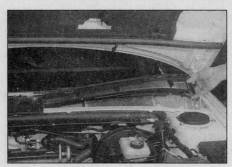

16.4 . . . and vent panels to gain access to the wiper motor

16.5 Depress the clip and disconnect the wiper motor wiring connector

16.6a Slacken and remove the mounting nuts and bolt (arrowed) . . .

16.6b . . . then manoeuvre the wiper motor out of position . . .

16.6c . . . and recover the spacers from the motor mounting rubbers

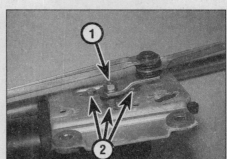

16.7 Wiper motor spindle nut (1) and mounting bolts (2)

4 Unclip the left- and right-hand inlet vent panels, and remove them from beneath the windscreen to gain access to the wiper motor (see illustration).
5 Trace the wiring back from the wiper motor and disconnect it at the wiring connector (see illustration).
6 Slacken and remove the wiper motor mounting nuts and bolt, and manoeuvre the wiper motor assembly out of position. Recover the spacers from the motor mounting rubbers (see illustrations).
7 If necessary, mark the relative positions of the motor shaft and crank, then unscrew the retaining nut and washer and free the wiper linkage from the motor spindle. Unscrew the motor retaining bolts, and separate the motor and linkage (see illustration).

Refitting

8 Refitting is the reverse of removal, ensuring all fasteners are securely tightened. Also ensure that the inlet vent panels are correctly clipped in position prior to refitting the wiper arms.

17 Rear screen/tailgate wiper motor - removal and refitting

Removal

1 Disconnect the battery negative terminal.
2 Remove the wiper arm as described in Section 15 and proceed as described under the relevant sub-heading.

Saloon models

3 Unscrew the nut from the motor spindle, and lift off the washer and rubber sealing ring.
4 From inside the luggage compartment, disconnect the wiring connector, then slacken and remove the nuts/bolts and manoeuvre the wiper motor assembly out of position.
5 Recover the inner seal from the wiper spindle and the spacers from the motor mounting rubbers.

Estate models

6 Open up the tailgate then prise out the retaining clips and remove the inner trim panel.
7 Slacken and remove the wiper motor retaining nuts and carefully manoeuvre the motor out of position, disconnecting its wiring connector as it becomes accessible. Note: It may be necessary to slide the spacer off the motor spindle to gain the necessary clearance required to withdraw the motor. Recover the

spacers from the motor mounting rubbers and remove the rubber sealing grommet from the tailgate glass (see illustrations).

Refitting

8 Refitting is the reverse of removal. Prior to refitting, check the mounting rubbers, washers and sealing grommet (as applicable) for damage and renew if necessary.

18 Washer system components - removal and refitting

1 The washer reservoir is located behind the right-hand front wing. On Estate models, the reservoir also supplies the tailgate washer. On models equipped with headlight washers, the reservoir also supplies the headlight washer jets via an additional pump.

17.7a On Estate models, slacken and remove the retaining nuts (arrowed) . . .

17.7b . . . then manoeuvre the motor out of position and disconnect the wiring . . .

Spare parts are available from many sources, including maker's appointed garages, accessory shops, and motor factors. To be sure of obtaining the correct parts, it will sometimes be necessary to quote the vehicle identification number. If possible, it can also be useful to take the old parts along for positive identification. Items such as starter motors and alternators may be available under a service exchange scheme - any parts returned should be clean.

Our advice regarding spare parts is as follows.

Officially appointed garages

This is the best source of parts which are peculiar to your car, and which are not otherwise generally available (eg, badges, interior trim, certain body panels, etc). It is also the only place at which you should buy parts if the vehicle is still under warranty.

Accessory shops

These are very good places to buy materials and components needed for the maintenance of your car (oil, air and fuel filters, light bulbs, drivebelts, greases, brake pads, touch-up paint, etc). Components of this nature sold by a reputable shop are usually of the same standard as those used by the car manufacturer.

Besides components, these shops also sell tools and general accessories, usually have convenient opening hours, charge lower prices, and can often be found close to home. Some accessory shops have parts counters where components needed for almost any repair job can be purchased or ordered.

Motor factors

Good factors will stock the more important components which wear out comparatively quickly, and can sometimes supply individual components needed for the overhaul of a larger assembly (eg, brake seals and hydraulic parts, bearing shells, pistons, valves). They may also handle work such as cylinder block reboring, crankshaft regrinding, etc.

Tyre and exhaust specialists

These outlets may be independent, or members of a local or national chain. They frequently offer competitive prices when compared with a main dealer or local garage, but it will pay to obtain several quotes before making a decision. When researching prices, also be sure to ask what "extras" may be added - for instance, fitting a new valve, balancing the wheel, and checking the tracking (front wheels) are all commonly charged on top of the price of a new tyre.

Other sources

Beware of parts or materials obtained from market stalls, car boot sales or similar outlets. Such items are not invariably sub-standard, but there is little chance of compensation if they do prove unsatisfactory. in the case of safety-critical components such as brake pads, there is the risk not only of financial loss, but also of an accident causing injury or death.

Second-hand components or assemblies obtained from a car breaker can be a good buy in some circumstances, but this sort of purchase is best made by the experienced DIY mechanic.

Vehicle identification

Modifications are a continuing and unpublicised process in vehicle manufacture, quite apart from major model changes. Spare parts manuals and lists are compiled upon a numerical basis, the individual vehicle identification numbers being essential to correct identification of the component concerned.

When ordering spare parts, always give as much information as possible. Quote the car model, year of manufacture and registration, chassis and engine numbers as appropriate.

The *Vehicle Identification Number (VIN)* plate is riveted to the right-hand end of the bonnet lock crossmember and is visible once the bonnet has been opened. The vehicle identification (chassis) number is also stamped onto the top of the right-hand side of the engine compartment bulkhead and is stamped on a plate attached to the top, left-hand end of the facia (visible through the windscreen) **(see illustrations)**. On certain models a *Homologation plate* is attached to the left-hand end of the bonnet locking crossmember.

The *engine number and code* can be found on the front of the cylinder block. On petrol engine models the number and code are stamped onto the cylinder block surface; on 1.6 and 1.8 litre models they can be found at the bottom, left-hand corner of the block, and on 2.0 litre models they are situated just to the left of the oil filter. On 1.9 litre diesel engine models the engine number and code are stamped onto a metal plate which is riveted to the centre of the block, directly behind the injection pump, and on 2.1 litre models the code and number are stamped on the centre of the cylinder block surface, just to the left of the oil filter **(see illustration)**.

The *paint code* is stamped onto the side of the left-hand front suspension strut mounting turret in the engine compartment.

The vehicle identification number (VIN) plate (arrowed) is riveted to the right-hand end of the bonnet lock crossmember

The chassis number (arrowed) is also stamped onto the top of the engine compartment bulkhead

The engine number and code can be found on the front of the cylinder block (2.0 litre petrol engine shown)

Whenever servicing, repair or overhaul work is carried out on the car or its components, observe the following procedures and instructions. This will assist in carrying out the operation efficiently and to a professional standard of workmanship.

Joint mating faces and gaskets

When separating components at their mating faces, never insert screwdrivers or similar implements into the joint between the faces in order to prise them apart. This can cause severe damage which results in oil leaks, coolant leaks, etc upon reassembly. Separation is usually achieved by tapping along the joint with a soft-faced hammer in order to break the seal. However, note that this method may not be suitable where dowels are used for component location.

Where a gasket is used between the mating faces of two components, a new one must be fitted on reassembly; fit it dry unless otherwise stated in the repair procedure. Make sure that the mating faces are clean and dry, with all traces of old gasket removed. When cleaning a joint face, use a tool which is unlikely to score or damage the face, and remove any burrs or nicks with an oilstone or fine file.

Make sure that tapped holes are cleaned with a pipe cleaner, and keep them free of jointing compound, if this is being used, unless specifically instructed otherwise.

Ensure that all orifices, channels or pipes are clear, and blow through them, preferably using compressed air.

Oil seals

Oil seals can be removed by levering them out with a wide flat-bladed screwdriver or similar implement. Alternatively, a number of self-tapping screws may be screwed into the seal, and these used as a purchase for pliers or some similar device in order to pull the seal free.

Whenever an oil seal is removed from its working location, either individually or as part of an assembly, it should be renewed.

The very fine sealing lip of the seal is easily damaged, and will not seal if the surface it contacts is not completely clean and free from scratches, nicks or grooves. If the original sealing surface of the component cannot be restored, and the manufacturer has not made provision for slight relocation of the seal relative to the sealing surface, the component should be renewed.

Protect the lips of the seal from any surface which may damage them in the course of fitting. Use tape or a conical sleeve where possible. Lubricate the seal lips with oil before fitting and, on dual-lipped seals, fill the space between the lips with grease.

Unless otherwise stated, oil seals must be fitted with their sealing lips toward the lubricant to be sealed.

Use a tubular drift or block of wood of the appropriate size to install the seal and, if the seal housing is shouldered, drive the seal down to the shoulder. If the seal housing is unshouldered, the seal should be fitted with its face flush with the housing top face (unless otherwise instructed).

Screw threads and fastenings

Seized nuts, bolts and screws are quite a common occurrence where corrosion has set in, and the use of penetrating oil or releasing fluid will often overcome this problem if the offending item is soaked for a while before attempting to release it. The use of an impact driver may also provide a means of releasing such stubborn fastening devices, when used in conjunction with the appropriate screwdriver bit or socket. If none of these methods works, it may be necessary to resort to the careful application of heat, or the use of a hacksaw or nut splitter device.

Studs are usually removed by locking two nuts together on the threaded part, and then using a spanner on the lower nut to unscrew the stud. Studs or bolts which have broken off below the surface of the component in which they are mounted can sometimes be removed using a stud extractor. Always ensure that a blind tapped hole is completely free from oil, grease, water or other fluid before installing the bolt or stud. Failure to do this could cause the housing to crack due to the hydraulic action of the bolt or stud as it is screwed in.

When tightening a castellated nut to accept a split pin, tighten the nut to the specified torque, where applicable, and then tighten further to the next split pin hole. Never slacken the nut to align the split pin hole, unless stated in the repair procedure.

When checking or retightening a nut or bolt to a specified torque setting, slacken the nut or bolt by a quarter of a turn, and then retighten to the specified setting. However, this should not be attempted where angular tightening has been used.

For some screw fastenings, notably cylinder head bolts or nuts, torque wrench settings are no longer specified for the latter stages of tightening, "angle-tightening" being called up instead. Typically, a fairly low torque wrench setting will be applied to the bolts/nuts in the correct sequence, followed by one or more stages of tightening through specified angles.

Locknuts, locktabs and washers

Any fastening which will rotate against a component or housing during tightening should always have a washer between it and the relevant component or housing.

Spring or split washers should always be renewed when they are used to lock a critical component such as a big-end bearing retaining bolt or nut. Locktabs which are folded over to retain a nut or bolt should always be renewed.

Self-locking nuts can be re-used in non-critical areas, providing resistance can be felt when the locking portion passes over the bolt or stud thread. However, it should be noted that self-locking stiffnuts tend to lose their effectiveness after long periods of use, and should then be renewed as a matter of course.

Split pins must always be replaced with new ones of the correct size for the hole.

When thread-locking compound is found on the threads of a fastener which is to be re-used, it should be cleaned off with a wire brush and solvent, and fresh compound applied on reassembly.

Special tools

Some repair procedures in this manual entail the use of special tools such as a press, two or three-legged pullers, spring compressors, etc. Wherever possible, suitable readily-available alternatives to the manufacturer's special tools are described, and are shown in use. In some instances, where no alternative is possible, it has been necessary to resort to the use of a manufacturer's tool, and this has been done for reasons of safety as well as the efficient completion of the repair operation. Unless you are highly-skilled and have a thorough understanding of the procedures described, never attempt to bypass the use of any special tool when the procedure described specifies its use. Not only is there a very great risk of personal injury, but expensive damage could be caused to the components involved.

Environmental considerations

When disposing of used engine oil, brake fluid, antifreeze, etc, give due consideration to any detrimental environmental effects. Do not, for instance, pour any of the above liquids down drains into the general sewage system, or onto the ground to soak away. Many local council refuse tips provide a facility for waste oil disposal, as do some garages. If none of these facilities are available, consult your local Environmental Health Department, or the National Rivers Authority, for further advice.

With the universal tightening-up of legislation regarding the emission of environmentally-harmful substances from motor vehicles, most vehicles have tamperproof devices fitted to the main adjustment points of the fuel system. These devices are primarily designed to prevent unqualified persons from adjusting the fuel/air mixture, with the chance of a consequent increase in toxic emissions. If such devices are found during servicing or overhaul, they should, wherever possible, be renewed or refitted in accordance with the manufacturer's requirements or current legislation.

OIL CARE
FOLLOW THE CODE
OIL BANK LINE
0800 66 33 66
www.oilbankline.org.uk

Note: It is antisocial and illegal to dump oil down the drain. To find the location of your local oil recycling bank, call this number free.

The jack supplied with the vehicle tool kit should only be used for changing the roadwheels - see *"Wheel changing"* at the front of this manual. When carrying out any other kind of work, raise the vehicle using a hydraulic (or "trolley") jack, and always supplement the jack with axle stands positioned under the vehicle jacking points.

To raise the front of the vehicle, position the jack head underneath the centre of the front suspension subframe. Lift the vehicle to the required height and support it on axle stands positioned underneath the vehicle jacking points on the sills **(see illustration)**.

To raise the rear of the vehicle, position the jack head underneath the rear suspension lower arm, directly beneath the coil spring. Lift the vehicle to the required height and support it on axle stands positioned underneath the vehicle jacking points on the sills **(see illustration)**.

The jack supplied with the vehicle locates with the jacking points on the sills. Ensure that the jack head is correctly engaged before attempting to raise the vehicle.

Never work under, around, or near a raised vehicle, unless it is adequately supported in at least two places.

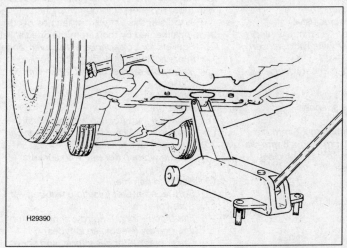

To raise the front of the vehicle, position the jack head underneath the centre of the subframe

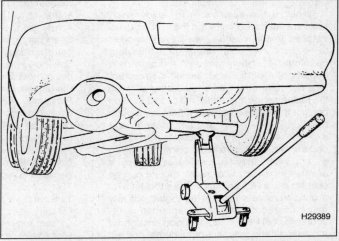

To raise the rear of the vehicle, position the jack head directly underneath one of the rear suspension lower arms

Radio/cassette unit anti-theft system - precaution

The radio/cassette/CD player/autochanger unit fitted as standard equipment by Peugeot is equipped with a built-in security code, to deter thieves. If the power source to the unit is cut, the anti-theft system will activate. Even if the power source is immediately reconnected, the radio/cassette unit will not function until the correct security code has been entered. Therefore if you do not know the correct security code for the unit, **do not** disconnect the battery negative lead, or remove the radio/cassette unit from the vehicle.

The procedure for reprogramming a unit that has been disconnected from its power supply varies from model to model - consult the handbook supplied with the unit for specific details or refer to your Peugeot dealer.

Introduction

A selection of good tools is a fundamental requirement for anyone contemplating the maintenance and repair of a motor vehicle. For the owner who does not possess any, their purchase will prove a considerable expense, offsetting some of the savings made by doing-it-yourself. However, provided that the tools purchased meet the relevant national safety standards and are of good quality, they will last for many years and prove an extremely worthwhile investment.

To help the average owner to decide which tools are needed to carry out the various tasks detailed in this manual, we have compiled three lists of tools under the following headings: *Maintenance and minor repair, Repair and overhaul,* and *Special.* Newcomers to practical mechanics should start off with the *Maintenance and minor repair* tool kit, and confine themselves to the simpler jobs around the vehicle. Then, as confidence and experience grow, more difficult tasks can be undertaken, with extra tools being purchased as, and when, they are needed. In this way, a *Maintenance and minor repair* tool kit can be built up into a *Repair and overhaul* tool kit over a considerable period of time, without any major cash outlays. The experienced do-it-yourselfer will have a tool kit good enough for most repair and overhaul procedures, and will add tools from the *Special* category when it is felt that the expense is justified by the amount of use to which these tools will be put.

Maintenance and minor repair tool kit

The tools given in this list should be considered as a minimum requirement if routine maintenance, servicing and minor repair operations are to be undertaken. We recommend the purchase of combination spanners (ring one end, open-ended the other); although more expensive than open-ended ones, they do give the advantages of both types of spanner.

☐ *Combination spanners:*
  Metric - 8 to 19 mm inclusive
☐ *Adjustable spanner - 35 mm jaw (approx.)*
☐ *Spark plug spanner (with rubber insert) - petrol models*
☐ *Spark plug gap adjustment tool - petrol models*
☐ *Set of feeler gauges*
☐ *Brake bleed nipple spanner*
☐ *Screwdrivers:*
  Flat blade - 100 mm long x 6 mm dia
  Cross blade - 100 mm long x 6 mm dia
  Torx - various sizes (not all vehicles)
☐ *Combination pliers*
☐ *Hacksaw (junior)*
☐ *Tyre pump*
☐ *Tyre pressure gauge*
☐ *Oil can*
☐ *Oil filter removal tool*
☐ *Fine emery cloth*
☐ *Wire brush (small)*
☐ *Funnel (medium size)*
☐ *Sump drain plug key (not all vehicles)*

Repair and overhaul tool kit

These tools are virtually essential for anyone undertaking any major repairs to a motor vehicle, and are additional to those given in the *Maintenance and minor repair* list. Included in this list is a comprehensive set of sockets. Although these are expensive, they will be found invaluable as they are so versatile - particularly if various drives are included in the set. We recommend the half-inch square-drive type, as this can be used with most proprietary torque wrenches.

The tools in this list will sometimes need to be supplemented by tools from the *Special* list:

☐ *Sockets (or box spanners) to cover range in previous list (including Torx sockets)*
☐ *Reversible ratchet drive (for use with sockets)*
☐ *Extension piece, 250 mm (for use with sockets)*
☐ *Universal joint (for use with sockets)*
☐ *Flexible handle or sliding T "breaker bar" (for use with sockets)*
☐ *Torque wrench (for use with sockets)*
☐ *Self-locking grips*
☐ *Ball pein hammer*
☐ *Soft-faced mallet (plastic or rubber)*
☐ *Screwdrivers:*
  Flat blade - long & sturdy, short (chubby), and narrow (electrician's) types
  Cross blade – long & sturdy, and short (chubby) types
☐ *Pliers:*
  Long-nosed
  Side cutters (electrician's)
  Circlip (internal and external)
☐ *Cold chisel - 25 mm*
☐ *Scriber*
☐ *Scraper*
☐ *Centre-punch*
☐ *Pin punch*
☐ *Hacksaw*
☐ *Brake hose clamp*
☐ *Brake/clutch bleeding kit*
☐ *Selection of twist drills*
☐ *Steel rule/straight-edge*
☐ *Allen keys (inc. splined/Torx type)*
☐ *Selection of files*
☐ *Wire brush*
☐ *Axle stands*
☐ *Jack (strong trolley or hydraulic type)*
☐ *Light with extension lead*
☐ *Universal electrical multi-meter*

Sockets and reversible ratchet drive

Brake bleeding kit

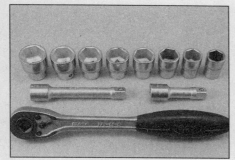
Torx key, socket and bit

Hose clamp

Angular-tightening gauge

Special tools

The tools in this list are those which are not used regularly, are expensive to buy, or which need to be used in accordance with their manufacturers' instructions. Unless relatively difficult mechanical jobs are undertaken frequently, it will not be economic to buy many of these tools. Where this is the case, you could consider clubbing together with friends (or joining a motorists' club) to make a joint purchase, or borrowing the tools against a deposit from a local garage or tool hire specialist. It is worth noting that many of the larger DIY superstores now carry a large range of special tools for hire at modest rates.

The following list contains only those tools and instruments freely available to the public, and not those special tools produced by the vehicle manufacturer specifically for its dealer network. You will find occasional references to these manufacturers' special tools in the text of this manual. Generally, an alternative method of doing the job without the vehicle manufacturer's special tool is given. However, sometimes there is no alternative to using them. Where this is the case and the relevant tool cannot be bought or borrowed, you will have to entrust the work to a dealer.

- ☐ *Angular-tightening gauge*
- ☐ *Valve spring compressor*
- ☐ *Valve grinding tool*
- ☐ *Piston ring compressor*
- ☐ *Piston ring removal/installation tool*
- ☐ *Cylinder bore hone*
- ☐ *Balljoint separator*
- ☐ *Coil spring compressors (where applicable)*
- ☐ *Two/three-legged hub and bearing puller*
- ☐ *Impact screwdriver*
- ☐ *Micrometer and/or vernier calipers*
- ☐ *Dial gauge*
- ☐ *Stroboscopic timing light*
- ☐ *Dwell angle meter/tachometer*
- ☐ *Fault code reader*
- ☐ *Cylinder compression gauge*
- ☐ *Hand-operated vacuum pump and gauge*
- ☐ *Clutch plate alignment set*
- ☐ *Brake shoe steady spring cup removal tool*
- ☐ *Bush and bearing removal/installation set*
- ☐ *Stud extractors*
- ☐ *Tap and die set*
- ☐ *Lifting tackle*
- ☐ *Trolley jack*

Buying tools

Reputable motor accessory shops and superstores often offer excellent quality tools at discount prices, so it pays to shop around.

Remember, you don't have to buy the most expensive items on the shelf, but it is always advisable to steer clear of the very cheap tools. Beware of 'bargains' offered on market stalls or at car boot sales. There are plenty of good tools around at reasonable prices, but always aim to purchase items which meet the relevant national safety standards. If in doubt, ask the proprietor or manager of the shop for advice before making a purchase.

Care and maintenance of tools

Having purchased a reasonable tool kit, it is necessary to keep the tools in a clean and serviceable condition. After use, always wipe off any dirt, grease and metal particles using a clean, dry cloth, before putting the tools away. Never leave them lying around after they have been used. A simple tool rack on the garage or workshop wall for items such as screwdrivers and pliers is a good idea. Store all normal spanners and sockets in a metal box. Any measuring instruments, gauges, meters, etc, must be carefully stored where they cannot be damaged or become rusty.

Take a little care when tools are used. Hammer heads inevitably become marked, and screwdrivers lose the keen edge on their blades from time to time. A little timely attention with emery cloth or a file will soon restore items like this to a good finish.

Working facilities

Not to be forgotten when discussing tools is the workshop itself. If anything more than routine maintenance is to be carried out, a suitable working area becomes essential.

It is appreciated that many an owner-mechanic is forced by circumstances to remove an engine or similar item without the benefit of a garage or workshop. Having done this, any repairs should always be done under the cover of a roof.

Wherever possible, any dismantling should be done on a clean, flat workbench or table at a suitable working height.

Any workbench needs a vice; one with a jaw opening of 100 mm is suitable for most jobs. As mentioned previously, some clean dry storage space is also required for tools, as well as for any lubricants, cleaning fluids, touch-up paints etc, which become necessary.

Another item which may be required, and which has a much more general usage, is an electric drill with a chuck capacity of at least 8 mm. This, together with a good range of twist drills, is virtually essential for fitting accessories.

Last, but not least, always keep a supply of old newspapers and clean, lint-free rags available, and try to keep any working area as clean as possible.

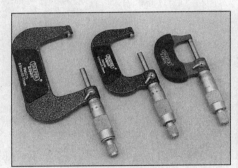
Micrometers

Dial test indicator ("dial gauge")

Strap wrench

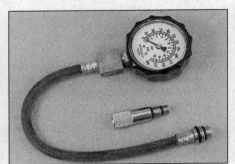
Compression tester

Fault code reader

This is a guide to getting your vehicle through the MOT test. Obviously it will not be possible to examine the vehicle to the same standard as the professional MOT tester. However, working through the following checks will enable you to identify any problem areas before submitting the vehicle for the test.

Where a testable component is in borderline condition, the tester has discretion in deciding whether to pass or fail it. The basis of such discretion is whether the tester would be happy for a close relative or friend to use the vehicle with the component in that condition. If the vehicle presented is clean and evidently well cared for, the tester may be more inclined to pass a borderline component than if the vehicle is scruffy and apparently neglected.

It has only been possible to summarise the test requirements here, based on the regulations in force at the time of printing. Test standards are becoming increasingly stringent, although there are some exemptions for older vehicles.

An assistant will be needed to help carry out some of these checks.

The checks have been sub-divided into four categories, as follows:

1 Checks carried out **FROM THE DRIVER'S SEAT**

2 Checks carried out **WITH THE VEHICLE ON THE GROUND**

3 Checks carried out **WITH THE VEHICLE RAISED AND THE WHEELS FREE TO TURN**

4 Checks carried out on **YOUR VEHICLE'S EXHAUST EMISSION SYSTEM**

---

1 Checks carried out **FROM THE DRIVER'S SEAT**

Handbrake

☐ Test the operation of the handbrake. Excessive travel (too many clicks) indicates incorrect brake or cable adjustment.
☐ Check that the handbrake cannot be released by tapping the lever sideways. Check the security of the lever mountings.

Footbrake

☐ Depress the brake pedal and check that it does not creep down to the floor, indicating a master cylinder fault. Release the pedal, wait a few seconds, then depress it again. If the pedal travels nearly to the floor before firm resistance is felt, brake adjustment or repair is necessary. If the pedal feels spongy, there is air in the hydraulic system which must be removed by bleeding.

☐ Check that the brake pedal is secure and in good condition. Check also for signs of fluid leaks on the pedal, floor or carpets, which would indicate failed seals in the brake master cylinder.
☐ Check the servo unit (when applicable) by operating the brake pedal several times, then keeping the pedal depressed and starting the engine. As the engine starts, the pedal will move down slightly. If not, the vacuum hose or the servo itself may be faulty.

Steering wheel and column

☐ Examine the steering wheel for fractures or looseness of the hub, spokes or rim.
☐ Move the steering wheel from side to side and then up and down. Check that the steering wheel is not loose on the column, indicating wear or a loose retaining nut. Continue moving the steering wheel as before, but also turn it slightly from left to right.
☐ Check that the steering wheel is not loose on the column, and that there is no abnormal

movement of the steering wheel, indicating wear in the column support bearings or couplings.

Windscreen, mirrors and sunvisor

☐ The windscreen must be free of cracks or other significant damage within the driver's field of view. (Small stone chips are acceptable.) Rear view mirrors must be secure, intact, and capable of being adjusted.

☐ The driver's sunvisor must be capable of being stored in the "up" position.

Seat belts and seats

Note: *The following checks are applicable to all seat belts, front and rear.*

☐ Examine the webbing of all the belts (including rear belts if fitted) for cuts, serious fraying or deterioration. Fasten and unfasten each belt to check the buckles. If applicable, check the retracting mechanism. Check the security of all seat belt mountings accessible from inside the vehicle.

☐ Seat belts with pre-tensioners, once activated, have a "flag" or similar showing on the seat belt stalk. This, in itself, is not a reason for test failure.

☐ The front seats themselves must be securely attached and the backrests must lock in the upright position.

Doors

☐ Both front doors must be able to be opened and closed from outside and inside, and must latch securely when closed.

2 Checks carried out WITH THE VEHICLE ON THE GROUND

Vehicle identification

☐ Number plates must be in good condition, secure and legible, with letters and numbers correctly spaced – spacing at (A) should be at least twice that at (B).

☐ The VIN plate and/or homologation plate must be legible.

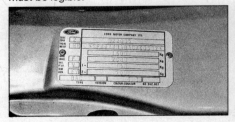

Electrical equipment

☐ Switch on the ignition and check the operation of the horn.

☐ Check the windscreen washers and wipers, examining the wiper blades; renew damaged or perished blades. Also check the operation of the stop-lights.

☐ Check the operation of the sidelights and number plate lights. The lenses and reflectors must be secure, clean and undamaged.

☐ Check the operation and alignment of the headlights. The headlight reflectors must not be tarnished and the lenses must be undamaged.

☐ Switch on the ignition and check the operation of the direction indicators (including the instrument panel tell-tale) and the hazard warning lights. Operation of the sidelights and stop-lights must not affect the indicators - if it does, the cause is usually a bad earth at the rear light cluster.

☐ Check the operation of the rear foglight(s), including the warning light on the instrument panel or in the switch.

☐ The ABS warning light must illuminate in accordance with the manufacturers' design. For most vehicles, the ABS warning light should illuminate when the ignition is switched on, and (if the system is operating properly) extinguish after a few seconds. Refer to the owner's handbook.

Footbrake

☐ Examine the master cylinder, brake pipes and servo unit for leaks, loose mountings, corrosion or other damage.

☐ The fluid reservoir must be secure and the fluid level must be between the upper (A) and lower (B) markings.

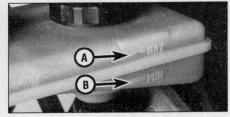

☐ Inspect both front brake flexible hoses for cracks or deterioration of the rubber. Turn the steering from lock to lock, and ensure that the hoses do not contact the wheel, tyre, or any part of the steering or suspension mechanism. With the brake pedal firmly depressed, check the hoses for bulges or leaks under pressure.

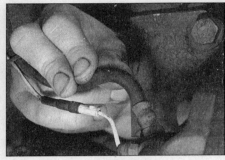

Steering and suspension

☐ Have your assistant turn the steering wheel from side to side slightly, up to the point where the steering gear just begins to transmit this movement to the roadwheels. Check for excessive free play between the steering wheel and the steering gear, indicating wear or insecurity of the steering column joints, the column-to-steering gear coupling, or the steering gear itself.

☐ Have your assistant turn the steering wheel more vigorously in each direction, so that the roadwheels just begin to turn. As this is done, examine all the steering joints, linkages, fittings and attachments. Renew any component that shows signs of wear or damage. On vehicles with power steering, check the security and condition of the steering pump, drivebelt and hoses.

☐ Check that the vehicle is standing level, and at approximately the correct ride height.

Shock absorbers

☐ Depress each corner of the vehicle in turn, then release it. The vehicle should rise and then settle in its normal position. If the vehicle continues to rise and fall, the shock absorber is defective. A shock absorber which has seized will also cause the vehicle to fail.

Exhaust system

☐ Start the engine. With your assistant holding a rag over the tailpipe, check the entire system for leaks. Repair or renew leaking sections.

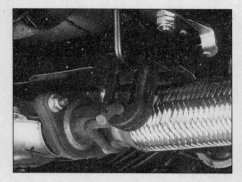

3 Checks carried out
WITH THE VEHICLE RAISED AND THE WHEELS FREE TO TURN

Jack up the front and rear of the vehicle, and securely support it on axle stands. Position the stands clear of the suspension assemblies. Ensure that the wheels are clear of the ground and that the steering can be turned from lock to lock.

Steering mechanism

☐ Have your assistant turn the steering from lock to lock. Check that the steering turns smoothly, and that no part of the steering mechanism, including a wheel or tyre, fouls any brake hose or pipe or any part of the body structure.
☐ Examine the steering rack rubber gaiters for damage or insecurity of the retaining clips. If power steering is fitted, check for signs of damage or leakage of the fluid hoses, pipes or connections. Also check for excessive stiffness or binding of the steering, a missing split pin or locking device, or severe corrosion of the body structure within 30 cm of any steering component attachment point.

Front and rear suspension and wheel bearings

☐ Starting at the front right-hand side, grasp the roadwheel at the 3 o'clock and 9 o'clock positions and rock gently but firmly. Check for free play or insecurity at the wheel bearings, suspension balljoints, or suspension mountings, pivots and attachments.
☐ Now grasp the wheel at the 12 o'clock and 6 o'clock positions and repeat the previous inspection. Spin the wheel, and check for roughness or tightness of the front wheel bearing.

☐ If excess free play is suspected at a component pivot point, this can be confirmed by using a large screwdriver or similar tool and levering between the mounting and the component attachment. This will confirm whether the wear is in the pivot bush, its retaining bolt, or in the mounting itself (the bolt holes can often become elongated).

☐ Carry out all the above checks at the other front wheel, and then at both rear wheels.

Springs and shock absorbers

☐ Examine the suspension struts (when applicable) for serious fluid leakage, corrosion, or damage to the casing. Also check the security of the mounting points.
☐ If coil springs are fitted, check that the spring ends locate in their seats, and that the spring is not corroded, cracked or broken.
☐ If leaf springs are fitted, check that all leaves are intact, that the axle is securely attached to each spring, and that there is no deterioration of the spring eye mountings, bushes, and shackles.

☐ The same general checks apply to vehicles fitted with other suspension types, such as torsion bars, hydraulic displacer units, etc. Ensure that all mountings and attachments are secure, that there are no signs of excessive wear, corrosion or damage, and (on hydraulic types) that there are no fluid leaks or damaged pipes.
☐ Inspect the shock absorbers for signs of serious fluid leakage. Check for wear of the mounting bushes or attachments, or damage to the body of the unit.

Driveshafts (fwd vehicles only)

☐ Rotate each front wheel in turn and inspect the constant velocity joint gaiters for splits or damage. Also check that each driveshaft is straight and undamaged.

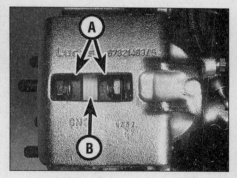

Braking system

☐ If possible without dismantling, check brake pad wear and disc condition. Ensure that the friction lining material has not worn excessively, (A) and that the discs are not fractured, pitted, scored or badly worn (B).

☐ Examine all the rigid brake pipes underneath the vehicle, and the flexible hose(s) at the rear. Look for corrosion, chafing or insecurity of the pipes, and for signs of bulging under pressure, chafing, splits or deterioration of the flexible hoses.
☐ Look for signs of fluid leaks at the brake calipers or on the brake backplates. Repair or renew leaking components.
☐ Slowly spin each wheel, while your assistant depresses and releases the footbrake. Ensure that each brake is operating and does not bind when the pedal is released.

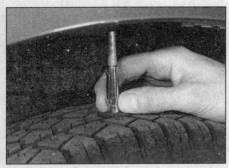

□ Examine the handbrake mechanism, checking for frayed or broken cables, excessive corrosion, or wear or insecurity of the linkage. Check that the mechanism works on each relevant wheel, and releases fully, without binding.

□ It is not possible to test brake efficiency without special equipment, but a road test can be carried out later to check that the vehicle pulls up in a straight line.

Fuel and exhaust systems

□ Inspect the fuel tank (including the filler cap), fuel pipes, hoses and unions. All components must be secure and free from leaks.

□ Examine the exhaust system over its entire length, checking for any damaged, broken or missing mountings, security of the retaining clamps and rust or corrosion.

Wheels and tyres

□ Examine the sidewalls and tread area of each tyre in turn. Check for cuts, tears, lumps, bulges, separation of the tread, and exposure of the ply or cord due to wear or damage. Check that the tyre bead is correctly seated on the wheel rim, that the valve is sound and properly seated, and that the wheel is not distorted or damaged.

□ Check that the tyres are of the correct size for the vehicle, that they are of the same size and type on each axle, and that the pressures are correct.

□ Check the tyre tread depth. The legal minimum at the time of writing is 1.6 mm over at least three-quarters of the tread width. Abnormal tread wear may indicate incorrect front wheel alignment.

Body corrosion

□ Check the condition of the entire vehicle structure for signs of corrosion in load-bearing areas. (These include chassis box sections, side sills, cross-members, pillars, and all suspension, steering, braking system and seat belt mountings and anchorages.) Any corrosion which has seriously reduced the thickness of a load-bearing area is likely to cause the vehicle to fail. In this case professional repairs are likely to be needed.

□ Damage or corrosion which causes sharp or otherwise dangerous edges to be exposed will also cause the vehicle to fail.

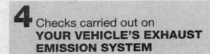

4 Checks carried out on **YOUR VEHICLE'S EXHAUST EMISSION SYSTEM**

Petrol models

□ Have the engine at normal operating temperature, and make sure that it is in good tune (ignition system in good order, air filter element clean, etc).

□ Before any measurements are carried out, raise the engine speed to around 2500 rpm, and hold it at this speed for 20 seconds. Allow the engine speed to return to idle, and watch for smoke emissions from the exhaust tailpipe. If the idle speed is obviously much too high, or if dense blue or clearly-visible black smoke comes from the tailpipe for more than 5 seconds, the vehicle will fail. As a rule of thumb, blue smoke signifies oil being burnt (engine wear) while black smoke signifies unburnt fuel (dirty air cleaner element, or other carburettor or fuel system fault).

□ An exhaust gas analyser capable of measuring carbon monoxide (CO) and hydrocarbons (HC) is now needed. If such an instrument cannot be hired or borrowed, a local garage may agree to perform the check for a small fee.

CO emissions (mixture)

□ At the time of writing, for vehicles first used between 1st August 1975 and 31st July 1986 (P to C registration), the CO level must not exceed 4.5% by volume. For vehicles first used between 1st August 1986 and 31st July 1992 (D to J registration), the CO level must not exceed 3.5% by volume. Vehicles first

used after 1st August 1992 (K registration) must conform to the manufacturer's specification. The MOT tester has access to a DOT database or emissions handbook, which lists the CO and HC limits for each make and model of vehicle. The CO level is measured with the engine at idle speed, and at "fast idle". The following limits are given as a general guide:

> At idle speed -
> CO level no more than 0.5%
> At "fast idle" (2500 to 3000 rpm) -
> CO level no more than 0.3%
> (Minimum oil temperature 60ºC)

□ If the CO level cannot be reduced far enough to pass the test (and the fuel and ignition systems are otherwise in good condition) then the carburettor is badly worn, or there is some problem in the fuel injection system or catalytic converter (as applicable).

HC emissions

□ With the CO within limits, HC emissions for vehicles first used between 1st August 1975 and 31st July 1992 (P to J registration) must not exceed 1200 ppm. Vehicles first used after 1st August 1992 (K registration) must conform to the manufacturer's specification. The MOT tester has access to a DOT database or emissions handbook, which lists the CO and HC limits for each make and model of vehicle. The HC level is measured with the engine at "fast idle". The following is given as a general guide:

> At "fast idle" (2500 to 3000 rpm) -
> HC level no more than 200 ppm
> (Minimum oil temperature 60ºC)

□ Excessive HC emissions are caused by incomplete combustion, the causes of which can include oil being burnt, mechanical wear and ignition/fuel system malfunction.

Diesel models

□ The only emission test applicable to Diesel engines is the measuring of exhaust smoke density. The test involves accelerating the engine several times to its maximum unloaded speed.

Note: It is of the utmost importance that the engine timing belt is in good condition before the test is carried out.

□ The limits for Diesel engine exhaust smoke, introduced in September 1995 are:

Vehicles first used before 1st August 1979:
> Exempt from metered smoke testing, but must not emit "dense blue or clearly visible black smoke for a period of more than 5 seconds at idle" or "dense blue or clearly visible black smoke during acceleration which would obscure the view of other road users".

Non-turbocharged vehicles first used after 1st August 1979: 2.5m-1

Turbocharged vehicles first used after 1st August 1979: 3.0m-1

□ Excessive smoke can be caused by a dirty air cleaner element. Otherwise, professional advice may be needed to find the cause.

Engine 1
- [ ] Engine fails to rotate when attempting to start
- [ ] Engine rotates, but will not start
- [ ] Engine difficult to start when cold
- [ ] Engine difficult to start when hot
- [ ] Starter motor noisy or excessively-rough in engagement
- [ ] Engine starts, but stops immediately
- [ ] Engine idles erratically
- [ ] Engine misfires at idle speed
- [ ] Engine misfires throughout the driving speed range
- [ ] Engine hesitates on acceleration
- [ ] Engine stalls
- [ ] Engine lacks power
- [ ] Engine backfires
- [ ] Oil pressure warning light illuminated with engine running
- [ ] Engine runs-on after switching off
- [ ] Engine noises

Cooling system 2
- [ ] Overheating
- [ ] Overcooling
- [ ] External coolant leakage
- [ ] Internal coolant leakage
- [ ] Corrosion

Fuel and exhaust systems 3
- [ ] Excessive fuel consumption
- [ ] Fuel leakage and/or fuel odour
- [ ] Excessive noise or fumes from exhaust system

Clutch 4
- [ ] Pedal travels to floor - no pressure or very little resistance
- [ ] Clutch fails to disengage (unable to select gears)
- [ ] Clutch slips (engine speed increases, with no increase in vehicle speed)
- [ ] Judder as clutch is engaged
- [ ] Noise when depressing or releasing clutch pedal

Manual transmission 5
- [ ] Noisy in neutral with engine running
- [ ] Noisy in one particular gear
- [ ] Difficulty engaging gears
- [ ] Jumps out of gear
- [ ] Vibration
- [ ] Lubricant leaks

Automatic transmission 6
- [ ] Fluid leakage
- [ ] Transmission fluid brown, or has burned smell
- [ ] General gear selection problems
- [ ] Transmission will not downshift (kickdown) with accelerator pedal fully depressed
- [ ] Engine will not start in any gear, or starts in gears other than Park or Neutral
- [ ] Transmission slips, shifts roughly, is noisy, or has no drive in forward or reverse gears

Driveshafts 7
- [ ] Vibration when accelerating or decelerating
- [ ] Clicking or knocking noise on turns (at slow speed on full-lock)

Braking system 8
- [ ] Vehicle pulls to one side under braking
- [ ] Noise (grinding or high-pitched squeal) when brakes applied
- [ ] Excessive brake pedal travel
- [ ] Brake pedal feels spongy when depressed
- [ ] Excessive brake pedal effort required to stop vehicle
- [ ] Judder felt through brake pedal or steering wheel when braking
- [ ] Brakes binding
- [ ] Rear wheels locking under normal braking

Suspension and steering 9
- [ ] Vehicle pulls to one side
- [ ] Wheel wobble and vibration
- [ ] Excessive pitching and/or rolling around corners, or during braking
- [ ] Wandering or general instability
- [ ] Excessively-stiff steering
- [ ] Excessive play in steering
- [ ] Lack of power assistance
- [ ] Tyre wear excessive

Electrical system 10
- [ ] Battery will only hold a charge for a few days
- [ ] Ignition/no-charge warning light remains illuminated with engine running
- [ ] Ignition/no-charge warning light fails to come on
- [ ] Lights inoperative
- [ ] Instrument readings inaccurate or erratic
- [ ] Horn inoperative, or unsatisfactory in operation
- [ ] Windscreen wipers inoperative, or unsatisfactory in operation
- [ ] Windscreen washers inoperative, or unsatisfactory in operation
- [ ] Electric windows inoperative, or unsatisfactory in operation
- [ ] Central locking system inoperative, or unsatisfactory in operation

Introduction

The vehicle owner who does his or her own maintenance according to the recommended service schedules should not have to use this section of the manual very often. Modern component reliability is such that, provided those items subject to wear or deterioration are inspected or renewed at the specified intervals, sudden failure is comparatively rare. Faults do not usually just happen as a result of sudden failure, but develop over a period of time. Major mechanical failures in particular are usually preceded by characteristic symptoms over hundreds or even thousands of miles. Those components which do occasionally fail without warning are often small and easily carried in the vehicle.

With any fault-finding, the first step is to decide where to begin investigations. Sometimes this is obvious, but on other occasions, a little detective work will be necessary. The owner who makes half a dozen haphazard adjustments or replacements may be successful in curing a fault (or its symptoms), but will be none the wiser if the fault recurs, and ultimately may have spent more time and money than was necessary. A calm and logical approach will be found to be more satisfactory in the long run. Always take into account any warning signs or abnormalities that may have been noticed in the period preceding the fault - power loss, high or low gauge readings, unusual smells, etc - and remember that failure of components such as fuses or spark plugs may only be pointers to some underlying fault.

The pages which follow provide an easy-reference guide to the more common problems which may occur during the operation of the vehicle. These problems and their possible causes are grouped under headings denoting various components or systems, such as Engine, Cooling system, etc. The Chapter and/or Section which deals with the problem is also shown in brackets. Whatever the fault, certain basic principles apply. These are as follows:

Verify the fault. This is simply a matter of being sure that you know what the symptoms are before starting work. This is particularly important if you are investigating a fault for someone else, who may not have described it very accurately. *Don't overlook the obvious.* For example, if the vehicle won't start, is there fuel in the tank? (Don't take anyone else's word on this particular point, and don't trust the fuel gauge either!) If an electrical fault is indicated, look for loose or broken wires before digging out the test gear.

Cure the disease, not the symptom. Substituting a flat battery with a fully-charged one will get you off the hard shoulder, but if the underlying cause is not attended to, the new battery will go the same way. Similarly, changing oil-fouled spark plugs for a new set will get you moving again, but remember that the reason for the fouling (if it wasn't simply an incorrect grade of plug) will have to be established and corrected.

Don't take anything for granted. Particularly, don't forget that a "new" component may itself be defective (especially if it's been rattling around in the boot for months), and don't leave components out of a fault diagnosis sequence just because they are new or recently-fitted. When you do finally diagnose a difficult fault, you'll probably realise that all the evidence was there from the start.

1 Engine

Engine fails to rotate when attempting to start

- [ ] Battery terminal connections loose or corroded (see *"Weekly checks"*)
- [ ] Battery discharged or faulty (Chapter 5)
- [ ] Broken, loose or disconnected wiring in the starting circuit (Chapter 5)
- [ ] Defective starter solenoid or switch (Chapter 5)
- [ ] Defective starter motor (Chapter 5)
- [ ] Starter pinion or flywheel ring gear teeth loose or broken (Chapters 2 and 5)
- [ ] Engine earth strap broken or disconnected (Chapter 5)

Engine rotates, but will not start

- [ ] Fuel tank empty
- [ ] Battery discharged (engine rotates slowly) (Chapter 5)
- [ ] Battery terminal connections loose or corroded (*"Weekly checks"*)
- [ ] Ignition components damp or damaged - petrol models (Chapters 1 and 5)
- [ ] Broken, loose or disconnected wiring in the ignition circuit - petrol models (Chapters 1 and 5)
- [ ] Worn, faulty or incorrectly-gapped spark plugs - petrol models (Chapter 1)
- [ ] Preheating system faulty - diesel models (Chapter 5)
- [ ] Fuel injection system fault - petrol models (Chapter 4)
- [ ] Stop solenoid faulty - diesel models (Chapter 4)
- [ ] Air in fuel system - diesel models (Chapter 4)
- [ ] Major mechanical failure (eg camshaft drive) (Chapter 2)

Engine difficult to start when cold

- [ ] Battery discharged (Chapter 5)
- [ ] Battery terminal connections loose or corroded (see *"Weekly checks"*)
- [ ] Worn, faulty or incorrectly-gapped spark plugs - petrol models (Chapter 1)
- [ ] Preheating system faulty - diesel models (Chapter 5)
- [ ] Fuel injection system fault - petrol models (Chapter 4)
- [ ] Other ignition system fault - petrol models (Chapters 1 and 5)
- [ ] Low cylinder compressions (Chapter 2)

Engine difficult to start when hot

- [ ] Air filter element dirty or clogged (Chapter 1)
- [ ] Fuel injection system fault - petrol models (Chapter 4)
- [ ] Low cylinder compressions (Chapter 2)

Starter motor noisy or excessively-rough in engagement

- [ ] Starter pinion or flywheel ring gear teeth loose or broken (Chapters 2 and 5)
- [ ] Starter motor mounting bolts loose or missing (Chapter 5)
- [ ] Starter motor internal components worn or damaged (Chapter 5)

Engine starts, but stops immediately

- [ ] Loose or faulty electrical connections in the ignition circuit - petrol models (Chapters 1 and 5)
- [ ] Vacuum leak at the throttle body or inlet manifold - petrol models (Chapter 4)
- [ ] Blocked injector/fuel injection system fault - petrol models (Chapter 4)

Engine idles erratically

- [ ] Air filter element clogged (Chapter 1)
- [ ] Vacuum leak at the throttle body, inlet manifold or associated hoses - petrol models (Chapter 4)
- [ ] Worn, faulty or incorrectly-gapped spark plugs - petrol models (Chapter 1)
- [ ] Uneven or low cylinder compressions (Chapter 2)
- [ ] Camshaft lobes worn (Chapter 2)
- [ ] Timing belt incorrectly fitted (Chapter 2)
- [ ] Blocked injector/fuel injection system fault - petrol models (Chapter 4)
- [ ] Faulty injector(s) - diesel models (Chapter 4)

Engine misfires at idle speed

- [ ] Worn, faulty or incorrectly-gapped spark plugs - petrol models (Chapter 1)
- [ ] Faulty spark plug HT leads (where fitted) - petrol models (Chapter 1)
- [ ] Vacuum leak at the throttle body, inlet manifold or associated hoses - petrol models (Chapter 4)
- [ ] Blocked injector/fuel injection system fault - petrol models (Chapter 4)
- [ ] Faulty injector(s) - diesel models (Chapter 4)
- [ ] Distributor cap cracked or tracking internally - petrol models (where applicable) (Chapter 1).
- [ ] Uneven or low cylinder compressions (Chapter 2)
- [ ] Disconnected, leaking, or perished crankcase ventilation hoses (Chapter 4)

Engine misfires throughout the driving speed range

- [ ] Fuel filter choked (Chapter 1)
- [ ] Fuel pump faulty, or delivery pressure low (Chapter 4)
- [ ] Fuel tank vent blocked, or fuel pipes restricted (Chapter 4)
- [ ] Vacuum leak at the throttle body, inlet manifold or associated hoses - petrol models (Chapter 4)
- [ ] Worn, faulty or incorrectly-gapped spark plugs - petrol models (Chapter 1)
- [ ] Faulty spark plug HT leads (where fitted) - petrol models (Chapter 1)
- [ ] Faulty injector(s) - diesel models (Chapter 4)
- [ ] Distributor cap cracked or tracking internally - petrol models (where applicable) (Chapter 1)

1 Engine (continued)

Engine misfires throughout the driving speed range (continued)

- ☐ Faulty ignition coil - petrol models (Chapter 5)
- ☐ Uneven or low cylinder compressions (Chapter 2)
- ☐ Blocked injector/fuel injection system fault - petrol models (Chapter 4)

Engine hesitates on acceleration

- ☐ Worn, faulty or incorrectly-gapped spark plugs - petrol models (Chapter 1)
- ☐ Vacuum leak at the throttle body, inlet manifold or associated hoses (Chapter 4)
- ☐ Blocked injector/fuel injection system fault - petrol models (Chapter 4)
- ☐ Faulty injector(s) - diesel models (Chapter 4)

Engine stalls

- ☐ Vacuum leak at the throttle body, inlet manifold or associated hoses - petrol models (Chapter 4)
- ☐ Fuel filter choked (Chapter 1)
- ☐ Fuel pump faulty, or delivery pressure low - petrol models (Chapter 4)
- ☐ Fuel tank vent blocked, or fuel pipes restricted (Chapter 4)
- ☐ Blocked injector/fuel injection system fault - petrol models (Chapter 4)
- ☐ Faulty injector(s) - diesel models (Chapter 4)

Engine lacks power

- ☐ Timing belt incorrectly fitted (Chapter 2)
- ☐ Fuel filter choked (Chapter 1)
- ☐ Fuel pump faulty, or delivery pressure low (Chapter 4)
- ☐ Uneven or low cylinder compressions (Chapter 2)
- ☐ Worn, faulty or incorrectly-gapped spark plugs - petrol models (Chapter 1)
- ☐ Vacuum leak at the throttle body, inlet manifold or associated hoses - petrol models (Chapter 4)
- ☐ Blocked injector/fuel injection system fault - petrol models (Chapter 4)
- ☐ Faulty injector(s) - diesel models (Chapter 4)
- ☐ Injection pump timing incorrect - diesel models (Chapter 4)
- ☐ Brakes binding (Chapters 1 and 9)
- ☐ Clutch slipping (Chapter 6)

Engine backfires

- ☐ Timing belt incorrectly fitted (Chapter 2)
- ☐ Vacuum leak at the throttle body, inlet manifold or associated hoses - petrol models (Chapter 4)
- ☐ Blocked injector/fuel injection system fault - petrol models (Chapter 4)

Oil pressure warning light illuminated with engine running

- ☐ Low oil level, or incorrect oil grade ("Weekly checks")
- ☐ Faulty oil pressure sensor (Chapter 5)
- ☐ Worn engine bearings and/or oil pump (Chapter 2)
- ☐ High engine operating temperature (Chapter 3)
- ☐ Oil pressure relief valve defective (Chapter 2)
- ☐ Oil pick-up strainer clogged (Chapter 2)

Engine runs-on after switching off

- ☐ Excessive carbon build-up in engine (Chapter 2)
- ☐ High engine operating temperature (Chapter 3)
- ☐ Fuel injection system fault - petrol models (Chapter 4)
- ☐ Faulty stop solenoid - diesel models (Chapter 4)

Engine noises

Pre-ignition (pinking) or knocking during acceleration or under load

- ☐ Ignition timing incorrect/ignition system fault - petrol models (Chapters 1 and 5)
- ☐ Incorrect grade of spark plug - petrol models (Chapter 1)
- ☐ Incorrect grade of fuel (Chapter 1)
- ☐ Vacuum leak at the throttle body, inlet manifold or associated hoses - petrol models (Chapter 4)
- ☐ Excessive carbon build-up in engine (Chapter 2)
- ☐ Blocked injector/fuel injection system fault - petrol models (Chapter 4)

Whistling or wheezing noises

- ☐ Leaking inlet manifold or throttle body gasket - petrol models (Chapter 4)
- ☐ Leaking exhaust manifold gasket or pipe-to-manifold joint (Chapter 4)
- ☐ Leaking vacuum hose (Chapters 4, 5 and 9)
- ☐ Blowing cylinder head gasket (Chapter 2)

Tapping or rattling noises

- ☐ Worn valve gear or camshaft (Chapter 2)
- ☐ Ancillary component fault (coolant pump, alternator, etc) (Chapters 3, 5, etc)

Knocking or thumping noises

- ☐ Worn big-end bearings (regular heavy knocking, perhaps less under load) (Chapter 2)
- ☐ Worn main bearings (rumbling and knocking, perhaps worsening under load) (Chapter 2)
- ☐ Piston slap (most noticeable when cold) (Chapter 2)
- ☐ Ancillary component fault (coolant pump, alternator, etc) (Chapters 3, 5, etc)

Title	Book No.
Peugeot 2.0, 2.1, 2.3 & 2.5 litre Diesel Engines (74 - 90) up to H	1607
PORSCHE 911 (65 - 85) up to C	0264
Porsche 924 & 924 Turbo (76 - 85) up to C	0397
PROTON (89 - 97) F to P	3255
RANGE ROVER V8 Petrol (70 - Oct 92) up to K	0606
RELIANT Robin & Kitten (73 - 83) up to A *	0436
RENAULT 4 (61 - 86) up to D *	0072
Renault 5 Petrol (Feb 85 - 96) B to N	1219
Renault 9 & 11 Petrol (82 - 89) up to F	0822
Renault 18 Petrol (79 - 86) up to D	0598
Renault 19 Petrol (89 - 96) F to N	1646
Renault 19 Diesel (89 - 96) F to N	1946
Renault 21 Petrol (86 - 94) C to M	1397
Renault 25 Petrol & Diesel (84 - 92) B to K	1228
Renault Clio Petrol (91 - May 98) H to R	1853
Renault Clio Diesel (91 - June 96) H to N	3031
Renault Clio Petrol & Diesel (May 98 - May 01) R to Y	3906
Renault Clio Petrol & Diesel (June 01 - 04) Y-reg. onwards	4168
Renault Espace Petrol & Diesel (85 - 96) C to N	3197
Renault Laguna Petrol & Diesel (94 - 00) L to W	3252
Renault Mégane & Scénic Petrol & Diesel (96 - 98) N to R	3395
Renault Mégane & Scénic Petrol & Diesel (Apr 99 - 02) T-reg. onwards	3916
Renault Mégane Petrol & Diesel (02 - 05) 52 to 55	4284
Renault Scénic & Grand Scénic Petrol & Diesel (03 - 06) 53 to 06	4297
ROVER 213 & 216 (84 - 89) A to G	1116
Rover 214 & 414 Petrol (89 - 96) G to N	1689
Rover 216 & 416 Petrol (89 - 96) G to N	1830
Rover 211, 214, 216, 218 & 220 Petrol & Diesel (Dec 95 - 99) N to V	3399
Rover 25 & MG ZR Petrol & Diesel (Oct 99 - 04) V-reg. onwards	4145
Rover 414, 416 & 420 Petrol & Diesel (May 95 - 98) M to R	3453
Rover 618, 620 & 623 Petrol (93 - 97) K to P	3257
Rover 820, 825 & 827 Petrol (86 - 95) D to N	1380
Rover 3500 (76 - 87) up to E *	0365
Rover Metro, 111 & 114 Petrol (May 90 - 98) G to S	1711
SAAB 95 & 96 (66 - 76) up to R *	0198
Saab 90, 99 & 900 (79 - Oct 93) up to L	0765
Saab 900 (Oct 93 - 98) L to R	3512
Saab 9000 (4-cyl) (85 - 98) C to S	1686
Saab 9-5 4-cyl Petrol (97 - 04) R-reg onwards	4156
SEAT Ibiza & Cordoba Petrol & Diesel (Oct 93 - Oct 99) L to V	3571
Seat Ibiza & Malaga Petrol (85 - 92) B to K	1609
SKODA Estelle (77 - 89) up to G	0604
Skoda Favorit (89 - 96) F to N	1801
Skoda Felicia Petrol & Diesel (95 - 01) M to X	3505
SUBARU 1600 & 1800 (Nov 79 - 90) up to H *	0995
SUNBEAM Alpine, Rapier & H120 (67 - 74) up to N *	0051
SUZUKI SJ Series, Samurai & Vitara (4-cyl) Petrol (82 - 97) up to P	1942
TALBOT Alpine, Solara, Minx & Rapier (75 - 86) up to D	0337
Talbot Horizon Petrol (78 - 86) up to D	0473
Talbot Samba (82 - 86) up to D	0823
TOYOTA Carina E Petrol (May 92 - 97) J to P	3256

Title	Book No.
Toyota Corolla (80 - 85) up to C	0683
Toyota Corolla (Sept 83 - Sept 87) A to E	1024
Toyota Corolla (Sept 87 - Aug 92) E to K	1683
Toyota Corolla Petrol (Aug 92 - 97) K to P	3259
Toyota Hi-Ace & Hi-Lux Petrol (69 - Oct 83) up to A	0304
Toyota Yaris Petrol (99 - 05) T to 05	4265
TRIUMPH GT6 & Vitesse (62 - 74) up to N *	0112
Triumph Herald (59 - 71) up to K *	0010
Triumph Spitfire (62 - 81) up to X	0113
Triumph Stag (70 - 78) up to T *	0441
Triumph TR2, TR3, TR3A, TR4 & TR4A (52 - 67) up to F *	0028
Triumph TR5 & 6 (67 - 75) up to P *	0031
Triumph TR7 (75 - 82) up to Y *	0322
VAUXHALL Astra Petrol (80 - Oct 84) up to B	0635
Vauxhall Astra & Belmont Petrol (Oct 84 - Oct 91) B to J	1136
Vauxhall Astra Petrol (Oct 91 - Feb 98) J to R	1832
Vauxhall/Opel Astra & Zafira Petrol (Feb 98 - Apr 04) R-reg onwards	3758
Vauxhall/Opel Astra & Zafira Diesel (Feb 98 - Apr 04) R-reg onwards	3797
Vauxhall/Opel Calibra (90 - 98) G to S	3502
Vauxhall Carlton Petrol (Oct 78 - Oct 86) up to D	0480
Vauxhall Carlton & Senator Petrol (Nov 86 - 94) D to L	1469
Vauxhall Cavalier Petrol (81 - Oct 88) up to F	0812
Vauxhall Cavalier Petrol (Oct 88 - 95) F to N	1570
Vauxhall Chevette (75 - 84) up to B	0285
Vauxhall/Opel Corsa Diesel (Mar 93 - Oct 00) K to X	4087
Vauxhall Corsa Petrol (Mar 93 - 97) K to R	1985
Vauxhall/Opel Corsa Petrol (Apr 97 - Oct 00) P to X	3921
Vauxhall/Opel Corsa Petrol & Diesel (Oct 00 - Sept 03) X-reg onwards	4079
Vauxhall/Opel Frontera Petrol & Diesel (91 - Sept 98) J to S	3454
Vauxhall Nova Petrol (83 - 93) up to K	0909
Vauxhall/Opel Omega Petrol (94 - 99) L to T	3510
Vauxhall/Opel Vectra Petrol & Diesel (95 - Feb 99) N to S	3396
Vauxhall/Opel Vectra Petrol & Diesel (Mar 99 - May 02) T-reg. onwards	3930
Vauxhall/Opel 1.5, 1.6 & 1.7 litre Diesel Engine (82 - 96) up to N	1222
VOLKSWAGEN 411 & 412 (68 - 75) up to P *	0091
Volkswagen Beetle 1200 (54 - 77) up to S	0036
Volkswagen Beetle 1300 & 1500 (65 - 75) up to P	0039
Volkswagen Beetle 1302 & 1302S (70 - 72) up to L *	0110
Volkswagen Beetle 1303, 1303S & GT (72 - 75) up to P	0159
Volkswagen Beetle Petrol & Diesel (Apr 99 - 01) T-reg. onwards	3798
Volkswagen Golf & Bora Petrol & Diesel (April 98 - 00) R to X	3727
Volkswagen Golf & Jetta Mk 1 Petrol 1.1 & 1.3 (74 - 84) up to A	0716
Volkswagen Golf, Jetta & Scirocco Mk 1 Petrol 1.5, 1.6 & 1.8 (74 - 84) up to A	0726
Volkswagen Golf & Jetta Mk 1 Diesel (78 - 84) up to A	0451
Volkswagen Golf & Jetta Mk 2 Petrol (Mar 84 - Feb 92) A to J	1081

Title	Book No.
Volkswagen Golf & Vento Petrol & Diesel (Feb 92 - Mar 98) J to P.	3097
Volkswagen Golf & Bora 4-cyl Petrol & Diesel (01 - 03) X to 53	4169
Volkswagen LT Petrol Vans & Light Trucks (76 - 87) up to E	0637
Volkswagen Passat & Santana Petrol (Sept 81 - May 88) up to E	0814
Volkswagen Passat 4-cyl Petrol & Diesel (May 88 - 96) E to P	3498
Volkswagen Passat 4-cyl Petrol & Diesel (Dec 96 - Nov 00) P to X	3917
VW Passat Petrol & Diesel (00 - 05) X to 05	4279
Volkswagen Polo & Derby (76 - Jan 82) up to X	0335
Volkswagen Polo (82 - Oct 90) up to H	0813
Volkswagen Polo Petrol (Nov 90 - Aug 94) H to L	3245
Volkswagen Polo Hatchback Petrol & Diesel (94 - 99) M to S	3500
Volkswagen Polo Hatchback Petrol (00 - Jan 02) V to 51	4150
Volkswagen Scirocco (82 - 90) up to H *	1224
Volkswagen Transporter 1600 (68 - 79) up to V	0082
Volkswagen Transporter 1700, 1800 & 2000 (72 - 79) up to V *	0226
Volkswagen Transporter (air-cooled) Petrol (79 - 82) up to Y *	0638
Volkswagen Transporter (water-cooled) Petrol (82 - 90) up to H	3452
Volkswagen Type 3 (63 - 73) up to M *	0084
VOLVO 120 & 130 Series (& P1800) (61 - 73) up to M *	0203
Volvo 142, 144 & 145 (66 - 74) up to N *	0129
Volvo 240 Series Petrol (74 - 93) up to K	0270
Volvo 262, 264 & 260/265 (75 - 85) up to C *	0400
Volvo 340, 343, 345 & 360 (76 - 91) up to J	0715
Volvo 440, 460 & 480 Petrol (87 - 97) D to P	1691
Volvo 740 & 760 Petrol (82 - 91) up to J	1258
Volvo 850 Petrol (92 - 96) J to P	3260
Volvo 940 Petrol (90 - 96) H to N	3249
Volvo S40 & V40 Petrol (96 - Mar 04) N-reg. onwards	3569
Volvo S70, V70 & C70 Petrol (96 - 99) P to V	3573
Volvo V70 / S80 Petrol & Diesel (98 - 05) S to 55	4263

AUTOMOTIVE TECHBOOKS

Title	Book No.
Automotive Air Conditioning Systems	3740
Automotive Electrical and Electronic Systems Manual	3049
Automotive Gearbox Overhaul Manual	3473
Automotive Service Summaries Manual	3475
Automotive Timing Belts Manual – Austin/Rover	3549
Automotive Timing Belts Manual – Ford	3474
Automotive Timing Belts Manual – Peugeot/Citroën	3568
Automotive Timing Belts Manual – Vauxhall/Opel	3577

DIY MANUAL SERIES

Title	Book No.
The Haynes Manual on Bodywork	4198
The Haynes Manual on Brakes	4178
The Haynes Manual on Carburettors	4177
The Haynes Manual on Diesel Engines	4174
The Haynes Manual on Engine Management	4199
The Haynes Manual on Fault Codes	4175
The Haynes Manual on Practical Electrical Systems	4267
The Haynes Manual on Small Engines	4250
The Haynes Manual on Welding	4176

* Classic reprint

All the products featured on this page are available through most motor accessory shops, cycle shops and book stores. Our policy of continuous updating and development means that titles are being constantly added to the range. For up-to-date information on our complete list of titles, please telephone: (UK) **+44 1963 442030** • (USA) **+1 805 498 6703** • (France) **+33 1 47 17 66 29** • (Sweden) **+46 18 124016** • (Australia) **+61 3 9763 8100**

CL19.10/05

Preserving Our Motoring Heritage

> The Model J Duesenberg Derham Tourster. Only eight of these magnificent cars were ever built – this is the only example to be found outside the United States of America

Almost every car you've ever loved, loathed or desired is gathered under one roof at the Haynes Motor Museum. Over 300 immaculately presented cars and motorbikes represent every aspect of our motoring heritage, from elegant reminders of bygone days, such as the superb Model J Duesenberg to curiosities like the bug-eyed BMW Isetta. There are also many old friends and flames. Perhaps you remember the 1959 Ford Popular that you did your courting in? The magnificent 'Red Collection' is a spectacle of classic sports cars including AC, Alfa Romeo, Austin Healey, Ferrari, Lamborghini, Maserati, MG, Riley, Porsche and Triumph.

A Perfect Day Out

Each and every vehicle at the Haynes Motor Museum has played its part in the history and culture of Motoring. Today, they make a wonderful spectacle and a great day out for all the family. Bring the kids, bring Mum and Dad, but above all bring your camera to capture those golden memories for ever. You will also find an impressive array of motoring memorabilia, a comfortable 70 seat video cinema and one of the most extensive transport book shops in Britain. The Pit Stop Cafe serves everything from a cup of tea to wholesome, home-made meals or, if you prefer, you can enjoy the large picnic area nestled in the beautiful rural surroundings of Somerset.

> John Haynes O.B.E., Founder and Chairman of the museum at the wheel of a Haynes Light 12.

< Graham Hill's Lola Cosworth Formula 1 car next to a 1934 Riley Sports.

The Museum is situated on the A359 Yeovil to Frome road at Sparkford, just off the A303 in Somerset. It is about 40 miles south of Bristol, and 25 minutes drive from the M5 intersection at Taunton.
Open 9.30am - 5.30pm (10.00am - 4.00pm Winter) 7 days a week, *except Christmas Day, Boxing Day and New Years Day*
Special rates available for schools, coach parties and outings Charitable Trust No. 292048